curned ~~ ~ ~-~
te be

D1150735

Social History in ~~P~~

General Editor: ~~I~~

Social History in Perspective is a se.   ~~studies~~ of the
many topics in social, cultural and relig.   ~~history~~ for students. They
also give the student clear surveys of the subject and present
the most recent research in an accessible way.

PUBLISHED

John Belchem *Popular Radicalism in Nineteenth-Century Britain*
Simon Dentith *Society and Cultural Forms in Nineteenth-Century England*
Harry Goulbourne *Race Relations in Britain since 1945*
Tim Hitchcock *English Sexualities, 1700–1800*
Sybil M. Jack *Towns in Tudor and Stuart Britain*
Helen M. Jewell *Education in Early Modern England*
Hugh McLeod *Religion and Society in England, 1850–1914*
Christopher Marsh *Popular Religion in the Sixteenth Century*
Michael A. Mullett *Catholics in Britain and Ireland, 1558–1829*
John Spurr *English Puritanism, 1603–1689*
W. B. Stephens *Education in Britain, 1750–1914*
David Taylor *Crime, Policing and Punishment in England, 1750–1914*
N. L. Tranter *British Population in the Twentieth Century*
Ian D. Whyte *Scotland's Society and Economy in Transition, c.1500–c.1760*

FORTHCOMING

Eric Acheson *Late Medieval Economy and Society*
Ian Archer *Rebellion and Riot in England, 1360–1660*
Jonathan Barry *Religion and Society in England, 1603–1760*
A. L. Beier *Early Modern London*
Sue Bruley *Women's Century of Change*
Andrew Charlesworth *Popular Protest in Britain and Ireland, 1650–1870*
Richard Connors *The Growth of Welfare in Hanoverian England,
1723–1793*
Geoffrey Crossick *A History of London from 1800 to 1939*
Alistair Davies *Culture and Society, 1900–1995*
Martin Durham *The Permissive Society*
Peter Fleming *Medieval Family and Household England*
David Fowler *Youth Culture in the Twentieth Century*
Malcolm Gaskill *Witchcraft in England, 1560–1760*
Peter Gosden *Education in the Twentieth Century*
S. J. D. Green *Religion and the Decline of Christianity
in Modern Britain, 1880–1980*

Titles continued overleaf

LIVERPOOL JMU LIBRARY

3 1111 00804 2036

Please note that a sister series, *British History in Perspective*, is available which covers all the key topics in British political history.

SOCIETY AND CULTURAL FORMS IN NINETEENTH CENTURY ENGLAND

SIMON DENTITH

First published in Great Britain 1998 by
MACMILLAN PRESS LTD
Houndmills, Basingstoke, Hampshire RG21 6XS and London
Companies and representatives throughout the world

A catalogue record for this book is available from the British Library.

ISBN 0–333–62014–3 hardcover
ISBN 0–333–62015–1 paperback

First published in the United States of America 1998 by
ST. MARTIN'S PRESS, INC.,
Scholarly and Reference Division,
175 Fifth Avenue, New York, N.Y. 10010

ISBN 0–312–21631–9

Library of Congress Cataloging-in-Publication Data
Dentith, Simon.
Society and cultural forms in nineteenth century England / Simon
Dentith.
p.   cm. — (Social history in perspective)
Includes bibliographical references (p.   ) and index.
ISBN 0–312–21631–9 (cloth)
1. England—Social conditions—19th century.   I. Title.
II. Series.
HN398.E5.D45   1998
306'.0942'09034—dc21   98–18587
                                                                               CIP

© Simon Dentith 1998

All rights reserved. No reproduction, copy or transmission of this publication may be made
without written permission.

No paragraph of this publication may be reproduced, copied or transmitted save with
written permission or in accordance with the provisions of the Copyright, Designs and
Patents Act 1988, or under the terms of any licence permitting limited copying issued by
the Copyright Licensing Agency, 90 Tottenham Court Road, London W1P 9HE.

Any person who does any unauthorised act in relation to this publication may be liable to
criminal prosecution and civil claims for damages.

The author has asserted his right to be identified as the author of this work in accordance
with the Copyright, Designs and Patents Act 1988.

This book is printed on paper suitable for recycling and made from fully managed and
sustained forest sources.

10   9   8   7   6   5   4   3   2   1
07   06   05   04   03   02   01   00 ˙ 99   98

Printed in Hong Kong

For Kath, as ever

CONTENTS

LIST OF ILLUSTRATIONS

Acknowledgements for Illustrations

For permission to reproduce pictures I gratefully acknowledge the fol-
lowing: the Earl of Mansfield for David Wilkie, *The Village Politicians*;
Birmingham Museums and Art Gallery for Henry Wallis, *The Stone-
breaker*; the British Library for *Illustrated Times* (13/4/1561), *Taking the
Census in the Dark Arches of the Adelphi*; the Bridgeman Art Library for
Sir Luke Fildes, *Applicants for Admission to a Casual Ward*; the E. T.
Archive for W. G. Joy, *General Gordon's Last Stand*.

PREFACE
AND ACKNOWLEDGEMENTS

In *Beyond a Boundary*, his immensely attractive and persuasive history of cricket in nineteenth-century England and the twentieth-century West Indies, the great Marxist historian C. L. R. James protests against the exclusion of W. G. Grace from all accounts of the social history of England. In his generous conception of such a history, a cricketer like W. G. Grace – not that there *was* anybody like him – could only be understood as bringing forward into the late nineteenth century some of the social energies of an earlier age. And for James, this is not only a matter of social history; as he remarks of the stroke-play of another, this time West Indian, cricketer, if this was not culture, then what was?

I regret to say that, despite C. L. R. James, this is the last time that the robust figure of W. G. Grace makes an appearance in these pages. He appears now to suggest something of the possible range of the book that follows. What might *not* be included in a book that sought to give an account of society and cultural forms in nineteenth-century England? The range of material that ought to be considered is so wide, the volume of 'evidence' so enormous, as to make any attempted overview like this one appear foolhardy. How could one set about writing a book which seeks to make sense of the cultural history of the nineteenth century in England in the context of its encompassing social history, when the range of what can be legitimately counted as 'culture' is... practically everything?

Though at times the book may read like a survey, it has certainly not been my intention to write one. On the contrary, what I have hoped to provide is rather a *way* of understanding the cultural material I discuss – to understand it as a way of negotiating the complex and changing social relationships of the nineteenth century. But to establish such a view of cultural objects requires in effect close and extended readings of them, compounding the difficulties created by the range of the material. In practice, this has meant that I have had to be very selective in the examples that I have discussed in any detail. It has also meant that I have tried to consider mostly familiar material, in the hope that in doing so I will be providing common reference-points for readers as the book proceeds. I certainly have not restricted my discussions to the 'canon', because part of my argument is that canonical material is drawn from cultural forms that represent only a proportion of the possible forms with which people in the nineteenth century made sense of their lives. However, in making that case I have alluded, wherever possible, to cultural objects that I have presumed to be relatively well known.

A further point follows from this, concerning the system of annotation and reference that I have adopted. Quotations and references are annotated in the usual way at the end of the book, though I have tried to keep annotation of this kind to a minimum. In addition, however, I have also provided a brief reading-list for the book as a whole, taken chapter by chapter, suggesting a small number of books that might be immediately turned to in order to pursue any of the points or arguments advanced. This seems to me to be more useful than an unwieldy bibliography, which like the very nineteenth-century material discussed, could have in principle (or in practice) no conclusion. I hope that readers of this volume will find this a helpful arrangement.

A prefatory word is also required about the restriction implied in my title, 'Society and Cultural Forms in Nineteenth-Century *England*'. The final chapter of the book discusses the embarrassment that attaches to the words 'Britain' and 'England' – how it is impossible to use the first without invoking a particular national and imperial history, while to use the second to include Scotland, Wales and Ireland is unforgivable. The cultural material that I discuss is, for the most part, English; since one of the central contentions of the book is that cultural objects emerge from specific social situations, it seemed best simply to signal in the title the real limits that actually control the book. The difficulties that surround this terminology are in fact intractable, because they emerge from still unresolved, and conflictual, national histories. These are not difficulties that can be overcome by a decision about terms, but the restriction implied in the title is to be understood as alluding to this awkward history, without, I hope, reproducing the awkwardness.

Finally, a brief outline is required of the matter of the book. The first, introductory, chapter suggests the more theoretical, or relatively abstract, considerations that underlie the book as a whole. One such is the idea of 'faultlines' – major structuring oppositions within the social order around which, or across which, cultural objects are constructed. The chapters that form the bulk of the book are concerned with a series of such faultlines. The second and third chapters discuss one principal axis of division in nineteenth-century England, the lines of authority that play across the divisions of social class. Chapters 4 and 5 are concerned with the faultline that runs between country and city, discussing in turn the cultural forms that are addressed to rural and urban life. Chapter 6 is concerned with the question of gender, and the centrality of the faultline of gender to nineteenth-century cultural production. Finally, Chapter 7 addresses the social and cultural divisions that formed around ethnicity and race in the nineteenth century. While these are real distinctions, I am conscious even as I list them of the artificiality of treating them separately – I shall be arguing, indeed, that these faultlines in social and cultural life both support and contradict each other in specific ways. Nevertheless, the necessity for such abstracting simplifications is evident if one is to make any effort at cultural description at all.

In this particular effort at cultural description, my warmest thanks are due to John Belchem and Peter Widdowson, who both generously agreed to read the manuscript, and managed to correct some at least of my errors. My thanks are due also to my colleagues in the Humanities Department at Cheltenham and Gloucester College of Higher Education, with whom I have enjoyed many a disagreement on the matters discussed in the book; and especially to Philip Martin, for creating an environment in which the book could be written. Finally, I wish to thank Kath and Imogen and Jack, who have helped me write the book in all sorts of ways which would be too numerous to mention.

LIVERPOOL JOHN MOORES UNIVERSITY
LEARNING SERVICES

1

INTRODUCTION: 'SOCIETY' AND 'CULTURAL FORM'

'Society' and 'cultural form' – the terms 'culture' and 'society' are not far to seek in my title. This book addresses culture and society in the nineteenth century, and its topic is essentially a *relationship*: between the realities of nineteenth-century society in England, and the extraordinary range of cultural objects, of all kinds, produced within that century. But this relationship is difficult to specify, for a variety of reasons. Firstly, it is a relationship between two entities which are constantly transforming themselves and whose definitions are, anyway, difficult and controversial. Secondly, the very effort to specify a relationship *between* 'society' and 'culture' tends to make both entities too rigid, to presuppose a separate reality for each – and thus to indicate a way of conceiving the relationship which ought precisely to be the matter for inquiry. Let me say immediately, then, that no society is conceivable without a culture, and indeed that no culture is conceivable without a society to sustain it. In fact, one of my central contentions in this book will be that social relationships are partly realised in culture, and that culture is a space in which such relationships are both cemented and contested. Moreover, my topic is historically located in the nineteenth century, in a country, England, undergoing remarkable transformations, so that social relationships were in a state of constant tension and renegotiation; culture is both one of the means of this renegotiation, and the particular valuations made within culture are some of its products.

Both these central terms will be the subject of further discussion and definition later in this introduction. However, it will be appropriate to

1

start the consideration of these matters with a brief overview of English social history in the nineteenth century, as a way of establishing a preliminary sense of at least one of the terms of the relationship.

English Social History in the Nineteenth Century

It is a commonplace of historical description to say that English society in the nineteenth century underwent a series of massive transformations. But for once this commonplace underestimates the extraordinary changes that overtook the first industrial nation between 1800 and 1900. At the beginning of the century, England was still a predominantly agricultural and rural society, with a population of approximately twelve million (albeit rapidly expanding). It was ruled by a landed elite, and its form of social organisation was predominantly vertical, with power and loyalties directed up and down the social scale. The predominance of London as an urban centre remained much as it had during the eighteenth century – the 'great wen', as Cobbett called it (itself a significant cultural evaluation), was by far the largest city. Transport and communications between the various parts of the country were slow and difficult, despite the recently established turnpike roads and stagecoaches, which made journeys possible, for those who could afford them, at the remarkable speed of twelve miles an hour. The majority of the population, however, had little experience of travel beyond their own locality. Literacy was confined to a small percentage of the population. Craft production permitted many women to enter the labour market, itself highly localised; but middle-class women were increasingly being confined by notions of respectability to a solely domestic sphere.

Contrast the position at the end of the century. The population had more than trebled, to approximately forty million, and by a large majority most of them now lived in towns. Large urban centres, in the North-West, the Midlands, the North-East, and South and Central Yorkshire – and also, of course, in Central Scotland and South Wales – had enormously expanded, with economies based on cotton, coal and iron. The governing role of that landed elite, though by no means entirely displaced, was at least challenged, not only by different centres of power and influence based upon finance and industry, but also by some genuine if limited democratic elements within British society and the state. The whole country was criss-crossed by railway lines, making travel and trade possible between different parts of the country at speeds unimaginable a hundred years earlier – indeed, the railway provided the most visible and dramatic symbol of the transition to modernity for those who witnessed the transformations it accomplished and accompanied. Above all this was a recognisably modern society, with horizontal loyalties of class and nation largely displacing the old vertical ones. This was a society whose traces we can still see around us in most of the big cities of contemporary Britain: in streets of terraced housing, in the churches and chapels built to accommodate this urban population, in the football teams established to entertain them, in the music-halls and parks that were built to occupy their leisure time. The overwhelming majority of the population was now literate, reading newspapers provided for them by press barons and sending their children to state-provided primary schools. Middle-class and lower middle-class women were beginning to enter the labour market in large numbers, to fill the expanding numbers of clerical jobs, travelling to work by mass public transport through large, socially zoned cities.

Even this impressionistic account indicates the scale of the changes between the beginning and the end of the century. Part of these changes can be accounted for by the industrialisation and urbanisation of Britain, processes obviously effected with different patterns of settlement, at different times and at different speeds, and with different intensities. Accompanying these evident and dramatic economic and social changes were perhaps less dramatic, but still substantial, political transformations; Parliament, the instrument of elite rule throughout the eighteenth century, could by 1900 boast some genuine democratic credentials, always tempered, of course, by the exclusion of half the adult population, the female half, from the franchise. Still more important, the transformations of social life brought with them, though not in any automatic or passive way, changes in social relationships, both at the wider level of relationships between classes, and at the most immediate level of daily interchange with one's neighbours and social superiors and inferiors.

It is possible to trace some of the faultlines of this social history – or rather, this series of complexly interlocking histories, driven by different divisions and contradictions and occurring at different tempos. One such division I have already hinted at: the question of class, without an understanding of which nineteenth-century culture and society are simply incomprehensible. One can see this history as a process of class simplification, in which the multiple *ranks* of pre-industrial society

were replaced by the large-scale *classes* of the end of the century. Those
ranks lived in surprising proximity to each other, not only in the country, where lines of deference and dependence were especially clearly
marked, but also in the towns; even in London, different ranks lived
in close proximity, sometimes actually in the same buildings, where different floors would be occupied by people of different wealth and rank.
But as the century progressed, these patterns were to be decisively disrupted, or, in the case of the new cities of the industrial Midlands and
North, were replaced by quite other patterns of settlement. At the end
of the century, England was zoned off and divided up by class to a
quite extraordinary degree; where people lived, what clothes they
wore, what accents they spoke in, what education they received, where
they took their holidays (even down to different areas in the same
resort), what entertainment they saw, where they sat in the music-hall
and when they sat there: all these things were determined by the social
class to which they belonged. Some of the profound cultural consequences of these acute and unprecedented social divisions are
addressed below, especially in Chapters 2 and 3.

But if class was one of the faultlines of nineteenth-century society, at
all times a matter of tension and anxiety, another was that of gender.
Feminism, after all, as much as socialism, is a product of the nineteenth
century. At first it may indeed seem a paradox that a period of history
which was most explicit in articulating an ideology of 'separate spheres'
for men and women should also be the age which produced large-scale
ascription to feminism and a militant suffrage movement. But far from
being paradoxical these are actually two sides of the same coin – repres-
sion and revolt produce each other, and their salience in the nineteenth
century results from the fraught and contested nature, both in practice
and in theory, of the 'Woman Question' almost throughout the century.
In part, this was because of the uneven exclusion of women from the
labour market, and their confinement to the domestic sphere – though
this was by no means universal and was sharply cut across by divisions
between and within classes, so that the domestic ideal was unattainable
for many during the century. This situation varied as the century went
on, so that the particular terms and conditions in which divisions of
labour were negotiated varied, and require close and careful attention.
At all events, questions of womanliness and manliness were endlessly
debated in the nineteenth century, and had an evident and central
cultural dimension. This whole matter forms the topic of Chapter 6 of
this book.

If the nineteenth century invented socialism and feminism – at least as coherent and explicit theories – it was also the century which, if it did not invent nationalism, certainly gave it unprecedented emphasis. Nationalism is the attempt to found a polity and indeed a politics on the support for, and resistance to, large 'national' entities based on community of ethnos, language, and, significantly, culture. To talk of it in the English context, however, is to point to a whole range of interlocking questions, which suggest not a single faultline like that of class or gender (though these of course are themselves complexly realised), but a number of varying divisions, antipathies and alliances. It also requires us to move beyond the focus upon England announced in my title, in order to see how wider British and imperial dimensions fissured English social history. In the preface I referred to the embarrassment which attaches to the word 'Britain' – though this name has a significant imperial history behind it, reaching well back in to the eighteenth century. This awkwardness itself points to a significant division. 'Britain' includes, of course, England, Wales, Scotland and, in the nineteenth century, Ireland, all assimilated to a greater or lesser degree into a single national polity. These differences mattered greatly, not only in the traditional Gaelic- or Welsh-speaking heartlands, but also in the great and growing urban centres. Large Irish emigration to Liverpool, Glasgow, South Wales, Tyneside; Welsh migration to Birmingham and Liverpool; Highland people moving to the Lowlands; all these evinced one aspect of the divisions along the line of ethnicity (not to mention language and religion) that characterised nineteenth-century life in these islands.

If there were significant divisions, along ethnic lines, within 'Britain', there were still more significant divisions, of increasing salience as the century went on, between Britain and the world that surrounded it. Yet another 'ism': imperialism. By the end of the nineteenth century, Britain ruled the greatest imperium of human history. This meant unprecedented contact with peoples of different races, including a small but significant number of black people within Britain. Not surprisingly, this situation produced various ideologies and self-identifications based around hierarchies of race; 'Anglo-Saxons' pitted against numerous others in the form of Celts, Asiatics, Negroes, and so on. Ethnicity and race, in other words, provided one of the most significant fractures of nineteenth-century society in Britain, given sharp and fundamental significance by movements of population and the massive repressive apparatus of empire.

All of these divisions have an evident and important cultural dimension, since all are intimately bound up with the question of identity
and the meanings which people find for their lives, or have given to
them, sometimes forcibly. But this is to anticipate somewhat our immi-
nent discussion of the meaning of 'culture'; before we turn to this
there are several outstanding questions which remain from the impressionistic survey I have given of nineteenth-century society. One principal question concerns the class nature of English society. I have
mentioned that at the beginning of the century England was ruled by
a landed elite. It should at once be added, of course, that their rule
was significantly buttressed by the bankers and merchants of the City
of London, but these groups greatly overlapped and shared comparable
social and political ideals. It is important to specify, however, exactly
what is meant when it is said that a country is 'ruled' by a particular
class within it. It certainly does not mean only that the rulers have control of the coercive and repressive powers of the state and that they are
prepared to use them against any challenges – though this certainly *was*
the case with the early nineteenth-century ruling elite, who had control
of the army and navy, and the various militia and yeomanry, and were
quite happy to deploy them in England just as much as Ireland. However, long-lasting and successful rule requires something more than
this; it requires a real element of consent on the part of the governed,
and thus requires to be buttressed by a wide panoply of ideological, political, ritual and intellectual supports. This enlarged notion of 'rule' has
been usefully distinguished by the notion of 'hegemony', which extends
the notion of rule to include not only the directly coercive means of
social control but significant intellectual and cultural aspects also.

It has been a matter of disagreement whether the character of hegemony in nineteenth-century England should be characterised broadly
as 'bourgeois' or 'aristocratic'. To support the former view, it is possible
to adduce all the tangible evidence of the 'industrial revolution', which
so evidently transformed English society and which must have put a
newly dominant class in control. After all, it was not the aristocracy
that ran the leading sectors of the economy, in cotton, iron and steel.
Moreover, the genuine if partial democratisation of the country in the
period seems evidence of bourgeois rather than aristocratic rule, for
the bourgeoisie is much less happy with the self-confessedly exclusive
forms of government practised by aristocracies. Are not those totemic
victories of the English middle class, the First Reform Act of 1832 and
the Repeal of the Corn Laws in 1846, sufficient evidence of the

dominance of the bourgeoisie, a dominance at least achieved by the middle of the century?

Against this, the atypical path of English development – the first industrial nation but with industrialisation achieved in a firmly entrenched aristocratic polity – seems to suggest the continuance of a hegemony of a decidedly more traditional kind. The actual staffing of the high offices of state remained in the hands of the landed elite and its allies in the City throughout the nineteenth century; sufficient to distort economic and social policy in a way that by the end of the century was already leading to relative industrial decline vis-à-vis Germany and America. And the cultural dominance of this landed elite remained important throughout the century, easily defeating the modest cultural challenges of a progressive bourgeoisie even in their urban strongholds.

I invoke this discussion here not with any ambition to decide the question one way or the other, but to suggest part of what is at stake in a discussion of 'culture and society' in the nineteenth century. If it seems reasonable to agree that hegemony is maintained by a wide variety of means, some cultural, then cultural objects begin to appear as not themselves above the social struggle but as an irreducible part of it. To say this is to make a claim quite at odds with the very nineteenth-century writer, Matthew Arnold, who did most to give centrality and significant political meaning to the separatist notion of culture. I shall certainly be understanding culture in a secular and thoroughly non-Arnoldian manner, as fully involved with the actualities and immediacies of social life.

However, even if a secular rather than a transcendent notion of culture is conceded, that leaves open the question of the role culture can be thought of as playing within the social order. This in turn requires a preliminary question: was this a society more characterised by conflict than co-operation between its classes? This too is not a matter to be settled here, and since it is an empirical question as much as a theoretical one, it could not possibly be decided without appeal to a substantial body of evidence and argument. Even if such an appeal were to be made, however, the evidence would appear awkward and contradictory. Take the comparatively delimited area of class relations in the cotton districts. At different times, and sometimes indeed at the same time, these were area of acute, intense and bitter industrial and social conflict. Yet these same districts could see the most remarkable examples of class harmony and bourgeois leadership acquiesced in on the part of the cotton workers. So the 'evidence' cannot be made to point simply to one answer rather than another.

Nevertheless, these alternatives ('consensual' or 'conflictual') are worth pursuing because they suggest fundamentally different ways of thinking about culture. In one respect, culture appears as integrative, as the realm of social life in which socially cohesive meanings are reaffirmed, as the realm which works to guarantee the reproduction of the currently existing and thus dominant order of society. If nineteenth-century society was marked by a high degree of class co-operation, then this is the notion of culture which we should invoke. But culture can also be conceived in opposite terms, as carrying with it, in many of its forms, an ideal or Utopian version of the very social relations from which it emerges. Thought of in this way, culture becomes potentially disruptive, carrying a promise to those who use it and make it that things might be otherwise. In situations of class conflict, culture is a realm in which contradictory and antagonistic meanings are developed and exploited. Thus, to give a nineteenth-century example, the decades of the 1830s and 1840s were a time of relatively prominent class conflict, symbolised above all by the emergence of Chartism. This had a significant cultural project, which involved both drawing on and renegotiating the meanings available in aspects of bourgeois culture, and in asserting, through ritual, dress, and use of the vernacular, a distinctive class identity. Culture, here, serves a function which at the very least challenges the dominant social order.

There are therefore several open questions about English social history in the nineteenth century which significantly affect the way one conceives of the relationship between society and culture in that century. These are partly empirical questions, though not the sort that can be immediately solved by an appeal to the evidence. But they are partly also questions of theory, or to put it less grandly, questions of definition: what exactly do we mean when we speak of 'society' and 'culture', for we need to attend to this matter more fully to have any chance of specifying their relationship more accurately? The following section provides a fuller account of these contentious and difficult terms.

'Society' and 'Culture'

The work of Raymond Williams is an inescapable starting point for thinking about these terms, both because of his substantive work on

British culture and society in the book of that title and subsequently, and because of the closely related work of definition that constantly accompanied that substantive work.[1] A crucial emphasis of Williams is that these terms, as terms, are not neutral, and have not been conceived apart from the social history to which they refer; the very meanings of 'society' and 'culture' have been determined, extended and challenged as a result of complex changes within society and culture. The crucial period in which these terms became prominent is precisely the nineteenth century, for it was then that the social changes occurred which were to make the substance of society and culture, and thus the terms, a matter for explicit reflection and conflict. Not that this is a process which in any way came to an end with the nineteenth century. When the Conservative Prime Minister in the 1980s, Mrs Thatcher, could assert that 'there is no such thing as society', we can see that these questions are still subject to sharp contention.

In fact, the notion of society is a key nineteenth-century discovery, along with its study, 'sociology', which was itself a nineteenth-century invention. It is possible to distinguish two wide currents of social thought for whom the notion of society was crucial. The first was broadly conservative, emphasising natural and even organic social ties, which it saw as a matter of tradition and custom. In this current, society is constituted from the loyalties, affections, deferences and responsibilities which bind people together in families, clans, and ultimately nations. George Eliot (1819–80), echoing the German social philosopher Riehl, described society as 'incarnate history'; it is a phrase which points to the way that society is conceived in this broad current, as a matter of largely pre-rational, customary and affective relationships.[2] The second tradition of thought was basically liberal, and started not from social relationships but from individuals. In this conception, which tended to *counterpose* the individual to society, society was a matter of the more or less rational collective arrangements that groups of individuals make to further their individual ends (this tradition of thought in part lies behind Mrs Thatcher's denial of the existence of society). John Ruskin (1819–1900) provides a powerful representative of the first current, while John Stuart Mill (1806–73) can serve as perhaps the leading figure in the second. They disagreed strongly on the nature of social relationships; Ruskin wished to assert the primacy of affective relationships over merely economic ones, while Mill emphasised the primacy of individuality in necessary conflict with an authoritarian or paternalistic social order.[3] These alternative views provide a paradigmatic instance of the disagreements over the nature of society within nineteenth-century social thought.

It may be that the very word 'society' carries with it inescapable connections with that broadly conservative, organicist tradition for whom it was so important – though it may be that given the very different social and economic conditions of the late twentieth century, the political direction of that organicist emphasis has now been radically transposed. At all events, a partially contrary stress upon economic self-interest, either of individuals or classes, is likely to undermine too organicist a notion of society and suggest instead a more conflictual model. For this reason, it will at times be preferable to refer to 'the social order' rather than 'society' to indicate that conflictual or tension-ridden aspect. But whether 'society' or 'social order' is used, the use of the term always implies an allusion to a level of explanation beyond the individual, in which the conditions for, and the realities of, human life are understood as being created between people, never in the singular but always in the plural.

Williams has provided a comparable range of meanings for culture, each of which emerges from a particular social and intellectual history at the end of the eighteenth and beginning of the nineteenth century.[4] He distinguishes three principal but related ways of using 'culture'. The first is a broadly anthropological usage, to mean a 'whole way of life'. This is an important way of using the term, for it encompasses the realisation that human societies are differentiated: equivalent in their capacity to learn, develop and reproduce skills, techniques and attitudes, but these will vary from one society to another, and that these learnt (not 'natural') aspects enter into the entirety of social life. In this definition, 'culture' alludes to the range of meanings with which and in which human beings live their lives. This is a sense for culture that has already informed my discussion of nineteenth-century social history and which will be crucial throughout the book.

A second principal meaning for the term carries a more evaluative charge, for the term can be used to denote a 'state of mind', as when people speak of a 'cultured individual', or of a person as someone of 'high culture'. This usage of the term suggests distinctions *within* culture, or at least draws attention to the possibility of culture as a learnt and therefore developmental process in which different people can attain different levels. Culture, in this sense, is certainly narrower than in that broadly anthropological usage of culture as a 'whole way of life', for it denotes the range of human achievement alluded to in the third usage, crudely and briefly: works of art. In this familiar usage of the word, culture simply subsumes the whole range of work which, in another vocabulary equally loaded with a social history, has been valued as demonstrating particular skill or deserving particular, aesthetic, attention. But this too is an evaluative category, for culture in this sense seeks to reserve that valued attention to a selection of all the 'cultural' objects which, in the wider anthropological sense, might come under the heading of culture. In this matter, as in so many others, questions of definition conceal substantive questions both of fact and of value.

Williams sought to contain some of this diversity, or to retain some of the emphases of each of these usages while evading the vagueness that besets the term by virtue of its very range, by offering his own definition of culture as a *realised signifying system*. In this definition, culture appears as the realm in which meanings are articulated and circulated between people. But the definition also permits some legitimate focusing of attention on those aspects of a 'whole way of life' in which the production of meaning is central or predominant. For the problem of too broad a definition of culture is just that *everything* can be shown to have a cultural aspect – not only 'works of art', but also more functional objects like buildings or washing machines; indeed 'culture' is an element in all aspects of human behaviour: the clothes we wear, the language we speak, the patterns of inflection we employ, even characteristic learnt gestures, expressions and physical attitudes. But clearly a study of all this is impracticable and requires some closer focus; Williams's definition permits us to direct our attention to those cultural forms and objects in which the production of significance is primary. This would be true, for example, of a painting or a novel, but not true of that characteristic product of the nineteenth century, the steam train, even though this has a cultural aspect in its very shape and design. Nevertheless, I will discuss some of the products of the century's material culture shortly.

Williams's definition of culture, then, as a 'realised signifying system', helps both to suggest the scope of culture, and also to give some grounds for focusing our attention within that large scope. What the definition fails to give, in using the passive participle ('realised') and in its stress upon a system, is sufficient sense of human activity and creativity in the production of meanings by means of a signifying system. This is not true of Williams's work as a whole; but to get a stronger and more active notion it is helpful to turn, not to other areas of Williams's writing, but to the work of a thinker to whom he became indebted late in his career, that is, to the work of the Russian writer Mikhail Bakhtin and his fellow Russian V. N. Vološinov.[5]

The problem with the notion of a 'system', for both Bakhtin and Vološinov, is that it too readily assumes that it is the system which produces meaning, rather than the people who use the system. In their accounts, cultural producers of all kinds draw upon the forms and conventions made available to them by the signifying systems within which they work, but they do not do so in any passive way; on the contrary, every new cultural product inflects its material in a new direction, gives a new stress or emphasis, redefines what is possible within a given form. In so doing, the system itself is reshaped, so that there is a constant renegotiation of the system even as it is being used. Cultural objects are thus not isolated one from another, and from the wider system of meanings within the general culture. Instead, they form part of an incessant dialogue, constantly agreeing, disagreeing, refuting, reshaping, parodying or celebrating other meanings. This is a never-ending process; cultural objects from the nineteenth century still speak to us now, but they pose very different challenges to the ones they did when they were first produced, since the context into which they now speak is so different from the context into which they were first addressed. But this is a matter of degree rather than of kind; no cultural object is addressed into a homogeneous and conflict-free situation, and it always presupposes difference and potential disagreement on the part of the people to whom it is addressed. Cultural objects, in short, are *interested*; that is, they are interventions into specific situations in which they are designed to make a difference, even if that difference is only to reinforce what everybody already knows and believes.

Moreover, the material with which cultural objects work is inescapably social. This is obviously true of the language which the novelist, for example, uses. At the simplest level, a novelist like Dickens makes use of a multiplicity of different accents, voices and sub-languages, all of which he recycles with varying degrees of parody, deference, irony and celebration. He is thus necessarily involved in the process of establishing and partially renegotiating the socially determined hierarchy into which those various 'languages' are sorted. But if the raw material with which a novelist works itself carries with it a social history, this is true also of the materials of all the other cultural practices with which this book is concerned. The very gestures of melodrama, for example, were part of an established repertoire of gesture which implied a set of social relationships in their usage. Or the different kinds of painting were carefully assorted, throughout the first half of the nineteenth century, into a hierarchy of genres, with history painting at the top, which implied that certain kinds of subject and topic – ultimately certain kinds of people – were more important than others. A painter (or group of painters like the Pre-Raphaelites) who challenged that hierarchy were thus necessarily renegotiating their social as much as their artistic attitudes.

We can thus agree with Williams that culture is indeed a realised signifying system, but we can add with Bakhtin that the people who inhabit and use that system do so in an active way, constantly renegotiating and reinflecting the forms and conventions of that system to their own ends. The immediate arena for that activity is the society they inhabit; it is only in the context of a particular set of social forces ('hegemony'), and against the background of other meanings which circulate within a particular social order, that cultural meanings take on their force and specificity – that they can 'mean' anything at all. The relationship that we wish to specify between culture and society is, therefore, naturally, a complex one. Cultural producers work with materials that are inextricably social. They inflect and reinflect their material in ways which only take on force and meaning in the context of the various conflicts and disagreements, across the different faultlines we have discussed, that characterise a society or social order, at any time. In this conception, society both provides the context in which cultural objects become meaningful, and culture provides one of the means by which social relationships are realised.

Substantial problems of definition remain, of course. One prominent difficulty concerns the relationship of the term 'culture' to adjacent terms, emerging from different conceptual systems and carrying with them their own freight of history. One such term is ideology, given special prominence by Marxism but figuring largely in liberal discourse also (as in such phrases as 'the end of ideology' used to greet the supposed demise of Marxism). Ideology also could be defined as a realised signifying system; certainly, given the emphasis that I have given to the *interested* nature of culture, it is hard to see how to distinguish the latter from a relatively broad, though not unusual definition of ideology. As ever, these are not problems of definition or designation alone, as though we could single-handedly agree to call particular topics or areas by whatever name we choose. Involved in all these problems are contested arguments, in this instance especially concerning the extent or penetration of social conflict, politics and/or ideas into the realm of meanings and values. In this light, 'ideology' appears the harder word than 'culture', making a greater claim for the penetration of politics or social conflict into the everyday production of meaning. Indeed, the choice between culture and ideology reflects again that conceptual (and political) split between consensual and conflictual models of society: culture, in its more anthropological sense of a 'whole way of life', being addressed to a society as a functioning whole; ideology, in its extended reference to the whole realm of values and meanings, insisting upon the wider conflicts that are always present in this realm. Since both contentions seem to me to be true, I shall use 'ideology' sparingly and, in effect, to indicate an emphasis where social conflict, or politics, or explicit and extended systems of ideas, are especially prominent.

We can begin to focus some of these definitions by considering a particular example. George Eliot published *The Mill on the Floss* in 1860. The novel draws upon established ways of writing, all inextricably laden with social meanings, and seeks to reinflect those ways of writing in order to generate new ways of seeing and understanding. George Eliot herself described one function of art to be 'the extension of our sympathies', across the artificial barriers of class. *The Mill on the Floss* can itself be described as engaged in the extension of our sympathies, and George Eliot has a very specific, middle-class readership in mind in this project. She seeks to bring the likes of the Dodsons and the Tullivers – the provincial lower middle class amongst whom the novel is set – into the orbit of readerly sympathy, treating them with a seriousness from which they had previously been excluded. But this aspect of her project is at best ambivalent, for she finally cannot decide whether the appropriate genre for such a task is tragedy or tragi-comedy. Tragedy, 'which sweeps the stage in regal robes', is a realm of high dignity; to claim tragedy for the sadnesses and disappointments of ordinary lives is to make a large claim indeed across the dividing-line of class. George Eliot does make such a claim, but at times she also sees the ordinary lives with which she deals as fit only for tragi-comedy, a genre which invites irony – sarcasm, even – at her characters' expense. The potentially inclusive and socially integrative project of the extension of sympathies is thus partially sabotaged by the persistence, within the novel, of an ironic attitude which depends upon the narrator's social distance from her characters rather than her solidarity with them. The novel itself, then, variously encodes social relationships – between writer, reader and characters – and thus enacts these social relationships as it is recuperated by its various and socially distinct readers.

The novel also draws upon well-established narratives of individual lives, especially concerning the heroine, Maggie Tulliver. One such is the narrative of escape, a prominent way of telling the story of an individual's life, and of recounting that person's relationship with their provincial childhood. Clearly, a narrative of escape can encode powerful valuations of provincial life, of the metropolis to which the escape is made, and of the family and class from which the escape is effected. George Eliot toys with such a narrative but finally rejects it for her heroine, in fact envisaging no socially typical outcome for the various dilemmas in which she is caught up. One reason for this is Maggie's gender; the novel prominently asks questions about women's education and destiny, and claims for women the right to a significant education. In invoking certain narratives, then, and in bringing them to the conclusions that she does, George Eliot is carrying forward and partially redirecting some socially laden meanings.

We can trace this process as much in the reactions to the novel as in the novel itself. Though I have described George Eliot as engaged in the extension of sympathy, I have also briefly suggested that this is an ambivalent project and that there are opposing currents running in the novel as well. In fact, one widespread reaction to the novel was that it was excessively hostile to provincial respectability and too sympathetic to adolescent and feminine rebelliousness. Likewise, for one reviewer, the novel posed the question of what to do with clever girls, 'born of uncongenial parents, hemmed in with unsympathising kindred'.[6] Both reactions demonstrate, though the point perhaps barely needs labouring, that the novel is engaged in an ongoing contention and negotiation of socially charged meanings.

However, this brief account of *The Mill on the Floss* has drawn on categories that themselves require further explication, particularly concerning the *forms* of culture. We require some intermediate categories between 'culture' and 'society', if we are to address the specificity and the historical persistence of these forms. This provides the topic of the next section.

The Forms of Culture

Culture, then, is a realm in which people actively produce meanings, working with and transforming their materials as they do so. They work in given forms, some of which have a very long history reaching well beyond the nineteenth century: at the broadest level, and alluding only to the narrower definition of culture as works of art, such forms as writing, painting, music, theatre and the design arts exist in long trajectories pointing backwards and forward in time. Nevertheless, all of these forms saw significant developments during the nineteenth century which reflect its transforming social changes.

As far as writing was concerned, the crucial transformation in England was from a society of minority literacy to one of mass literacy. This process had fundamental effects as much on the forms of high written culture as it did on the popular culture on which the effects might be thought to be most evident. Naturally, in this latter area, the changes were remarkable. The beginning of the century – and indeed some considerable time into it – was a period of broadside ballads and chapbooks, traditional stories and songs printed and distributed by networks of penny capitalists. Newspapers were taxed, and subject to ferocious censorship. The end of the century saw a mass reading public catered for by highly capitalised cheap newspapers and magazines – exemplary cases, the *Daily Mail* and *Tit-Bits* – and provided also with cheap novels and magazine stories distributed through station bookstalls and newsagents. The relatively unified written culture at the beginning of the century, with its small-scale publishing both of books and magazines, was strikingly fissured by the end of the century, with magazines increasingly divided into specialist audiences, and books increasingly finding either elite or popular readerships. The history of *writing* in the nineteenth century, then, is one both of a massive extension of readership, but also of exploitation of that readership in ways that reflected the class composition and mutual class isolation of late nineteenth-century England.

A not dissimilar story can be told about painting in the nineteenth century, affected not least by inventions and technical innovations, both in the production of images through photography (invented in the middle of the century), and in the means of reproduction and distribution of images. Once again the contrast between the beginning and the end of the century is remarkable. In the early nineteenth century, painting still enjoyed something of a craft status, with highly specialised genres and ways of working; it was still largely reliant on patronage. At one end of the scale, the nineteenth century witnessed the establishment of the National Gallery and a number of important municipal galleries throughout England; at the other end, a series of technical innovations made the reproduction of images on a mass scale possible and cheap, and a variety of publications, most notably the *Illustrated London News*, developed to exploit these new technologies. By the end of the century, though the prestige of the Royal Academy was still intact, there were certainly challenges to the forms of academic art it fostered, and there was a mass of commercial art which meant that most people were surrounded by reproduced images, of one sort or another, to a wholly unprecedented degree.

The history of music shows a similar pattern of institutional extension, commercialisation, and division into class-segmented forms – though it is certainly possible to exaggerate this last assertion, for there was throughout the nineteenth century a significant working-class audience and readership for the products of high culture across all its forms. In the case of music, this is apparent in the traditions of choral singing established in many working-class communities in the north of England and in South Wales in the late nineteenth century, and of the working-class patronage of the provincial symphony orchestras that were also established at the same period. But perhaps the most remarkable musical fact of the nineteenth century was the piano, which was produced in its millions. By the end of the century there was no middle-class or lower middle-class household that was complete without a piano; no child of these classes, girls especially, who was not required at least to attempt some music. This too was a market catered for by mass, highly capitalised publishing, providing the sheet music that these domestic musicians consumed in vast quantities.

Finally, nineteenth-century theatre evinces a comparable extension of audience (through an unprecedented and subsequently unsurpassed programme of theatre building throughout the century), and a break-up of that audience into elite and popular forms. At the beginning of the century London and some provincial centres possessed large theatres showing a predominantly classic repertoire to a mixed and sometimes rowdy audience. By the end of the century this classic repertoire had been partially renewed but also largely replaced by popular forms, above all melodrama, whose origins were in fact outside the licensed theatres. At the same time, the growth of music-halls from the mid-century, and of popular theatre from still earlier, fostered a variety of popular forms such as pantomime, burlesque, and popular spectacle, in addition to melodrama: theatre in one form or another formed a staple of popular entertainment at the end of the century. In addition, self-conscious efforts at renewal of the elite theatres, through artistically ambitious forms such as *realism* and *naturalism*, were beginning, by the 1880s and 1890s, to produce a small but artistically significant audience. At the end of the century London contained a number of commercial theatres producing a repertoire of melodrama and other plays (the 'West End'); some two or three more experimental theatres playing to small, elite audiences; and a massive number of suburban theatres and music-halls playing to lower middle-class and working-class audiences. This pattern was reproduced, with evident differences of scale, in all the large urban centres of England.

Such descriptions, though obviously painted with a very broad brush, do something to suggest the imbrication of cultural forms with the social transformations of the nineteenth century. These accounts are not merely external to the cultural forms described; such matters as audience, context of consumption, and relationship to other adjacent forms, enter into the very meanings of the individual cultural object. Nevertheless, such general accounts do not go far enough in describing the social nature of form; there are forms, genres and conventions *within* those broad distinctions of writing, music, etc., which themselves entail a social history and sets of social relationships.

The multiplicity of written forms immediately suggests the complexity of the relationships to be described: essays, 'news', novels, poems, short stories, sketches – each themselves further divisible into genres and conventions. It is actually at this lower level of analysis that some of the most significant social relationships are mediated. For example, the conventions governing the writing of articles in the great national reviews, *The Edinburgh Review* (founded 1802), *The Quarterly Review* (founded 1809) and *The Westminster Review* (founded 1824), are telling. The anonymity of the reviewers, the use of the presumptive 'we' to introduce judgements, the very categories into which books for review were sorted, all point to a relatively homogeneous reading public, admittedly divided by political allegiance, being addressed in the accents of authority by other members of the same class. Similarly, the conventions governing the descriptions of working-class life that are to be found in the mid-century 'Condition-of-England' novel entail specific assumptions about topic and readership. In effect, these novels are governed by the sympathetic downward glance, in which a member of the middle class explains to other members of her own class the conditions under which the poor are living. These relationships are present in the very texture of the prose, governing such matters as the forms of address ('Imagine, dear reader, if you can . . .'), the levels of irony against either the topic of the novel or its reader, and the management of sympathy and pathos. Dickens standing over the corpse of Jo the crossing-sweeper in *Bleak House*, admonishing his readers on the typicality of such deaths ('Dead, my lords and gentlemen... and dying thus around us, every day!'[7]), is only the most extreme example of such conventionally realised social relationships.

It follows from this that these forms, genres and conventions change with the social relationships that they entail. Conventions can be described as precipitated forms of social understanding, which encode specific relationships between reader (or spectator), author and topic. Given the high rate of transformation of social relationships in the nineteenth century, it is not surprising to find a constant process of discarding or transformation of old forms, and creation of new forms, in all cultural spheres. In the theatre, for example, we have already noted the dominance of melodrama from the beginning of the century onwards. This form, springing from the popular theatres of London and Paris, travelled up the cultural hierarchy to invade the licensed theatres and eventually to become in effect the dominant theatrical mode of the century. Melodrama deals in 'legible symbolic configurations' in which the relative moral positions of the characters are made manifest by a highly conventional language of gesture, action and music.[8] It sought, not to extend the forms of tragedy to the popular classes, but to displace tragedy with a mode which dealt in high moral seriousness, in a way that could carry popular social aspirations to a triumphant conclusion. Comparable transformations, displacements and inventions mark all cultural forms in the nineteenth century, as the social relationships encoded in older and previously dominant forms break down, and require new conventions, new genres, to be adequate to transformed social relationships.

However, cultural forms have their own particular specificities, their own rhythms and their own internal laws. They have a history, in other words, which is not solely determined by the wider society they inhabit. Another way of saying this is that they have their own historical gravity, and continue to suggest powerful ways of understanding and *being* long after the social moment which produces them has passed. The historical persistence of cultural forms means that at any given moment in history there is in effect an available repertoire of socially laden forms within which the cultural producer must work, or which she or he must transform. This is perhaps more obviously visible in quotidian cultural forms, like language and dress and the design of material objects, as is it in the predominantly artistic forms which this book is mostly addressing. The sometimes inappropriate persistence of particular forms was one of the most noticeable aspects of the Great Exhibition of 1851, for example, with sometimes ludicrous results, with exhibits including the 'Elizabethan New Patent Grand Oblique Pianoforte', the 'Patent bright steel reflecting Stove-grate, with Gilt Ornaments, in the Renaissance Style', and the 'Four-post Stretched Bedstead of Brass, in the Ionic Style'.[9] But we should not be too distracted by these sometimes incidental absurdities. The Great Exhibition also displayed a number of objects made out of new materials like gutta-percha and papier mâché, and the numerous official and semi-official commentaries on the exhibits themselves repeatedly advocated simpler and more functional designs. One way of understanding the design history of the nineteenth century is as an effort both to settle on those styles from the repertoire which carried the right historical and social connotations (Gothic, perhaps, rather than Rococo), and to find appropriate styles for the massive array of new technologies, objects and devices that were produced in the course of the century.

To speak of a 'repertoire' is perhaps to make it sound too much a matter of conscious choice; we cannot choose but to speak or act in ways which are formally or generically shaped. But in a socially diverse and complex society like England in the nineteenth century, there was a constant process of clash and competition between opposing forms, often with the most interesting culture emerging from the tension-point between different or opposed forms.

The Locations of Culture

Forms, conventions, genres: these are all essential intermediate terms for understanding the socially laden meanings carried by culture. But 'society' also needs to be analytically broken down to give a more precise sense of the social location of culture, in more institutionally specific ways than the broad faultlines of class, gender and ethnos that I indicated earlier. Substantial institutions – some transformed and developed in the nineteenth century, some entirely new – provided the immediate social location for much cultural production and reception. Above all, the institution of the market increasingly dominated cultural production in the course of the century, with a particularly significant impact on popular culture. But other institutions, marked by varying links with those pervasive, ruthless and seemingly inexorable market relations, continued to be sites, of varying degrees of authority, for the production and circulation of cultural meanings. Such institutions included the churches; the educational system; publishing houses; municipal galleries, museums, libraries and orchestras; a variety of metropolitan and provincial academies, institutes, lyceums, athenaeums, and literary and philosophical societies; a multitude of masonic, friendly and mutual clubs and associations of all kinds; trade unions; and the various institutions of popular theatre, spectacle and music-hall, ranging from the smallest travelling menagerie or waxworks, to the great circus spectacle of Astley's, or to the seaside spectacles of the end of the century. In short, the nineteenth century witnessed the growth of a civil society of quite remarkable depth and variety.

In the following two chapters I discuss more fully the roles of some of these institutions, as the sites of significant cultural production. Some of them were thoroughly transformed in the nineteenth century. The various institutions of the educational system, for example, all underwent root-and-branch changes, while retaining in some cases the outward show of tradition and continuity. The ancient universities of Oxford and Cambridge, in particular, began the century as clerically dominated and intellectually conservative backwaters; they ended the century showing some traces at least of their modern function as elite research and training institutions. Similarly the public schools, and more unevenly the old grammar schools, became geared in the course of the century to the needs of systematic public examinations – though still with a syllabus that was overwhelmingly classical, literary, and non-scientific or technical. By contrast, the churches were much less successful in adapting themselves, or being adapted, to the requirements of an industrial and urban England. There were indeed tremendous efforts at church building, the results of which are still visible all around us in every inner-city area of England. In rural areas also, the church continued to provide cultural leadership for substantial sections of the population. But by the end of the century, England was no longer, in the majority, a churchgoing population. Churches and chapels were still full on Sundays, and generated a host of activities with a significant cultural element: Sunday schools, chapel teas, walks and processions; teetotal and rechabite meetings; church and chapel bands and choirs. But while this affected significantly the cultural formation of the urban working class (with wide regional variations), it was only one cultural institution among several and did not command majority allegiance.

Many of the other institutions were themselves products of the nineteenth century, rather than older institutions which underwent substantial transformation. Such institutions as municipal art galleries, museums, literary and philosophical societies, mechanics' institutes, and libraries, were part of an ambitious effort of cultural and social leadership on the part of sections of the provincial middle class; they sought to provide rational recreation for a population whose cultural resources they minimised or misunderstood, and whom they believed to be unruly because of this. An 'improving' ambition of this kind is perhaps ambivalent; it springs both from genuinely benevolent intentions, and from the desire to retain order and appropriate social deference. And its results were certainly ambivalent; both in terms of the success of the whole enterprise of rational recreation when it was in competition with old and new forms of popular entertainment – and in terms of the multiple and unpredictable uses a population might make of a library, an art gallery or a museum.

Many of the other institutions of civil society have a less evident cultural dimension: masonic lodges, societies of elks and oddfellows, even friendly and savings clubs and trade unions. Nevertheless, their functions in establishing significant patterns of mutuality and neighbourliness – sometimes of class exclusiveness or solidarity – are clearly important in giving shape and meaning to lives. And at times even their more recognisably cultural dimension is apparent, in trade-union banners, or in codes of dress and behaviour (trade-union efforts to improve standards of speech, for example).

But all of these institutions were faced with competition, sometimes direct, from multiple, commercially driven institutions reliant on the market, ranging from the smallest-scale penny-capitalist venture through to the large publishing houses and the theatrical chains. Take the case of the local pub. It is not simply that it could prove more attractive than a visit to the library or the mechanics' institute – though this was doubtless the case. But the pub itself could be a cultural centre, if that description does not sound too pretentious. Enterprising landlords could encourage the practice of traditional popular cultural forms, even if it was only a skittle alley; in another direction, the music-hall itself grew out of forms of conviviality practised in public houses. Furthermore, there was often an intimate connection between the public house and forms of working-class (usually masculine) sociality, the pub providing the meeting-place for trade unions, debating clubs, odd-fellows and masons. Moving beyond this local commercialism, it was the market which determined the ways in which written cultural forms were published. Commercial publishing, commercial entertainment, commercial recreation – all operated in competition with, and sometimes replaced, the traditional cultural institutions.

Institutions are easily recognisable: they leave substantial material traces, such as Oxbridge colleges, Victorian Gothic churches, and pubs with names like 'The Freemason's Arms'. They have their histories written; some of them survive across long stretches of time, albeit in transformed ways. But we need to consider a less easily specifiable cultural location, or site of significant production, what Raymond Williams has called 'fractions': intermediate groups or sub-groups, with a more or less articulate sense of self-definition, within which much cultural production occurs, and within which it takes on its particular density and specificity.[10] The main nineteenth-century example that Williams provides is the Pre-Raphaelites, a fraction that came to have a real sense of its own distinctiveness with respect to the academic painting of the day, and managed a distinctive aesthetic theory and practice. A fraction, in this sense, is something more than a 'school', and something less than a class or even a generation, though education, class and generation might all be significant in the making of a such a grouping. The Pre-Raphaelites provide an especially visible and culturally recognisable example; but the history of nineteenth-century poetry has also been written in cognate terms.[11] Alfred Tennyson (1809–92) and the Cambridge Apostles; Robert Browning (1812–89) and the Unitarian Radicals around William J. Fox; these are both fractions, in the light of which the particular characteristics of the poetry become manifest. In both cases it is at the level of the fraction that connections can be made between the particular intellectual and aesthetic properties of the cultural object, and some wider social and political project.

Institutions and fractions, then, provide useful mediating terms between those larger terms 'society' and 'culture'. They too are subject to the broad divisions of the nineteenth-century social order; some of the institutions we have discussed have a very specific class character and serve very specific class ends. The class character of the rural Church of England, for example, is evident enough; the rector who was connected to the landowning elite by birth or marriage, who served as a magistrate, and who exacted deference from his parishioners, has a substantial basis in history as well as the novels of Trollope. Similarly, the class character of the formations we have discussed is important, often because such formations end up in conscious revolt against the class from whom they have divided. (The opposite cases of Millais and William Morris are instructive here. Both starting with similar aesthetic objectives, the former could readily accommodate them to purely decorative and even commercial purposes, while the latter developed Pre-Raphaelite aestheticism into a fully-blown critique of nineteenth-century industrialism and capitalism). We can generalise from this fact of the centrality of class for a further point about the location of culture in the nineteenth century, namely its broad division into elite and popular forms. But we must be wary of projecting back on to the nineteenth century the cultural conditions of the late twentieth century. Elite culture could and did speak in significant ways to significant sections of the working class throughout the nineteenth century, and some of this book will discuss the ways in which it did so. The rural cottager at the beginning of the century was not only an impoverished figure equipped with shreds and tatters of popular song to go with the shreds and tatters that he wore on his back – he might also have a copy of *Pilgrim's Progress* on his shelf, and find it essential to him as he made his way through the world. The skilled artisan of the 1820s and 1830s, with his Shakespeare, Milton and Burns, and his knowledge of Robert Owen and Saint-Simon – he too could draw on the resources of 'high culture' to make some sense of the world around him. Finally, the skilled trade-unionist at the end of the century, committed to self-education via cheap editions of the works of Ruskin and Carlyle, and a regular attender at his town's choral society – he too found much in the realm of high culture that spoke immediately and directly to him. I discuss this working-class culture of self-improvement further in Chapter 3, below. Nevertheless, it is doubtless fair to say that these figures were exceptional, and that in broad terms culture was divided along class lines in the nineteenth century.

Nineteenth-century England, then, possessed a culture with multiple institutional locations, increasingly mediated by the market, and fissured along class lines. But that market was a *national* market, and it is with a sense of the national location of culture that I wish to conclude this section, noting again that neither 'England' nor 'Britain' adequately express the necessary shape. It was a culture supported by national institutions, national publishing companies, national newspapers and national networks of entertainment in music-hall and theatre – all relying on a national railway network. Of course regional and, within

'Britain', national distinctions persisted: cultural institutions in Wales, Scotland and Ireland remained distinctive in significant respects, or their cultural institutions were invented (or reinvented) in national guise in the course of the century. 'Britain' was the name given to that constructed national space; however ersatz, it was a genuine cultural reality at the end of the century, and it extended far beyond the shores of the British Isles, to take in a large, diverse (and still expanding) empire. Many of those national institutions of culture, like the universities, publishing houses, and even theatres, had developed important outposts in the British colonies by the end of the century. English culture was emphatically an imperial culture, and we will be examining some of the effects of this in Chapter 7.

The Diversity of Cultural Forms

I draw the following general conclusions from these brief introductory remarks, conclusions that will inform all the discussions that follow. Cultural objects, I shall be arguing, emerge from and speak to particular forms of life. A social form of life, however, does not simply pre-exist the culture which emerges from it; on the contrary, a social form of life is both material and ideal; that is, it exists in its imagined forms as well as in its material social relations (the phrase 'imagined communities', coined by Benedict Anderson to describe the life of the nation, is very appropriate for other forms of life as well[12]). 'Culture' is then the space in which this imaginary social life is continued; social relations are in part constituted in particular cultural forms.

However, the word 'society' or the phrase 'a social form of life' too easily suggest homogeneity in a social organism. But, actually, social life is complex: it is divided upon different axes, and across differing lines of authority – what I have been calling 'faultlines' – to form an 'open totality'. That is to say, the multiple divisions of social life are interconnected, but not in any way that makes *one* of these divisions the master-key or fundamental division. This open totality is subject to varying and interconnected authorities; the combination of these authorities constitutes 'hegemony'. Hegemony in this sense is fluid, and is always being negotiated and renegotiated.

If 'society' too readily suggests an organic whole, then 'culture' likewise can too easily imply an undifferentiated or non-contradictory entity, especially in usages which talk of 'a culture' as 'a whole way of life'. For this reason, I shall be constantly referring in what follows to 'cultural forms'. Cultural forms, and related formulations like genres and conventions, represent distinctive ways of understanding and addressing social relations; culture itself, like 'society', is thus not unitary, but cut across and divided along different faultlines and divisions. It is the diversity, heterogeneity and even contradictoriness of cultural forms that I wish to emphasise – the availability of multiple ways of understanding social life, and of negotiating relationships within it.

If 'society' and 'culture' are not to be thought of as uniform, but rather as complex, diverse and internally divided, then the same can be said of individual cultural objects also – especially some of the large and complex nineteenth-century cultural objects that I shall discuss in this book. The repertoire of cultural forms needs to be thought of as in some sense internal to individual cultural objects, which draw upon differing forms and conventions, all with their own histories. Thus the great panoramic mid-century novels of Dickens, Thackeray, George Eliot or Trollope all contain within them diverse and even contradictory modes of writing, providing alternative ways to make sense of the world, and for the novels themselves to be made sense of. It is this internal complexity which, in part, contributes to the fluidity and instability of meaning that characterises cultural objects. Though particular cultural objects contribute to, or can be made to challenge, the always- to-be-reconstituted hegemony of any particular moment, that does not exhaust their meaning, and such readings always constitute only provisional resolutions of the cultural object's complexity.

Finally, culture is at once social and individual; that is, it exists both in the social world, between people, and reaches into and constitutes subjectivity. It follows from what I have said about the diversity of cultural forms that subjectivity must also be thought of as diverse and multiple, formed in the differing and often contradictory invitations of competing cultural forms. Subjectivity is thus profoundly historical – that is, it is made up out of historically contingent cultural materials, combined in various and individually specific ways. Especially in a period of rapid and dramatic social change like the nineteenth century, the cultural resources upon which individuals drew were subject to change also. To draw once again on the vocabulary of Mikhail Bakhtin, the process of becoming a subject is one in which the individual assimilates the words of social authority and makes them 'internally persuasive'.[13] In a period of unprecedented social transformations, people in the

nineteenth century had to find the means to render multiple and sometimes contradictory cultural forms internally persuasive.

In Chapters 2 and 3 of this book, I will be examining culture in two contradictory aspects; first in its capacity to act as a kind of social cement,
articulating the meanings which held nineteenth-century English
society together; second as a realm of contestation, articulating alternative possibilities which challenge or look beyond the immediate social
order. To that extent, these two chapters are both implicitly and explicitly concerned with the major dividing-line of class – how, in a very
patchily democratic society, the vast majority of the population either
accepted or contested their subordination. In the space of culture, this
may seem a crude or perhaps an artificial distinction: many cultural
objects do both of these things, or can be made to serve either end in
the multiple negotiations and renegotiations of their meaning that characterises their actual history. And it is finally this above all that I wish to
stress: that cultural objects of all kinds, from novels to paintings to articles of clothing, emerge from a particular history, from a particular
site within a society – and that they return to particular places also, so
that there is no space, no cultural realm, above the heat and dust of
social conflict. Cultural statements are not, nevertheless, the victims of
history, but active carriers of it, inflecting inherited meanings in new
directions and sometimes even inventing new meanings altogether.
The multiple social transformations of the nineteenth century meant
that it was a century especially rich in such new inflections and new
inventions.

2

CONNECTIONS – CULTURE AND THE SOCIAL ORDER

Nineteenth-century England was a social order undergoing rapid transformation, and one split along multiple different and overlapping lines of fissure. In this chapter I examine those cultural institutions, intellectual positions, and cultural forms, which acted cohesively, as a kind of social cement – which sought to counteract some at least of those lines of division. Above all, this chapter will be concerned with authority, with the attempt to sustain authority in its crucial social sites. Accordingly, I start with religion, the importance of which in nineteenth-century England can hardly be overestimated. I move on from there to consider some of the intellectual alternatives that were proposed to religion when its authority came to be questioned in the course of the century. In effect I argue that the collapse of the intellectual and social authority of religion posed a crisis of hegemony for the social order, which different intellectuals sought to solve in different ways. A crucial figure in the chapter is therefore Matthew Arnold (1822–88), whose project was explicitly to sustain the social authority of religion by refiguring it as 'culture'. But I conclude in a rather different vein, by considering those cultural forms – the large multi-plot novel, above all – which sought to encompass the whole social order. The very capacity to imagine a whole social order is radically extended via such cultural forms, and the chapter ends with a brief consideration of the political ambivalence of such acts of imagination.

Religion in Society

I wish to begin by considering the central role of religion in nineteenth-century society – or rather, the role of the churches, for I wish to look into how these various institutions acted as locations of social and cultural authority. This entails approaching the churches from a one-sidedly social, and even political, direction, in a manner that is bound to provoke a charge of reductiveness. Let me say, then, that I do not believe that the meaning of religious activity is to be reduced to the needs of social order. In this belief, I will not be following a line of somewhat cynical nineteenth-century conservatives, who precisely believed that religion was to be encouraged as a useful support of good order and government – witness the words of the Duke of Wellington: 'I consider that the attendance at divine service in publick is a duty upon every individual in high station, who has a large house and many servants, and whose example might influence the conduct of others.'[1] But I *will* be considering the churches as often competing locations of social and cultural power and authority; what is at stake in the many and furious nineteenth-century theological debates is the large question of how that authority is to be secured and renewed. Thus, these debates often revolved around the relation of church and state, the authority of the priest or minister within the church, and around the role of the godly in wider secular society. In reviewing some of the movements of renewal and defence that sought to transform the churches in the nineteenth century, I shall be stressing the social visions, the imaginative social relations, which appear to me to be animating them.

This may not seem to approach the essence of Christianity. Let me compound my mistake, then, by asserting that part of the peculiar power of religion and of religious experience is its capacity to reach into the soul (I speak metaphorically) of those who assent or are brought to assent to it. Thus when, from the 1830s and 1840s onwards, the intellectual and philosophical grounds of Christianity became increasingly insecure, this was not a matter, for many people, of painless loss and transfer to some other system of belief. On the contrary, it could provoke acute and intimate reassessments, involving sometimes debilitating doubts and anxieties. Part of the cultural history of the nineteenth century is the story of these reassessments, from the poetry of Tennyson (1809–92), Arthur Clough (1819–61) and Matthew Arnold, to the writings of Thomas Carlyle (1795–1881), the novels of George Eliot

(1819–80) and indeed innumerable other writers and novelists. This is a history of reimagined social relations, but one with searching personal reach.

In the first place, then, I wish to examine the social visions that are present in all forms of religious practice, and which were indeed at the heart of many of the disputes both within the Church of England in the nineteenth century, and between the Church of England and Nonconformity. But I also wish to examine the churches as locations of cultural production, both narrowly (in terms of the cultural forms which were literally located in church buildings), and more widely (in terms of the massive production of magazines, newspapers, tracts, polemics and religious books associated with the churches).

At the beginning of the nineteenth century, in a predominantly rural country, there was indeed a network of parishes which, with varying degrees of efficiency, meant a network of clergy distributed across the country. The Church of England could perhaps claim majority allegiance among English people, but it faced competition from a variety of different Nonconformist denominations, some recent, like Methodism, and some, like the Quakers and the Independents, with histories reaching back into the seventeenth century. These denominations had differing regional strengths, and as the century progressed, began to become increasingly differentiated in class terms. By the end of the century, the churches still retained much of their authority in rural England, but the massive growth of urban England had substantially defeated them. Despite extraordinary efforts at church building and parochial reorganisation, neither the Church of England nor the Dissenting churches captured the allegiance of the majority of the urban working class. Moreover, the intellectual prestige of religion was largely broken. It is in this broad context that the following account of the churches and religion in nineteenth-century England is offered.

Owen Chadwick, a twentieth-century historian largely sympathetic to nineteenth-century Anglicanism, begins his chapter on the village church in the following way:

> In 1860 the idea of a village church was still embodied in some country parishes. The squire was in his pew, his friend the parson was in his stall, respectable farmers in pews, and on benches the labourers in smock frocks, delicately embroidered in front and back, their wives often in scarlet flannel shawls. The men sat passive, some unable to read, but silent with a stolid attentiveness, not liking to be

absent because of the squire or the farmer or habit, but in no way sorry to be there, men without hostility and with quiet acceptance.[2]

This is a view of the village church which captivated the nineteenth century, and continued to captivate Chadwick as he wrote some seventy years after the nineteenth century was over. It is more of a vision of the social hierarchy than a strictly religious vision, and of course it makes massive suppositions about the attitudes of the labourers as they sit on the benches at the back of the church. But read in a sceptical or uncharitable spirit, it surely does reveal a fundamental truth about the rural church – as an institution in which the social hierarchy is precisely reproduced in the layout of the church, and in which patterns of social command and patronage are reinforced on a weekly basis.

To describe the church in this way is to concede the fundamental Erastianism of the Church of England; that is, it is to agree that the purposes of religion have been subordinated to purposes of state. The Church of England is indeed, historically, Erastian, inasmuch as the head of the Church is also the head of state. But the varieties of church renewal and reform that galvanised the Church in the nineteenth century sought to remedy a much more widespread and commonplace Erastianism as it characterised the eighteenth-century and Regency Church. This was a church dominated by pluralism (the practice of the same individual accumulating multiple church offices), and where the status of the clergy as a simple arm of the governing class was only too apparent – clergy often served as magistrates, were overwhelmingly drawn from gentry families, and formed an obvious alliance with the squire as figures of authority. In the early part of the century clergy participated happily in a range of activities later thought inappropriate, so that the image of the fox-hunting vicar came to sum up the problems with an unreformed church. The various religious movements that swept the Church, some much more profoundly than others, all sought to resecure the authority of religion in social life in ways that would protect it from the reproaches caused by that worldly eighteenth-century inheritance.

The first such movement is Evangelicalism, a rediscovery of serious or Gospel-based religion that began as early as the mid-eighteenth century, but which reached the height of its influence in the early nineteenth century. This was a movement that swept through both the Dissenting churches and sections of the Church of England. Though later it became associated with dogmatic conservatism, in the early nineteenth century it is perhaps better thought of as indicating a cultural and social

style and ambition, rather than any specific doctrinal positions. Evangelicalism was characterised by the discovery of seriousness, a desire to give
first place to religious concerns in all the affairs of life, an insistence on
the experience of conversion as an aspect of personal religious life, an
avoidance of profane and secular pursuits, and a sometimes militant
desire to see such codes carried into all aspects of life. As such it might
be thought to be hostile to non-religious cultural forms, and indeed at
the doctrinal level Evangelicals often found it hard to reconcile an interest in secular culture with their dogmatic convictions.[3] But we must also
see Evangelicalism as the driving energy behind much cultural production, for Evangelicals were the principal movers in such ventures as the
British and Foreign Bible Society (founded 1804), the Church Missionary Society (founded 1797), and a variety of other charitable and religious societies. So successful were the efforts of the former that the
Oxford press became the largest printers of bibles in the world by
mid-century, producing over a million bibles in 1860; a Bible Society
New Testament cost one penny, and sold eight million copies between
1884 and 1903.[4] Quite apart from this obvious form of cultural reproduction, Evangelicals were prominent in the writing and distribution
of tracts, in the founding and editing of magazines and reviews of various shades of religious opinion and denominational allegiance, and in
some appropriate political campaigns, most notably the campaigns for
the abolition of the slave trade and then slavery itself.

If there was a social and political vision at the heart of all this, it is not
always apparent – or not always as apparent as in the following quotation from a tract by one of the famous early nineteenth-century Evangelical clergymen, Legh Richmond (1772–1827):

> . . . how comfortable is the lot of the industrious poor, whose hearts
> have learned the lesson of gratitude in the school of heavenly wisdom.
> For them, as mercifully as for their richest neighbour, the sun shines,
> the rain descends, the earth brings forth her increase, the flower
> blossoms, the birds sing; their wants are few, and contentment
> makes them less. How great the blessing of being poor in this world,
> but rich in faith, and a chosen inheritance in a better![5]

It is not difficult to decode this as motivated at least as much by a vision
of social deference as by religion. Certainly the political allegiance of
Dissenting Evangelicalism was likely to vary from that of the grandees
of the Clapham Sect (men like William Wilberforce [1759–1833] and

John Venn [1759–1813]), a writer like Hannah More (1745–1833) – whose tract *The Shepherd of Salisbury Plain* (1810) is a nauseous homily, like Legh Richmond's, in favour of thrift and social deference – and the editors of the *Christian Record*, an ultra-Evangelical newspaper founded in 1825 which 'regarded theological and political liberalism as two facets of one ill'.[6] The crucial point is perhaps not so much the explicit social vision, as the capacity of Evangelicalism to perform two essential tasks: to refound the legitimacy of the leaders of society, by contrast with the flagrant unseriousness of the lives of many such leaders during the early nineteenth century; and to provide a defining sense of social and cultural identity for substantial sections of the English middle class in the same period.[7] If such a thing as Victorianism existed – and the question is controversial[8] – then Evangelicalism is the best candidate to serve as its parent.

The Oxford Movement, though theologically contrasted with Evangelicalism, was similarly a call to seriousness, and likewise sought to re-establish the authority of the Church – though this time, very explicitly the Church of England (to begin with) and not Dissent. Beginning in Oxford in the 1830s, it remained rooted in Oxford in terms of its principal characters, and appealed especially to the rural clergy. Its theological distinctiveness lay in its claim of apostolic succession for the clergy of the Church of England, but it was prompted into existence by what it saw as the attacks upon the authority of the Church by a Reformed Parliament. So it is not difficult to see this as an essentially reactionary movement, and it was not difficult to do so in the nineteenth century itself – John Tulloch, looking back in 1885, could say that 'it was a new Toryism, or designed to be such, as well as a new Sacerdotalism'.[9] Indeed, leading figures in the movement such as John Henry Newman (1801–90) and John Keble (1792–1866), not to mention lesser figures such as Richard Hurrell Froude (1803–36), proclaimed their hostility to liberalism as one of their main principles. Thus Newman could proclaim, in a sermon from the early 1830s, that:

> Here I will not shrink from uttering my firm conviction, that it would be a gain to this country, were it vastly more superstitious, more bigoted, more gloomy, more fierce in its religion, than at present it shows itself to be. Not, of course, that I think the tempers of mind herein implied desirable, which would be an evident absurdity; but I think them infinitely more desirable and more promising than a heathen obduracy, and a cold, self-sufficient, self-wise tranquillity.[10]

The analogies with other, more obviously secular social movements of the 1830s are apparent – notably with 'Young England', a social and political movement which sought to revive the paternalistic and authoritarian social relations of the Middle Ages as an antidote to contemporary liberalism and laissez-faire. But Newman's sermons perhaps do not provide the most characteristic expression of the Oxford Movement. Neither perhaps do the Tracts themselves, the series of theological pamphlets published in the early 1830s by Newman and his fellow 'Tractarians', which served to make the movement a party within the Church and then a recognisable social and cultural force. For the most typical spirit of the Oxford Movement, we should perhaps look to the volume of poems that Keble published in 1827 called *The Christian Year*. These poems, characterised by mild piety and designed to give imaginative support to the rituals of the Christian liturgy as realised in the Anglican Prayer Book, are premised on the passing seasons as observed in a rural parish. That seductive vision of the village church, set out by Owen Chadwick above, pervades the Oxford Movement, and Keble's own ministry to the village of Hursley in Hampshire provided a model of paternal care and parochial piety.

The theology of the Oxford Movement – its insistence on the *Catholic* nature of the Church of England, and on the apostolic authority of its bishops and clergy, almost immediately laid it open to charges of sympathy with Rome; and these charges were soon to be given credence. Indeed, the story of Newman's secession to Rome is one of the great personal and theological dramas of the nineteenth century, though he was only one of many high-placed converts to Roman Catholicism from the 1840s onwards. But the Oxford Movement appeared Romanising in other ways as well, for the second generation of the movement was responsible for a revival of ritualism in church services which eventually spread to areas of the Church and Dissent theologically very distinct from Anglo-Catholicism itself. Such was the persistent anti-Catholicism of England that the introduction of the wearing of a surplice could cause rioting in Exeter in 1845;[11] but later in the century more elaborate rituals became widespread, along with more elaborate vestments for the clergy, decorated church furniture, and the revival of stained glass. The Oxford Movement thus contributed very directly to much characteristic nineteenth-century cultural production

The Oxford Movement, then, contained a deeply conservative social vision, imaginatively centred on the village priest, and theologically rooted in the apostolic authority of the Church. As a particular social and cultural formation, it was based very strongly in Oxford, the old unreformed clerical Oxford hostile to liberalism and many of the signs of modernity. Like Evangelicalism before it, it too sought to bolster the authority of religion, but it sought to do so by insisting on the authority of the Church of England; for those to whom ultimately this seemed insufficient, then a suitable home appeared in the Church of Rome. As I have suggested, the vision of authority and society that it offered was cognate with other versions of paternalism available in the 1830s and 1840s, notably 'Young England', Carlyle's *Past and Present* (1844) and the Catholic and Gothic romanticism expressed in *Contrasts* (1836) by Augustus Pugin (1812–52).

The social location of the Oxford Movement, and its conservative political agenda, are readily apparent. From the 1840s onwards, other movements within the Church of England drew on very different theological inspirations, seeking in some cases to renew the appeal of the Church and to make it more inclusive. Thus the Broad Church Movement, associated with Thomas Arnold (1795–1842), the headmaster of Rugby school, and Arthur Stanley (1815–81), the Dean of Westminster, sought to enlarge the scope of the Church of England by insisting that it was a national church and ought thus to find ways to reinclude the nonconforming churches. The perceived social and political crisis of the late 1840s provoked a small group within the Church of England to proclaim themselves Christian Socialists. Taking theological inspiration from F. D. Maurice (1805–72), men such as Charles Kingsley (1819–75) and Thomas Hughes (1822–96) combined Christian moralism with hostility to the miseries created by the operations of crude market forces – a generous and inclusive vision for the Church, marred at times by paternalism and didacticism. Still later in the century, in the 1880s, another period of perceived social crisis produced a comparable effort to extend and renew the influence of religion in the direction of social responsibility, the so-called 'Settlement Movement' associated with Samuel Barnett (1844–1913) and Arnold Toynbee (1852–83). Like the Christian Socialist Movement of thirty years earlier, this too emphasised the social responsibilities of the Church, especially to the crying evils of poverty and misery that characterised the modern city; but here too there was a definite element of paternalism mixed in with the social responsibility, as groups of Oxford undergraduates were recruited for social work in settlements in the East End.

Implicit in all these efforts at renewal in the Church of England is a sense of the Church as a national church – a belief that the Church either is, or ought to be, the natural centre of religious authority in society. No such belief ever characterised the Dissenting churches, though in differing ways they also provided locations of cultural and social authority, capable of becoming real centres of class leadership. It is important, of course, to recognise the tremendous variety of the Non-conformist churches, both in their theology and in their social constituencies. It is important too to recognise their sense of exclusion from national life – they were excluded from holding parliamentary or municipal office until the repeal of the Test and Corporation Acts in 1828, were excluded from the universities of Oxford and Cambridge until the 1850s, but had nevertheless to get married in the parish church, register the baptisms of their children in the church baptismal register, bury their dead in the church graveyard, and pay church rates. While all of these grievances were gradually addressed, they jointly contributed to a sense of exclusion, to a sense of the Nonconformist churches forming a separate connection within society. For some this sense of separateness from and opposition to the established Church was just the point of belonging to a Nonconformist chapel; Joseph Arch (1826–1919), union leader of the agricultural workers, who grew up in rural Warwickshire in the 1830s, consciously rejected the Church of England because of its association with the oppressive paternalism of parson and squire, and joined instead a small local dissenting congregation.[12] But for others, membership of the Baptist or Independent church was a badge of middle-class respectability, especially in provincial towns and cities; such churches could provide the basis for a regulated social and cultural life, and the history of the nineteenth century was the history of their gradual recognition by, and inclusion in, the state. John Bright (1811–89), for example, was the first Nonconformist to enter the Cabinet, in 1868. When Joseph Chamberlain (1836–1914), a Unitarian, preached the 'social gospel' in Birmingham in the 1860s and 1870s, he was in effect announcing the social coming of age of provincial Nonconformity.

Unitarianism, however, was untypical of Nonconformity, and in an account of the social location of culture deserves a special mention. For Unitarianism, a small sect descended from eighteenth-century Presbyterianism, provided what was in effect a kind of intellectual and cultural leadership for the middle classes of many provincial cities, and indeed for sections of London middle-class radicalism. In many provincial cities like Manchester, Liverpool, Newcastle, Norwich, Leicester and Birmingham, it was Unitarians – often wealthy, and recruited from

leaders of cultural production such as journalists, lawyers and writers –
who were especially active in the promotion of such activities as
athenaeums, literary and philosophical societies, museums, municipal
libraries and orchestras. In London, the Radical circle around W. J.
Fox (1786–1864) and the Unitarian magazine the *Monthly Repository*
extended to John Stuart Mill (1806–73) and Harriet Taylor, Harriet
Martineau (1802–76), Robert Browning (1812–89) and R. H. Horne
(1803–84). Though such a circle included those who were either not
Unitarians or who, like Fox himself, moved away from Unitarianism,
the sect itself provided its organising core. In short, Unitarianism, in
both its London and its provincial forms, was a distinct formation within
nineteenth-century society, which provided intellectual and cultural
leadership for the progressive middle class well beyond what its numerical membership would suggest.

Religion and 'Culture'

Religion, then, provided one of the centres of authority in nineteenth-
century society – literally so in its institutional form, though these varying churches were to some extent in competition with each other, but
also more generally in terms of the intellectual and spiritual authority
of a traditional religious faith. So what happened when that faith
began to be threatened from a variety of different directions – as was
the case in mid-century? For many intellectuals of this period, the question posed itself as the search for an alternative ground of justification
for both personal and social life.

This is a dilemma articulated acutely by Matthew Arnold, writing in
1873, in what was to prove his most popular book during his lifetime,
Literature and Dogma:

> When our philosophical Liberal friends say, that by universal suf-
> frage, public meetings, Church-disestablishment, marrying one's
> deceased wife's sister, secular schools, industrial development, man
> can very well live; and that if he studies the writings, say, of Mr.
> Herbert Spencer into the bargain, he will be perfect, he 'will have in
> modern and congenial language the truisms common to all systems of
> morality,' and the Bible is become quite old-fashioned and super-
> fluous for him;-when our philosophical friends now say this, the

masses, far from checking them, are disposed to applaud them to the echo. Yet assuredly, of conduct, which is more than three-fourths of human life, the Bible, whatever people may thus think and say, is the great inspirer; so that from the great inspirer of more than three-fourths of human life the masses of our society seem now to be cutting themselves off. This promises, certainly, if it does not already constitute, a very unsettled condition of things. And the cause of it lies in the Bible being made to depend on a story, or set of asserted facts, which it is impossible to verify; and which hard-headed people, therefore, treat as either an imposture, or a fairy-tale that discredits all which is found in connexion with it.[13]

In *Literature and Dogma*, Arnold sets out to rescue the Bible, but he adopts an extraordinary plan for doing so; he concedes all the criticism of it as a set of supernatural beliefs, or 'set of asserted facts', but seeks to retain it as literature – that is, read properly and not literally, the Bible animates and inspires profound moral truths whose truth is independent of the particular stories to which they are attached. In the passage I have quoted, it can be seen what is at stake in this strategy. On the one hand Arnold is contemptuous of the efforts of secularising liberalism to provide any comparably animated or emotionally attractive basis for morality. But on the other hand, no effort to retain the authority of the Bible, and religion with it, will survive if that authority is seen to depend on the literal truth of what is asserted in it. To retain the affective power of religion, therefore – to retain its capacity to regulate the conduct of 'the masses', to speak to them in tones at once moral and emotionally rich – it has to be seen to depend, not on its 'fairy-tale' elements, but on the underlying moral truths for which the fairy-tale is unessential. In short, it has to be re-presented as 'culture'.

Arnold's purpose in *Literature and Dogma* is consistent with attitudes and purposes expressed across the range of his writings: the authority of the centralising and unifying institutions of the state is to be re-established on surer grounds than the more short-sighted officers and beneficiaries of that authority themselves recognise. Institutions which get in the way of such central authority, notably the Dissenting churches, are signal embarrassments to this project, and Arnold accordingly waged a lifelong campaign of denigration against them. The fundamental recognition, for Arnold, is that the old unquestioned sources of authority and cohesion are now in the past; as he writes in *The Popular Education of France* in 1861, 'we in England have had, in our great aristocratical and ecclesiastical institutions, a principle of cohesion and unity';[14] the problem now is to find ways of rediscovering some such principle based on something other than mere authority, and which will have an affective reach comparable to that of religion. Arnold himself was a great educationalist; but the overarching principle which informed both his educational ideas and his writing was the notion of 'culture' as a way of combating 'anarchy'.[15]

This was only one way in which one of the central social and intellectual problems of the nineteenth century was sought to be resolved, though it is especially notable in the context of the present study in that Arnold placed such an emphasis upon the central place of 'culture' as a way of addressing the dissolution of authority in nineteenth-century society. Other great intellectuals addressed it in cognate ways, though of course with very different solutions. Thomas Carlyle, described by his biographer Froude as a 'Calvinist without the theology', carried the accents of religion into his secular writings; though he preached a secular message of duty, work and social responsibility, this was secured by a religious attitude which metaphorically 'translated' the supernatural, and apprehended it in the operations of history.[16] By contrast John Stuart Mill welcomed the demise of paternalism and all forms of arbitrary authority, including religion; but he was prepared to trust to the workings of education and the growth of sympathy and feelings of sociality to supplement and counteract the operations of the market. Finally, Herbert Spencer (1820–1903), and with him a group of mid-century intellectuals attracted to Positivism and the philosophical and social promise of science, came to believe that there were laws of social development that were intrinsic to the working and progress of society, which needed no external or religious sanction, but need only to be consciously adhered to by all members of the social order. Such ideas are discussed more fully below.

Political Economy, Positivism and Darwinism

Religion had a particular importance in the nineteenth century, as a force, to use Matthew Arnold's words, for 'cohesion and unity', because it took obvious institutional form. But it was by no means the only intellectual system which sought to provide explanations for the way a whole society operated, and, with this, the capacity to think through the duties and responsibilities of individuals and groups within society. Other, more secular conceptions of the social order took shape alongside religion in the early nineteenth century. As I suggested in Chapter 1, hegemony is not necessarily a matter of consistent and non-contradictory elements, but rather a matter of the always provisional construction of a sense of cohesion. So in considering the essentially secular ideas of political economy, Utilitarianism, Positivism and Darwinism, we need not assume that they fall into any logical or consistent relation with religion – or indeed with each other. On the contrary, such logical and consistent positions are just what require to be achieved, whether by the great institutions of the state – as they manufacture legislation, pronounce judicial sentence, and thunder in leading articles and reviews – or by individuals, as they struggle to make sense of the world and their place in it. Naturally enough, such struggles were conducted with more or less success, as people and institutions brought the multiple and disparate ideologies that assailed them into more or less consistent shape.

The most important of these secular conceptions of society was political economy, which achieved the status of a social and intellectual orthodoxy at the beginning of the nineteenth century, and retained it right through until the 1880s. Though modern economics are descended from political economy, the latter was rather more ambitious, since it sought to explain the whole movement of society in terms of the economic behaviour of its members. Looking back to Adam Smith and the *Wealth of Nations* of 1776, political economy was developed as an intellectual system above all in David Ricardo's *Principles of Political Economy and Taxation* (1817), Thomas Malthus's *Essay on the Principle of Population* (1798; revised in later editions) and John Stuart Mill's *Principles of Political Economy* (1848). In these texts, of various degrees of technical difficulty, there emerged a conception of society as governed by a series of 'laws' which could not be meddled with; attempts to do so by governments, trade unions or even well-meaning individuals were bound to be unsuccessful or even harmful. Political economy, however, is important above all because of the way it gained an extraordinary ascendancy over the English middle-class mind – it was influential, for example, on such key legislative acts as the New Poor Law of 1834, which sought to abolish outdoor relief to the able-bodied poor, and which marks the end of what has been called the 'moral economy' governing the social relations between rich and poor in the countryside.[17] Crude forms of political economy led to the notion of 'laissez-faire', or to such ideas as the 'iron law of wages', by which the level of wages was solely determined by the ratio of capital to population: that is, if you want to increase the level of wages, you have to change the ratio by decreasing the population. Indeed, it was probably Malthus's doctrines on the expansion of population, and its tendency to outgrow its means of subsistence, that had the widest popular resonance. This was a doctrine explicitly advanced by Malthus as a corrective to what he took to be Utopian ideas of human improvement, and throughout the nineteenth century his principle of population continued to provide a kind of model for the secular and law-governed understanding of human society. Such was the continuing efficacy of political economy as a kind of secular orthodoxy that when John Ruskin published *Unto this Last* in the *Cornhill Magazine* in 1860 – essays that attacked political economy – the outcry was so great that the editor, the novelist W. M. Thackeray (1811–63), was forced to discontinue it.

Political economy may appear unpropitious ground for culture, if by culture is meant that narrower definition of essentially imaginative aesthetic forms. And indeed, apart from the explicitly didactic *Illustrations of Political Economy* (1832–34) which Harriet Martineau wrote to give fictional form to its central doctrines, it is hard to point to much culture in this narrower sense which animated it. But the characteristic cultural forms in which its laws and doctrines were embodied were rather different. We have already noticed the great textbooks in which the principles were established; in addition, there were innumerable pamphlets, magazine articles and reviews by which simplified versions were circulated. But political economy was at work, too, in the government reports – the so-called Blue Books – which formed an increasing part of state business from the 1830s onwards, pioneered indeed by the *Poor Law Report* which preceded the Act of 1834. So while political economy may appear hostile to 'culture', it was actually itself responsible for, or part of, the massive panoply of state textual production in the nineteenth century, and to that extent can be seen as one of the century's most characteristic cultural forms.

Nevertheless, it could hardly, on its own, serve as the basis for any moral, personal or social system that would be at all affectively satisfying. This remained the case even when its tenets were buttressed by the moral system known as Utilitarianism, which sought to measure all human actions not by any absolute standard, in the manner of religion, but by the simple test of whether they contributed more or less good to the sum of human happiness. Jeremy Bentham (1748–1832) is the philosopher most closely associated with Utilitarianism, but John Stuart Mill subscribed to a modified version of it throughout his life. Mill's breakdown as a young man in the 1820s – finely described in his *Autobiography* – precisely focused on the aridity of political economy and Utilitarianism as they proposed themselves as whole guides to life.[18]

It is often said that political economy, and with it Utilitarianism, are the natural accompaniments of the new industrialism of the late eighteenth century and nineteenth century. In fact, however, the capitalist economy of the English countryside provided the most important model for a mode of thought whose power lay in its capacity to conceive of social life as a whole system in which the various parts interrelated with each other, so that as one varied, the others varied in proportionate ways. Ricardo's *Principles of Political Economy and Taxation* (1817) is the book which thought through this systematicity most rigorously; in it, the tripartite organisation of English agriculture into landlord, farmer and labourer reappears as the mutually varying values of rent, profit and wages. Both the attractiveness of political economy, and its insufficiency as a hegemonising cultural form, lay in its success in theorising so powerfully and elegantly this economic aspect of social life, while leaving other aspects of life untouched.

I am suggesting that there was in effect a strategic difficulty for nineteenth-century intellectuals in constructing a hegemonic cultural and intellectual system that might replace religion. This is precisely the difficulty that Arnold confronts in the long extract I have quoted from *Literature and Dogma*. Political economy, the most distinctive early nineteenth-century mode of thought, with large pretensions to explaining the whole operations of the social order, was nevertheless transparently incapable of real hegemonic reach, if only because it lacked the affective power of religion. Intellectuals sought a variety of other ways to ground their accounts of everyday life in satisfying general accounts of the social life and of its ultimate destination. At stake in such attempts was the capacity to find a basis for socially and ethically responsible behaviour – for 'conduct, which is more than three-fourths of human life', to use Arnold's phrase. I want briefly to consider two such attempts – Positivism and Darwinism.

Positivism is a system of thought which attracted a wide variety of thinkers from the 1830s onwards, most prominently John Stuart Mill and George Eliot. It was set out at large and in dogmatic form by the French philosopher Auguste Comte (1798–1857), but its appeal was much wider than its dogmatic form. At its most ambitious, it offered a vision of social reorganisation based upon positively known scientific laws, and drawing affective inspiration from a so-called 'Religion of Humanity'. In fact it is best to think of it as a version of humanism; that is, a belief that human behaviour is ultimately to be explained by an account of human nature, and that the ultimate grounds for moral and social action are human and not supernatural. Though Comte and other English writers sought to systematise the sciences, this is only really a preliminary moment in the effort to provide systematic and scientifically based accounts of social life. There were Positivist churches, with newly invented liturgies drawing upon a calendar of secular saints. George Eliot's poem 'O may I join the choir invisible' was used in the Positivist rite. Positivism, in this particular sense, looked back to the Catholic Church as a model of social organisation that was at once practical and affective; Positivists sought to reinvent such a social organisation but this time based not on the authority of religion but on the more certain – positive – authority of science.

If we think of Positivism as a version of humanism, then the solution it provides to the strategic difficulty posed by the weakness of religion becomes clearer. For George Eliot, a writer profoundly influenced by Positivism, humanism meant a translation of religious categories into the human terms which she saw as underlying them. In her novels she could thus retain the affective reach of religious experience – even allow it to continue to be thought of as religious experience – while seeking to ground it on the actual affective and emotional life of human beings. What at first appears to be the most radical aspect of her writing, her atheism, turns out rather to be a fundamental way of refounding the affective and moral cement of social life. Reading the novels reinforces this bracing of social ties, because in reading them we are led to feel for others elsewhere in the social scale from ourselves; we learn, in that telling phrase from one of George Eliot's essays, the 'extension of our sympathies'.[19]

Positivism attracted a number of intellectuals, from George Eliot and her partner George Henry Lewes (1817–78), to John Stuart Mill, Harriet Martineau and Frederic Harrison (1831–1923). It is important because it represents one of the most significant nineteenth-century attempts explicitly to base an alternative religion on science. But there were many, less dogmatically developed efforts to base ethical behaviour on science; the affective thinness of these efforts is just what Arnold mocked when he contemptuously referred to the writings of Herbert Spencer as forming the basis for a renovated ethical life. Spencer

LIVERPOOL JOHN MOORES UNIVERSITY
LEARNING SERVICES

might indeed be taken as the exemplary nineteenth-century instance of a more widespread positivism, understood as meaning the belief that moral and social life can be based upon the operations of the natural and biological world. It was in fact Spencer, not Darwin, who coined the phrase 'the survival of the fittest' to characterise the processes of evolution; more importantly, his system worked by a series of analogies between organic and social life that sought to regulate social life by its obedience to natural law.

Spencer was already an established intellectual by the time Charles Darwin (1809–82) published *The Origin of Species* in 1859, but he went on to incorporate a version of evolutionism in his intellectual system. Evolutionary theory is undoubtedly the single most important intellectual achievement of nineteenth-century England, but here I want to draw attention to two aspects of the Darwinian revolution. First, Darwin's theory was not unexpected. Quite apart from the numerous anticipations of evolutionary thought from the late eighteenth century onwards, the theory sprang directly from currents of thought already well established before the 1850s – notably Malthusian population theory, and even the natural theology which Darwin's theories displaced ('natural theology' is the widespread belief, or habit of mind, which discovers evidence of God's design in the workings of nature). In addition, the theory of evolution was dependent upon the discovery of geological time, firmly established in England by Sir Charles Lyell (1797–1875) in the 1830s; the antiquity of the earth was henceforth understood to be sufficiently great to allow the processes of natural selection to effect evolutionary change. So the publication of *The Origin of Species*, along with the simultaneous work of Alfred Russell Wallace (1823–1913), marks an epoch in nineteenth-century thought because of the stamp of authority that was given to ideas which were already widely current. But this leads to the second point. Evolutionary theory in biology rapidly established such prestige that it came to be used as a model for social thought also. From the 1870s onwards, Social Darwinism could serve as the intellectual basis for a number of socially conservative political ideas, providing them with an apparently unassailable sanction in natural law. Spencer's phrase 'the survival of the fittest' could be used – and was – to justify, for example, competition within the market both between individuals and between firms, justifying the ferocity of the most naked market forces as serving the higher goal of evolutionary progress. Or it could equally be used to justify colonial and imperial aggression, since the 'fittest' here could be interpreted to mean competing races.

By the end of the century, Social Darwinian ideas were thoroughly naturalised as ways of understanding social relations, and provided the opportunity both for triumphalism and profound anxiety: social forces – the expansion of the Empire, or the expansion of the slums – seemed to suggest either a higher evolutionary destiny for the English or the spawning of an underclass of the evolutionary unfit.

Social Darwinism was not the only way in which Darwinian ideas had an impact upon social thought. Indeed, many Darwinians, notably Thomas Huxley (1825–95) in *Ethics and Evolution* (1893), denied any connection between biological evolutionary processes and human morality. In the context of this chapter, however, the point of invoking such notions is that they provided one secular model of the way social life worked, which extended to compelling if rebarbative ethical and political positions. The consequences of Social Darwinian ideas with respect to the Empire are touched upon in Chapter 7 below.

Imagining the Social Whole

So far in this chapter, I have been considering the way that the cohesion and unity of social life could be maintained – how, that is, at the intellectual level, some foundational conception of coherent social life, and of people's ethical responsibilities in it, could be secured. In the remainder of this chapter I wish to discuss the very capacity to conceive of society as a whole, a capacity which actually became current in the nineteenth century, and was dependent upon certain nineteenth-century social developments.

Both political economy and Social Darwinism share the capacity to conceive of society as a system of interrelated parts. In the case of political economy, these various aspects of the system are such matters as rents, wages, profits; capital and labour. These are understood to be disposed in a set of complex mutually determining relationships; as one element of the system alters, so do the others in determinate ways. Similarly, Social Darwinism understands society as a dynamic system, in which the various elements are in mutual relationships of competition, adaptation and survival; the action of each individual can be understood as contributing to the wider progress of the whole. But these are by no means the only nineteenth-century systems of thought or cultural forms which succeed in imagining society in this systematic or totalising way.

Sociology was a nineteenth-century invention; the word was coined (by both Auguste Comte and Herbert Spencer) by analogy with biology, and the new study was premised on the belief that it was possible to study society in the same scientific way. The analogy with biology goes deeper than this, however; in the work of Herbert Spencer especially, society is conceived as an organism, and its various parts have analogies with various organic functions. Contemporaneous with this emergence of sociology, Karl Marx was developing a systematic way of thinking about the social order, drawing upon political economy to do so. And this same period at mid-century also produced a series of great panoramic novels in English, which, though proceeding differently, sought to conceive society inclusively, with its various parts mutually interconnected in significant ways. One might add to this the panoramic pictures of W. P. Frith (1819–1909); canvases such as *Derby Day* (1857) and *The Railway Station* (1863) similarly sought to provide inclusive metaphors of the whole social order. In short, the nineteenth century produced a number of powerful modes of representation in which the totality of the social order was imagined, and in which the various parts of society were conceived as acting together in mutually connected and defining ways.

These are all intellectual and cultural achievements that are characteristic of the nineteenth century. It seems worth asking, then, what nineteenth-century *social* developments underlay them. Though national political union in England long predated the nineteenth century, there were certainly a series of unifying factors in the social life of the century which can be considered to underpin these achievements. In what ways was nineteenth-century English society developing towards a more unified and coherent social system?

First, the transport system shrunk distances in dramatic ways in the course of the century. National systems of canals and tarmacadamed roads were succeeded from the 1830s onwards by a national network of railways; journeys that had only recently taken days could now be made in a matter of hours. By the end of the 1840s there was a recognisable national system by which all parts of Britain were connected. The railways brought with them other kinds of standardisation, most notably 'railway time' – though this was anticipated by the requirements of the stagecoach; timetables meant that all the clocks in the different parts of the country had to be set to the same standard (Greenwich Mean Time was established as an international standard in 1885). Other national systems followed, notably in education from 1870; in addition, national newspapers, national circuits for entertainment, nationally devised systems of policing were all either nineteenth-century innovations, or achieved a depth and penetration unprecedented before.

But perhaps the most important gauge of a new national cohesion, even homogeneity, was the establishment, during the nineteenth century, of a national standard in language. At the beginning of the nineteenth century England was a country of mutually incomprehensible dialects; when Harriet Martineau, for example, travelled as a young woman from Norwich to visit relations in Newcastle upon Tyne, she was unable to understand the speech of agricultural labourers in the grounds of Burleigh House in Stamford, Lincolnshire – a distance of less than one hundred miles. Even the members of the governing class spoke with strong regional accents. By contrast, at the end of the century the educational system and ease of transport had quite transformed this situation. The governing class now spoke with a distinctive 'public-school accent'; and while regional *dialects* certainly survived, they were being supplanted or modified by strong local *accents*, based on the great urban industrial conurbations of the West Midlands, Tyneside, Manchester, and of course London. The regional dialectal diversity of the beginning of the century had been replaced by a broadly class-related system of regional accents in relation to a strong and nationally homogenising standard enforced in part by the education system. These transformations within English were accompanied by the secular decline of Welsh, and Irish and Scottish Gaelic. Certainly at the end of the nineteenth century, England at least was an exceptionally monoglot country.

It may be, then, that the capacity to think about society as a unified system, whose parts are coherently and systematically interrelated, depended upon these objective transformations, which made clear the actual interconnections and increasing homogeneity in English society. Whether this was the case or not, there is no doubt that this capacity was a distinctive nineteenth-century achievement, though an ethically and politically ambivalent one. On the one hand it entails the ability to think, in rational and secular ways, about the movements of a whole society, and to recognise the interrelatedness of the people who make up that society – a recognition that can have positive and benign ethical consequences. On the other hand, it may be that the assumption of the unifying overview, the perspective from which 'society' appears as coherent and interrelated, is an assumption of a position of authority – indeed, that the very insistence upon this coherence falsifies a much messier reality and encourages a sense of the very homogenisation which it seeks only to describe.

The cultural form to which these questions apply most acutely in mid-century is the novel, especially a number of the ambitious and all-embracing novels from the 1840s, 1850s and 1860s which attempted to figure the range and movement of a whole society. Novels such as those of Dickens's maturity, from *Dombey and Son* (1846–48), to *David Copperfield* (1849–50), *Bleak House* (1852–53), *Little Dorrit* (1855–57) and *Our Mutual Friend* (1864–65); Thackeray's *Vanity Fair* (1847–48) and *The Newcomes* (1853–55); George Eliot's *Middlemarch* (1871–72) and *Daniel Deronda* (1876), all sought to encompass the social and geographical spectrum of English life. Naturally, the particular ways that they do so vary, and the kinds of connection that they seek to establish between the different parts of society vary also.

One primary way of figuring social inteconnectedness is the use of the encompassing metaphor, such as the fog in the opening paragraphs of *Bleak House,* or the repeated use of the prison in *Little Dorrit.* Consider these paragraphs from the opening of *Bleak House*:

Fog everywhere. Fog up the river, where it flows among green aits and meadows; fog down the river, where it rolls defiled among the tiers of shipping, and the waterside pollutions of a great (and dirty) city. Fog on the Essex marshes, fog on the Kentish heights. Fog creeping into the cabooses of collier-brigs; fog lying out on the yards, and hovering in the rigging of great ships; fog drooping on the gunwales of barges and small boats. Fog in the eyes and throats of ancient Greenwich pensioners, wheezing by the firesides of their wards; fog in the stem and bowl of the afternoon pipe of the wrathful skipper, down in his close cabin; fog cruelly pinching the toes and fingers of his shivering little 'prentice boy on deck. Chance people on the bridges peeping over the parapets into a nether sky of fog, with fog all round them, as if they were up in a balloon, and hanging in the misty clouds.

Gas looming through the fog in divers places in the streets, much as the sun may, from the spongey fields, be seen to loom by husbandman and ploughboy. Most of the shops lighted two hours before their time – as the gas seems to know, for it has a haggard and unwilling look.

The raw afternoon is rawest, and the dense fog is densest, and the muddy streets are muddiest, near that leaden-headed old obstruction, appropriate ornament for the threshold of a leaden-headed old corporation: Temple Bar. And hard by Temple Bar, in Lincoln's Inn Hall, at the very heart of the fog, sits the Lord High Chancellor in his High Court of Chancery.[20]

These are striking paragraphs, and represent a considerable effort of the imagination, at the same time as they draw upon socially established modes of perception. The fog is being used here, initially, as a figure of *connection*; it is a way of imaginatively drawing together people from the extremes of London. This requires an especially mobile narrative perspective, which enables us to hold together the city of London, to conceive of it from end to end, and at the same time to view up close the diverse figures who are picked from it. But if the fog is initially a metaphor of connection, it is also a metaphor of obstruction; the last paragraph associates it most strongly with just those unreformed institutions against which the novel has been written – the Corporation of London, and above all, the Court of Chancery. Figuratively, then, the fog both acts to connect the disparate parts of society, embracing them in one encompassing act of metaphoric connection, and also to assert the leaden and obfuscatory character of the institutions that actually rule contemporary England.

Dickens is the master of such acts of grand figurative encompassment. But his novels are notable also for their efforts to connect disparate social classes by means of multiple and densely connected narratives. The novels of his maturity are distinguished by this effort at connection, this attempt to reveal the social and affective bonds that bind people together, but which remain obscured by the alienating dissociation of the classes from each other, and by the obfuscating power of blocked and unregenerate institutions and social attitudes. The narrative connections which bind people together – in *Bleak House*, for example, Lady Dedlock with Jo the crossing-sweeper, the highest and the lowest in the land – are simultaneously assertions of the obligations and relationships that *ought* to bind together the social classes.[21] The cultural form of the novel, as inflected in these ambitious novels of Dickens's maturity, becomes a form which can comprehensively imagine social cohesion, and in doing so can offer itself as the sphere in which that cohesion is imaginatively achieved.

George Eliot's novels work by very different means, but they too, and *Middlemarch* especially, seek to imagine the social world as an interconnected totality. The metaphor that she uses is that of the 'web', by which she suggests the multiple ties and filiations that connect people with one another in the ordinary course of life. In this she differs from Dickens, in insisting on the *ordinariness* of these connections; Eliot is not characteristically a melodramatic writer, unlike Dickens, who relishes the extraordinary revelation of unexpected ties. But in her case also there is the effort to imagine, or to trace, myriad narrative interconnections which link person to person, so that the account of the provincial town, Middlemarch, becomes an account of how lives act and react upon one another. That density of narrative interconnections is exactly what George Eliot means by society, for social life entails multiple connections which imply obligation, affection, sympathy, responsibility, mutuality. This is what the social organism *is*. The novel as cultural form, with its capacity to bring together accounts of diverse and super-ficially unconnected lives, is here again being used to imagine, and thus partially create, the 'imagined community' of which it speaks.

Thackeray's use of the form is different again, and is more sceptical than either Dickens's or George Eliot's. Yet he too writes novels which provide a conspectus of the social world, not only in the historical novel *Vanity Fair* (1847–48), but also in the unjustly neglected *The New-comes* (1853–55). *Vanity Fair* begins with a sort of prologue, entitled 'Before the curtain'; it suggests the notion of life as Vanity Fair, inhabited by a series of moral and social types jostling together in no coherent con-nection with each other. And indeed this contributes to the effect of the novel itself; although it brings together a wide variety of different peo-ple's stories, it does not seek to force them into connection and cohesion as Dickens and George Eliot do, in their different ways. This is figured metaphorically in *The Newcomes* in a passage in which the various narrat-ives of the novel are imagined as ships that pass each other at sea:

> In such a history events follow each other without necessarily having a connection with one another. One ship crosses another ship, and, after a visit from one captain to his comrade, they sail away each on his course. The *Clive Newcome* meets a vessel which makes signals that she is short of bread and water; and after supplying her, our captain leaves her to see her no more. One or two of the vessels with which we commenced the voyage together, part company in a gale, and founder miserably; others, after being woefully battered in the tem-pest, make port, or are cast upon surprising islands where all sorts of unlooked-for prosperity await the lucky crew.[22]

Here Thackeray explicitly eschews the attempt to make 'connection' between the multiple stories that he is telling, since the encounters between people are often random, and their destinies governed by luck. This does not mean, however, that his use of the cultural form of the inclusive multi-plot novel quite rejects the potential that we saw realised in the examples of *Bleak House* and *Middlemarch*. Rather, while Thackeray's novels certainly imagine the social totality, they do so in a more open and less cohesive way than the works of the other two novelists. But the form itself remains the bearer of an understanding of social life in which multiple, disparate life-histories must be imagined together.

Other novelists, at mid-century and later, sought to use the powerful cultural form of the multi-plot novel to imagine complex and diverse social relationships – naturally with very different ideological inflections. The novel is a mobile form which was put to very different uses by novelists bent on different ends. Though I have emphasised its totalising ambition, it was always an act of imagination, involving the imposition of unity and coherence on multiple and disparate phenomena. The imaginative effort involved is apparent from the novels themselves, which are always in danger of outrunning the order which writers seek to impose upon them. Reading these novels, then, can often provoke the sense that the parts are greater than the whole, or rather that the posited unity and coherence is actually defeated by the disparate and intractably diverse materials of which it is made. In this, the novels reproduce, in their own formal enactments, the tensions, fissures and force-fields of the society from which they emerge. The unity and coherence of nineteenth-century society were, likewise, always only posited, always a matter of continuous construction and imposition. Tugging against these centripetal forces, there were always a host of recalcitrant and resistant oppositional voices that resisted the assimilation to unity.

In the next chapter I will discuss some of those resistant voices, and the cultural forms in which they were articulated. But we must be beware of resolving too readily the ambivalent ethics and politics of the totalising ambitions of the novel. The mid-nineteenth-century novel takes its place, I have suggested, alongside other nineteenth-century efforts at imaginative social synthesis. It may be the case that these efforts at systematic social thought, and at imaginative synthesis, are in one respect forms of policing, which exclude the diversity that they cannot contain. In another respect, however, they are efforts at moral and social connection, which strive to bring together falsely obfuscated relationships and obligations. Because Esther and Inspector Bucket, the figures of affective connection and supervisory policing respectively, go hand in hand in *Bleak House*, we need not assume that they need always do so.

This chapter has considered some diverse cultural forms, and some diverse institutions also. Its starting point was institutional religion and the cultural forms associated with it. I have argued that the secular decline of religion posed a challenge to nineteenth-century intellectuals, to find other intellectually and affectively powerful sources of authority. I have reviewed, however briefly, some of the answers that were proposed. The unity and cohesion of society is as much an imaginative as an 'objective' fact, and in intellectual and imaginative conceptions of the social whole, social relations are in part realised. The ambivalence of nineteenth-century visions of the whole social order leads me to consider, in the next chapter, the cultural forms in which oppositional forces were articulated.

3

DIVISIONS: CULTURAL AND SOCIAL CHALLENGES

In the previous chapter, I discussed the ways in which people in the nineteenth century sought to imagine and to hold together a whole social order, conceived as it were from the top down. In this chapter I wish to consider matters from the opposite perspective, from the bottom up; that is, I will be discussing the cultural forms available to the various subordinated classes of nineteenth-century England, and assessing the ways in which these cultural forms constituted challenges to the dominant social order. In other words, we will be considering the central faultline of nineteenth-century life, *class*, and the oppositional cultural forms available to the popular classes. In addition, we shall examine how the writings of some dissident intellectual groups were both made available to, and assimilated by, popular culture.

Working-class and Popular-cultural Forms

In Volume III of Henry Mayhew's *London Labour and the London Poor* (1861–62), Mayhew includes an interview with a Punch performer, who is, unsurprisingly, knowledgeable about good 'pitches' in London:

> '...where there's many chapels Punch won't do at all. I did once, though, strike up hopposition to a street preacher wot was a holding forth in the New-road, and did uncommon well. All his flock, as he

called 'em, left him, and come over to look at me. Punch and preaching is two different creeds – hopposition parties, I may say'.[1]

This little episode in the politics of street-theatre bears dwelling on. In the first instance, it tells us of the bustling and competitive life of the London streets at the middle of the century, populated by myriads of hucksters, small tradesmen, and petty capitalists of popular culture – not just Punch, but also jugglers, acrobats, vendors of broadside ballads, street bands, fire-swallowers, and so on. It is important not to romanticise all this; some of these performers, such as the malnourished and ragged crossing-sweepers also recorded by Mayhew, who tumbled pathetically for a few coppers, were very miserable performers indeed. But in general we can see a multiple and heteroglot popular culture jostling for pennies and attention across the streets of London. In the second place, this popular culture was in direct competition with popular religion; in that witty phrase of the Punch performer, they were 'hopposition parties'. In the anecdote recorded by Mayhew, that competition is of the most direct and immediate kind: Mr Punch manages to pinch his audience from the preacher. But in more general terms we can see a century-long opposition between, on the one hand, the apostles of good order, religion, and, in a different key, rational recreation, and on the other, the promoters and entrepreneurs of a vulgar and disorderly popular culture, whether it take the form of this penny-capitalist kind or whether it were the survival of traditional and indigenous activities and pastimes. The incident recalled by Mayhew's informant was but one tiny episode in that secular competition.[2]

It is impossible to speak, then, of any uniform 'working-class culture' in the nineteenth century, and for a variety of reasons. The working class was itself so various, differentiated both between regions and between different points in the social scale: respectable skilled workers were profoundly different from the ragged children, hucksters and costermongers interviewed by Mayhew. But in the context of Mayhew's anecdote, we can see another reason for recognising the heterogeneity of English popular-cultural life in the nineteenth century – the jostling competition among cultural forms which sought to give shape and meaning to working people's lives, and within which such people sought to give their own lives shape and meaning. It seems to me to be impossible, in the face of this heterogeneity, to give a single narrative of the coming-to-consciousness of that class, or to see that consciousness as anything other than fluid, subject to constant renegotiation and change.[3] Within those various cultural possibilities, a variety of different stories about themselves and their place in the world was circulated among the popular classes, in which 'class' was occasionally dominant, but so also were other self-definitions – as self-improvers, as Christians, as 'the people', as national, and eventually imperial, subjects. Yet we can, nevertheless, survey both the field of cultural possibilities available at various moments in the nineteenth century, and see how that secular struggle over popular-cultural forms developed over the course of it.

Let us begin with that traditional popular culture, still dominant at the beginning of the century. England, as I have repeatedly observed, was still predominantly a rural country; its popular-cultural forms naturally reflected that, and were linked both to the cycle of the agricultural year, and, to a lesser extent, to the liturgical year. The rhythms of work provided the basic rhythms of non-agricultural sections of the population also, both the rhythms of the working week, and of a working lifetime – apprenticeship, journeyman, and perhaps the cycle of production. Customary cultural forms accompanied the high points in these work-related cycles; hiring-fairs, rites of passage in the workshop, harvest-home suppers, the celebration of Saint Monday when workers in different trades would drink over Monday (and sometimes Tuesday and Wednesday too) before resuming the weekly tasks of production. These customary cultural forms were both traditional, and provided by small-scale enterprises like Mayhew's Punch performer or the myriad showmen who traipsed around the differing regional 'circuits' to take in the different local fairs. This was altogether an unruly, noisy, often violent, and usually drunken popular culture. Its great festivals, the annual fairs such as Nottingham's Goose Fair or Bartholomew Fair in London, were unruly occasions, causing great anxiety to many in authority. The violence of some of its cultural forms, especially violence against animals, is still sufficient to give pause to any too-sentimental retrospect – the widely popular game of cock-throwing, for example, involved tethering a cockerel and then throwing stones at it until it was killed – while other more familiar animal sports included bear-baiting, dog-fighting, badger-baiting and ratting. But this was also a culture suffused with notions of what has been well named the 'moral economy' – suffused, that is, with sometimes conservative notions of what constitutes the respective rights and responsibilities of one class to another, and prepared to enforce those rights. So the various Christmas and New Year ceremonies of Waits, Carols and mumming-plays, found in many parts of the country, characteristically involved some enforcement and ritual enactment of the paternalist relations of landlords and employers, by the collection of alms and drink, both in town and country. More spectacularly, the disruption of this traditional notion of a moral economy could be violently resisted, as in Luddite machine-breaking (targeting machines correctly perceived as destroying traditional patterns of work and rates of pay), or in the Captain Swing riots that swept across the south of England in 1831–32, which similarly appealed to traditional notions of responsibility between farmers and their labourers.

This traditional and customary popular culture came under attack from a variety of different directions in the course of the century, ensuring its partial suppression and transformation. It was assailed in the first place by sections of the Church, who could not tolerate its disorderliness, its drunkenness, its sheer plebeian disregard for the seemly and prudential virtues. So both the great and the minor festivals of this culture were policed, overseen, transformed, and if necessary suppressed – an emblematic moment here being the suppression of Bartholomew Fair in the 1850s, which ended a traditional celebration that extended back several hundred years. Numerous Societies for the Suppression of Vice, for Temperance, for the Suppression of Cruelty to Animals, for Lord's Day Observance, all combined to seek to tame the obvious excesses of these traditional popular-cultural forms, with considerable success on the whole. But equally, many practices were reinvented and transformed into practices at once more decorous and less threatening (as, for example, sports such as pugilism and football, which were tamed and brought under the control of codes and rules); or simply ousted by 'invented traditions', such as the Harvest Service devised in many country parishes in mid-century to replace the traditionally drunken harvest-homes and harvest-suppers.

Another enemy of this customary and unruly popular culture was, naturally enough, the employer, especially the employer of the more highly capitalised machinery of the factory system. In an industrialising country, new and more regulated work-discipline was evidently essential – no large employer was going to tolerate the celebration of Saint Monday, or the mass decamping of his workforce to witness a footrace or a boxing-match. The extraordinarily long hours of work demanded by the new factories (and vociferously defended by their owners) simply required a work-discipline inimical to the rhythms of an older popular culture, and replaced them instead with the more apparently 'rational' rhythms of the six-day working week and a working year barely interrupted by those intolerably unproductive holidays.

Though of course the factories of the industrial system developed their own workplace culture, and their own rituals of initiation and accommodation between employers and employed, these were not by and large the traditional workplace rituals, which survived rather in those centres of craft and small workshop production that persisted throughout the nineteenth century.

In one respect, then, popular and traditional cultural forms were obviously conservative, looking back to what were conceived as traditional norms and mutual responsibilities; these forms made up a culture that was sometimes prepared to take violent action to resist the depredations of an innovative and rationalising capitalism, both industrial and rural. This culture could also be violent, drunken, inward-looking, misogynist, antipathetic to strangers and hostile to change. We can contrast this with the very different social and cultural situation at the end of the century, after three generations of industrial transformation – a contrast between the customary and penny-capitalist popular culture at the beginning of the century, and the much more highly capitalised and nationally based mass culture at its end. The inhabitants of the working-class zones of London and the industrial cities (discussed more fully in Chapter 5 below) were more literate, more decorous, more disciplined and more entertained than their grandparents. The popular culture which they enjoyed was sold to them by the new entrepreneurs of the music-hall and the national newspapers and magazines. The men went drinking in the local pub, certainly, but this was now the 'local' for a neighbourhood and no longer the place where their wages were distributed or the 'house of call' for a trade. Their working hours were significantly shorter, and the institution of the Saturday half-holiday had become widespread from the 1870s onwards. This permitted the efflorescence of a range of cultural forms, most notably the extraordinary spread of professional sport, especially football; the Saturday match became instituted at the end of the century as a fixture of the (male) working-class week. Where his grandparents had enjoyed the boisterous pleasures of badger-baiting and cock-throwing, the 'hobbies' of the late nineteenth-century working-class man stretched to the gentler (though still fiercely competitive) pastimes of pigeon-fancying and canary-breeding. The cross-class enjoyments at the beginning of the century of horse-racing and pugilism had given way to the regularised pleasures of off-course betting, supported by a popular racing press. In short, in the popular-cultural forms of the late nineteenth century can be traced the outlines of a settlement, a still contested but relatively

stable way of life, that was to remain intact until well into the middle of
the twentieth century.

The dominant, or at least most widespread, culture of this settlement
was local and defensive in character, even when it drew upon national
and mass-provided institutions like the Sunday papers (at the end of
the century the *News of the World* had the largest of any circulation in
the world) and the nationally or regionally famous stars of the music-
hall. The horizons of the working-class areas of the industrial cities
were often very circumscribed, confined essentially to the immediate
neighbourhood – Robert Roberts, talking of his area of Salford at the
beginning of the twentieth century, refers to it as a 'village'.[4] In such
localities, though there were certainly other cultural possibilities available, popular-cultural forms provided ways of negotiating the difficult
realities of everyday life, but in ways that were accommodatory and
defensive, and which took the limits imposed upon that life for granted.
Exploiting the mass literacy more or less ensured by the Education Act
of 1870, Sunday papers like the *News of the World* and cheap periodicals
like *Tit-Bits*, *Answers* and *Ideas* provided short and easily assimilated
news and information. The *Daily Mail*, founded in 1896, was the first
national daily paper to aim at a similar mass public, though it did not
in fact achieve a mass *working-class* readership. Even the popular theatre
and the music-hall followed a pattern of re-presenting a version of this
local life back to those who lived it – Roberts describes how those commercially successful songs were in turn copied and parodied by the
inhabitants of his part of Salford. All in all, though this predominantly
commercial culture perhaps continued to draw on some of the old
popular-cultural energies (in comic magazines like *Ally Sloper's Half-
Holiday*), at the level of mass allegiance the social and cultural formation
of working-class life at the end of the century was defensive and
sometimes inward-looking.

The Culture of Self-improvement

However, this is to assess a social and cultural formation at the level of its
most visible and statistically dominant characteristics alone. We have to
consider, in addition, the competing forces that were contending
amongst the popular classes in the nineteenth century, and the popular
culture that I have just been surveying did not provide the only cultural

forms available to working people. There was, for example, a persistent indigenous strain of self-improvement amongst working-class people throughout the century, which overlapped to some extent with the movements for 'rational recreation' spearheaded by middle-class philanthropy, but whose meanings and purposes were by no means identical. And of course, Church and Chapel continued throughout the century to provide significant cultural centres for sections of the popular classes as well. The historian David Vincent, writing of that first tradition of working-class self-improvement through reading, has described it as a culture 'in the sense of a social entity which existed as a distinct element within the culture of the working class as a whole'.[5] I wish to consider what uses might be made of the elite cultural forms assimilated – often at heroic personal cost – by working-class readers.

There is no doubting the heroism. Here is Thomas Cooper, admittedly an extreme case, describing his self-educating regime of study while working as a shoemaker in Leicester in the 1820s:

Historical reading, or the grammar of some language, or translation, was my first employment on week-day mornings, whether I rose at three or four, until seven o'clock, when I sat down to the stall.

A book or a periodical in my hand while I breakfasted, gave me another half-hour's reading. I had another half-hour, and sometimes an hour's reading, or study of language, at from one to two o'clock, the time of dinner – usually eating my food with a spoon, after I had cut it in pieces, and having my eyes on a book all the time.

I sat at work till eight, and sometimes nine; and, then, either read, or walked about our little room and committed 'Hamlet' to memory, or the rhymes of some modern poet, until compelled to go to bed from sheer exhaustion – for it must be remembered that I was repeating something, audibly, as I sat at work, the greater part of the day – either declensions and conjugations or rules of syntax, or propositions of Euclid, or the 'Paradise Lost', or 'Hamlet', or poetry of some modern or living author.[6]

People like Thomas Cooper are of course quite exceptional, and courses of study like the one he describes here are (one presumes) very difficult to sustain. Nevertheless, there was a significant strand of working-class readers – a culture within a culture, to use Vincent's phrase – which remained an important presence throughout the century. Though reading was a solitary activity, such readers often supported themselves by forming little 'mutual improvement societies', meeting regularly to discuss worthwhile topics and painstakingly gathering together prized collections of books. What could those forms themselves mean in the realities of their lives?

Naturally enough, a programme of self-education could lead them to be sharply distinguished from their neighbours and workmates. This was not without its absurd aspects, as when Cooper took to speaking in 'the best and most refined English' to his customers at the shoe-maker's stall, which 'raised positive anger and scorn in some, and amazement in others' (pp. 56–7). There are several related questions here which need to be distinguished. For some self-educators, doubt-less, their pursuit of knowledge under difficulties was a form of self-help of the kind advocated by Samuel Smiles, and it led to their eventual translation out of their class. For others again, like Thomas Cooper himself in some respects, self-education led to political leadership – Cooper became one of the national Chartist leaders; and on a less exalted level, self-educated working people became the natural leaders of their class in trade unions, Co-operative Societies, and the many forms of mutual self-helping societies that characterised nineteenth-century working-class life. But there is a third question, to do with the meanings to the people themselves of these elite cultural forms so pain-fully acquired. Vincent suggests that 'the primary attraction of the world of literature was that it offered the working-class reader a limited but very real area of independence'.[7] Access to these elite cultural forms provided the self-educators with perspectives from which to make sense of their own lives, as well as perspectives in which those lives might be imaginatively escaped. Competence in these forms provided a self-esteem which was denied to them as members of subordinated or just impoverished sections of society. To quote Cooper again: 'The wondrous knowledge of the heart unfolded by Shakespeare, made me shrink into insignificance; while the sweetness, the marvellous power of expression and grandeur of his poetry seemed to transport me, at times, out of the vulgar world of circumstances in which I lived bodily' (p. 64). This 'vulgar world of circumstances' has a particular force for a working-class writer which lifts the phrase out of the realm of cliché and suggests something of the leverage provided for these readers by the culture which they took such pains to acquire.

When these self-taught readers themselves became writers, they per-force drew upon genres of writing – mostly poetry and autobiography – which were in some respects quite conservative. Especially in writing about their own class, their experience could be re-presented through relatively old-fashioned modes of writing, in which the presumed narrative position was one of downward-looking sympathy, and which could be used only with some awkwardness by working-class writers who wished to make themselves present in their verse. Despite this, one anthologist of nineteenth-century self-taught poets, Brian Maidment, has argued that 'in the absence of easily available radical or oppositional literary genres, the continuing use of eighteenth-century modes of moral indignation by ambitious self-taught writers, and the use of near-oral, communal, simple lyric forms and literary occasions by politically or communally motivated writers, both suggest regard for poetic possibility, and a clear awareness of the nature of literary form.' While many of these writers did attempt to write in the more self-consciously expressive modes of Romanticism, older neoclassical modes were in fact more congenial, and Maidment has indicated that 'the pastoral mode is endemic in the work of self-taught writers'.[8] In other words, the cultural forms to which many of these writers felt themselves to be drawn, and in which they chose to demonstrate their hard-won competence – which, moreover, they felt were best suited to express their sense of themselves and their relationship to their own experience – frequently carried with them particular consequences in terms of address and idiom. Take, for example, the following poem by Samuel Bamford, the Lancashire Radical and poet:

> God help the poor, who, on this wintry morn,
>   Come forth from alleys dim and courts obscure.
> God help yon poor pale girl, who droops forlorn,
>   And meekly her affliction doth endure;
> God help her, outcast lamb; she trembling stands,
> All wan her lips, and frozen red her hands;
> Her sunken eyes are modestly downcast,
> Her night-black hair streams on the fitful blast;
> Her bosom, passing fair, is half revealed,
> And oh! so cold, the snow lies there congealed;
> Her feet benumbed, her shoes all rent and worn,
> God help thee, outcast lamb, who stands forlorn!
>   God help the poor![9]

The poem here constructs the poor as objects of pathos in a genuinely affecting and accomplished way, which draws on the perspective and diction of neoclassical models, as well perhaps of Shakespeare ('her night-black hair streams on the fitful blast'). But the perspective is essentially that of the observer viewing the 'poor' from outside, even though this is a poem written by a poet who was himself 'poor'. The ideological power of a particular cultural form is seen strongly here, and it contrasts markedly with other modes which Bamford could himself use – dialect poetry and poems of political indignation and inspiration.

At all events, self-education, and the elite cultural forms to which it led, remained an important set of cultural possibilities within the working class throughout the nineteenth century and beyond. Certainly it was not rendered obsolete by the 1870 Education Act, which provided only a very basic primary education. As the century progressed, more opportunities for working-class higher education became available through university extension lectures and the Workers' Educational Association; but this takes us into the area of cultural provision *for* the popular classes, rather than the indigenous pursuit of education that people like Cooper and Bamford represent.

I have been emphasising the heterogeneity of working-class culture in the nineteenth century, a contested space in which differing cultural forms jostled for supremacy. We need finally to consider some of the 'top-down' efforts to fill this space, to provide rational and improving alternatives to the unruliness of popular culture, and to the autonomy provided by successful self-education. In the previous chapter we considered the success of the various religious denominations in providing cultural institutions for the popular classes; with some significant exceptions (Primitive Methodism, especially among miners and sections of the southern agricultural labouring class), both the Church and Dissent lost the battle to win over the mass of the population, though they did provide significant cultural leadership for sections of the upper working class. Here, I want to consider briefly the success of the secular movement for rational recreation – the effort to provide sober and improving alternatives to the disorderly and potentially threatening pleasures of the pub, the prize-fight, and the racecourse. The promoters of such endeavours sought to make available pastimes for the working classes that frequently had a large educational content, and many of the results of these efforts are still standing today – in the network of public libraries that, at different times, were established by local authorities from mid-century onwards; in civic museums; in choral societies and public orchestras, many of which have nineteenth-century pedigrees. Often, the recreation offered was more physical than educational – one of the roots of Association Football is such an effort at paternalist recreation. This was seized upon by the working class and given quite a different, more competitive and professional character than that intended by its philanthropic and gentlemanly advocates; while Rugby Football, similarly promoted, broke into quite separate amateur and professional codes. Libraries, museums and orchestras clearly did not penetrate the mass of the working-class population, though they certainly appealed to and were used by its respectable and self-improving sections, and in certain parts of the country could point to a genuine popular following.

Recalling the social and political mobility of cultural forms and institutions, it is not surprising that 'rational recreation' could serve needs unanticipated by its promoters, including on occasions the requirements of people interested in explicit opposition to the current constitution of the social order. It is to such explicit oppositional movements that we now turn.

Explicit Oppositional Movements

The heterogeneity of working-class culture included, as we have seen, customary cultural forms, a tradition of strenuous reading in partial opposition to those forms, and some reliance on elite forms and institutions provided from above. There were many other more obviously oppositional elements within the popular classes, which all sought, in different ways, to establish distinctive associational and cultural forms. Starting with the remnants of the Radical and even insurrectionary movements of the 1790s, through post-Napoleonic War Radicalism, Owenism and Socialism in the 1830s and 1840s, Chartism in the same decades, Trade Unionism, Co-operation, Secularism, and the newer Socialism of the 1880s and 1890s, it is possible to trace a succession of oppositional movements, all with significant working-class ascription or leadership. What intellectual and cultural resources did these movements draw upon? And what kinds of cultural and associational life did they encourage?

These are large questions; I wish to approach them by asking how readily these explicitly contentious political movements could speak to, or draw from, the conditions of life of those whose condition they sought to ameliorate. What was the connection, in other words, between, on the one hand, working-class conditions of work and of settlement, with their accompanying habitual cultural assumptions, and, on the other hand, these explicit movements of social and ideological improvement, with their languages of political rights, mutual support and solidarity, and of class against class?

This is a crucial question, taking us to the heart of the problem addressed by this book – the relationship between society and cultural forms. Such forms, I am arguing, do not spring spontaneously from people's conditions of life, but come from multiple different histories and social locations; their appropriateness to particular people in particular circumstances is always a matter of negotiation, accommodation, sometimes imposition or struggle. Nevertheless, at times there can be a quite remarkable fit between cultural forms and the conditions of life to which they are addressed; and in one sense, the history of these nineteenth-century radical movements is precisely a search to find the right kind of fit. For example, when Samuel Bamford and the other Radical leaders in Middleton in Lancashire rallied the crowds that were to march on Manchester on 16 August 1819, they sought very consciously – at least according to Bamford's retrospective report – to indicate their peaceable intentions. This is Bamford's account of the matter:

> First were selected twelve of the most comely and decent-looking youths, who were placed in two rows of six each, with each a branch of laurel held presented in his hand, as a token of amity and peace,- then followed the men of several districts in fives,-then the band of music, an excellent one,-then the colours; a blue one of silk, with inscriptions in golden letters, 'UNITY AND STRENGTH.' 'LIBERTY AND FRATERNITY.' A green one of silk, with golden letters, 'PARLIAMENTS ANNUAL.' 'SUFFRAGE UNIVERSAL'; and betwixt them on a staff, a handsome cap of crimson velvet, with a tuft of laurel, and the cap tastefully braided with the word, LIBERTAS, in front. Next were placed the remainder of the men of the districts in fives, – the districts being as follows. Middleton proper, or that part of the town next to the Church,-Back-o'-th'-Brow,-Barrowfields,-Boarshaw,-Stakehill and Thornham,-Hopwood,-Heabers-Birch,-Bowlee,-Heatons,-Rhodes,-Blackley,-Alkrington,-Little Park,-Tonge,-Parkfield,-Wood-street, and Middleton Wood. Some hundreds also joined us from Heywood.[10]

Bamford is here recalling a coherent and homogeneous-seeming political moment. The men of Middleton are about to march, in orderly fashion, to Manchester, to assert their political rights and to claim an extension of them. Yet we can also see a variety of cultural forms operating in this passage, even distinguishing as far as we can between the language that Bamford is retrospectively using to describe what he recalls, and the cultural forms adopted by the marchers themselves. The banners, for instance, are drawing upon a political vocabulary which is that of Radicalism, though, if Bamford's recollection is correct, that vocabulary is given a sought-for extra dignity by the inversions ('PARLIAMENTS ANNUAL', 'SUFFRAGE UNIVERSAL'), and even the use of Latin ('LIBERTAS'), while the Liberty bonnet is a symbol, however tasteful, that looks directly back to the insurrectionary tradition of the French Revolution. On the other hand, the leading marchers are carrying laurel branches 'as a token of amity and peace' – what customary 'folk' tradition is being pressed into service here? And that remarkable roll-call of the districts of Middleton is symptomatic also – of a mode of sociality which emerges very directly from immediate neighbourhood and locality as a profound source of meaning and self-identification. These are not districts of Manchester, they are districts of *Middleton* – a small weaving town about five miles from Manchester, now long since swallowed up into the Manchester 'conurbation'. Furthermore, the military order and discipline of the marchers is no accident either; it was the direct result of drilling, practised on the moors above Middleton and led by veterans of the Napoleonic Wars. So this apparently self-consistent display in fact emerges from multiple different social, political, cultural and historical experiences, and draws upon cultural forms that emerge from different histories but combine here and on this occasion. Bamford's own language, written some twenty-five years after the incidents he relates, avails itself of a vocabulary ('comely and decent-looking youths', 'tastefully braided') designed to give dignity and respectability to these potentially subversive activities.

The language of Radicalism, as here manifested in the very dispositions of the marchers who were setting off, as it turned out, to the massacre of Peterloo, seems to me, in this instance, to be remarkably close to the forms of life which it sought to champion. In the course of the nineteenth century, various such 'languages' became available, which were capable, with more or less degrees of success, of achieving similar accommodations and assimilations with quotidian forms and modes of understanding – or, in some other instances, such as Owenism, sought to distance themselves altogether from such quotidian forms. At the same time as Bamford was helping to organise the people of Lancashire in their pursuit of 'LIBERTAS', the journalist William Cobbett was articulating quite another vocabulary in his *Political Register*, a vocabulary that drew on the cadences of plain common sense, but which put these customary valuations to trenchant radical purposes.[11] By contrast, another section of the Radical press in the 1810s and 1820s sought to carry forward the tradition of Tom Paine and, with him, of the Enlightenment into the nineteenth century; Richard Carlile, originally a Devon tinsmith, was sent to prison for publishing Paine's *Age of Reason* in 1819, but widespread working-class support kept his bookshop open in the face of repeated arrests, and he was also supported by numerous Freethinkers' Societies in other towns and cities. The tradition of Paine and Carlile – rationalistic, freethinking, sometimes Deistic and sometimes atheistical, provided one distinctive language for working-class radicalism throughout the century.[12]

This tradition was partly taken up by Owenite Socialism, which flourished from the 1820s through to the 1840s. This movement drew directly on the perfectibilist language of the Enlightenment, as articulated by Robert Owen (1771–1858); excited by the success of his forms of management at New Lanark mills, Owen believed that it would be possible to replace the competition and destructiveness of the contemporary economic and social order by a morally superior system of co-operation and harmony. In short, it would be possible to supersede the Old Immoral World by the New Moral World. Owenite Socialism achieved a remarkable following among working people, which issued both in ambitious unionism, retail and productive co-operative schemes, and several communitarian experiments. It was remarkable also for the way it combined feminism with its socialism – the emancipation of women was seen, within Owenism, as equally important as the emancipation of men. When Owenite Socialism eventually fell apart in the 1840s, its Enlightenment vocabulary persisted in various fragments; in the Secularist movement; in feminism; in sections of the Union and Co-operative movements. For a brief moment in the 1830s, this vocabulary had been very successful in speaking to the lives and experiences of many working-class women and men.[13]

However, by far the most important of the working-class oppositional movements of the nineteenth century was Chartism, which was at its strongest in the late 1830s and early 1840s, and revived again at the end of the 1840s. This too used the language of Radicalism, and indeed its Six Points were all directed towards *political* reform. This was certainly a language capable of mobilising a mass working-class movement.

The success of Chartism, however, relied as much on its capacity to draw on customary traditions and solidarities, as upon this language of radicalism with its appeal to political solutions, and its identification of the enemy as Old Corruption. In what was anyway a regionally and politically varied movement, different traditions, solidarities and political memories combined, but always with different strategies and conceptions of what constituted 'legitimate' politics – most notably in the divide between 'moral force' and 'physical force' Chartism.

The variety of the ideological and cultural forms that Chartism had recourse to can be seen, for example, in the following two contrasting stanzas of Chartist poetry – Chartist papers such as *The Northern Star* published quantities of such poetry. The first is by William S. Villiers Sankey, and comes from a poem called 'Rule Britannia!', published in *The Northern Star* in 1840:

> Let Britain's heralds take their stand,
>   And loudly through the isle proclaim,
> This is the Charter of the land;
>   While million voices shout the same.
> Hail, Britannia! Britannia's sons are free!
> Suffrage guards their liberty.[14]

This is a parody, or perhaps simply a rewriting, of 'Rule Britannia'. It does not, however, rewrite the song in an entirely sardonic register; on the contrary, the poem here seeks to take over the patriotic reference and the somewhat inflated vocabulary of the original. What it alters is the political content, of course – in a radical-democratic direction, where, in some future state, the guardian of the freedoms of 'Britannia's sons' will be universal suffrage. Both the force of this as a mobilising strategy, and its limitations, are immediately apparent; this takes up and redirects traditional patriotic sentiments, but remains within a vocabulary that is at once patriotic and limited to male emancipation ('Britannia's *sons*') – though it should be said that in the two subsequent stanzas the poem anticipates a more general international (though not gendered) emancipation. Compare this with the far fiercer rhetoric of the Chartist poet Benjamin Stott, also published in *The Northern Star*, in 1842:

> How long will the millions sweat and toil,
>   To pamper the lordlings' bastard brats;

How long will they till the fruitful soil,
　To be starved by the base aristocrats?
How long will they bear the galling yoke,
Ere their bones shall burst, their chains be broke,
And vengeance comes down like a thunderstroke?

Bondsmen and slaves in every clime,
　Your voices raise in freedom's cause;
Despots, be wise; be wise in time,
　Remember it is Nature's laws
　That make men equal; and dare ye,
　In hellish conclave met, agree
To alter Nature's wise decree?[15]

In some respects, this is similar to Sankey's poem above in using the same vocabulary of indignant public address. But it articulates a very different ideological position, taking the sanction for its political egalitarianism from 'Nature' and not from any more specifically national notion of British liberties; indeed, the second stanza is explicitly internationalist in import. In addition, the violence of the vocabulary, in the first stanza, appeals not only to the radical-democratic tradition of hostility to *aristocrats*, but in invoking vengeance, is perhaps appealing also to the insurrectionary tradition in working-class politics which physical-force Chartism was heir to.

These two quotations are cited to suggest the variety of Chartism's intellectual and cultural resources. Uniquely among nineteenth-century oppositional movements, it managed to combine its various inheritances to mobilise substantial sections of the working classes to become a genuinely mass movement. This, in turn, left an inheritance amongst subsequent working-class political movements in the second half of the nineteenth century, an inheritance that was important both for the radical-democratic strand, and for Trades-Unionism, and eventually for Socialism, when it revived in the last two decades of the century.

Trades-Unionism, like other institutions of working-class self-help such as Friendly Societies, had an evident cultural dimension. The typical craft unionism of the mid-nineteenth century, with its rituals of initiation and strong respectable and improving ethos, had clear connections with the traditional craft rituals of the various trades; even the New Unionism of the 1890s, which organised for the first time the unskilled masses of dockers and transport workers, reflected and made use of currents within popular culture. These were important associational forms, which gave meaning and direction to some of the lives which were lived through them; in this sense they can be thought of as 'culture'.

Finally, in this brief survey of oppositional cultural forms as they appealed to the popular classes in the nineteenth century, we should consider Socialism as it reappeared in the last two decades of the nineteenth century, but now separated from its Owenite provenance. While Socialism certainly appealed to sections of the middle class in the 1880s and 1890s, it also had a significant appeal to sections of the working class, especially the upper skilled sections. Like Owenite Socialism before it, this late nineteenth-century variety had a profound ambivalence towards the institutions and habits of popular culture; in one version, the 'conversion' to Socialism was indeed equivalent to a religious conversion, and was accompanied by a similar repudiation of the habits and practices of the past. The 'religion of socialism' was thus characterised by adherence not only to a certain political and economic doctrine, but also to a transformed way of relating to one's fellows. This transformation naturally had recourse to the distinctive cultural achievements of Socialists like William Morris and Walter Crane, but also, in varying degrees, to the intellectual and cultural forms of a wide number of nineteenth-century writers, such Thomas Carlyle, John Ruskin, Edward Carpenter and John Stuart Mill. Thus, for some members of the working class, Socialism combined the traditions of self-improvement with ambitions for more general class and indeed national improvement.

We can get a sense of the associational culture characteristic of Socialism in the following description of a Socialist meeting in the early 1890s:

> ...in the Albion Halls last Saturday, owing to the unavoidable absence of William Nairn, Mr J. Bruce Glasier reviewed 'News from Nowhere', an ideal of socialism by William Morris. The meeting was one of the strangest I have seen since the lectures began. Quite a religious feeling seemed to pervade the hall, and you could have heard the proverbial pin drop while Comrade Glasier was reading some of the passages from the book. Not that the meetings have been noisy hitherto, but the silence at the last one was so still and death-like that it shows a wonderful power in the book.[16]

As the writer of this report himself makes clear, this was an exceptional meeting. Nevertheless, it suggests the religious intensity that could accompany the Socialist movement, and how the movement could both produce and assimilate high cultural forms – in this case, Morris's Utopian romance *News from Nowhere*, first published in fact in the newspaper of the Socialist League, *Commonweal*, between January and October 1890. While the impact of Socialism may have been small in numerical terms among the working class at the end of the century, it certainly provided a distinctive set of cultural possibilities for the class as a whole, and effected a significant juncture between that class and some of the intellectual and cultural resources of the classes above it.

Dissident Cultural Fractions

In the final section of this chapter, I shall consider further how such conjunctions might come to be made; that is, I want to consider the various strands of middle-class oppositional culture and how they managed to get any purchase among the popular classes, if at all. I take as my guide through this large topic Raymond Williams's notion of the 'cultural fraction';[17] that is, that in the course of the nineteenth century a number of distinct groups split off from the middle class and articulated their opposition to the dominant social order, though in very different ways. The groups that I wish to pass under review are the Philosophical Radicals of the first thirty years of the century; the group of mildly Bohemian writers and artists gathered around comic journalism in the 1840s and 1850s, including Henry Mayhew, Douglas Jerrold, *Punch* magazine, and even Charles Dickens; the Pre-Raphaelite Brotherhood; the Arts and Crafts movement of the end of the century; and the significant middle-class ascription to Socialism.

We can distinguish between these groups, in a very broad way, by considering the differing and even contradictory nature of their projects. Philosophical Radicalism, and indeed a whole tradition of middle-class intellectual effort through the century, sought in effect to reformulate the grounds of the social order and to place them on a more rational footing. To this extent they were the heirs of the Enlightenment, and couched their critiques of the prevailing social world in terms of its irrationality and unnaturalness. By contrast, the other groups characteristically stressed not the irrationality of the social world but its heartlessness; their opposition to the world as constituted in the 1840s, for example, was not that it was irrational but, on the contrary, that it was if anything *too* rational – that it obeyed unfeelingly the laws of political economy and thus condemned the majority to poverty and the remainder to an affective desert. Dickens's *A Christmas Carol* (1843) is the most striking and well-known expression of this attitude. Both these broad dispositions were capable of being inflected in very different ways, and each could likewise be assimilated towards defence of the social order. But both spoke to what appeared to be profound inadequacies in nineteenth-century social life. On the one hand, this social life was irrational, bore with it too many traces of its unreformed aristocratic history, bearing fruit in corruption, patronage, muddle, administrative stupidity and inefficiency. To remedy this what was required was rationality, a knowledge of the laws governing social life, perhaps democratic controls. On the other hand, social life was heartless, brutal, corrosive of the affective bonds that should bind society together; what was needed to remedy it was a bracing of the affective bonds, a rediscovery of mutual responsibilities, the inhabiting of an affective and aesthetic realm beyond the mere 'cash nexus' (to use Carlyle's telling phrase, coined in *Past and Present* [1843]).

The Philosophical Radicals were a group which provided intellectual leadership to sections of the middle class in the 1810s and 1820s; we can get a sense of the plasticity of intellectual and cultural forms from the fact we have already discussed their philosophical position – the secular moral code known as Utilitarianism – in the previous chapter, as an intellectual position potentially cohesive of the social order rather than disruptive of it. If Philosophical Radicalism was corrosive of some of the dominant social institutions of the early part of the century, this was because those institutions appeared to be founded on habit and arbitrary authority; men such as Jeremy Bentham and James Mill (1773–1836) sought to refound them on sounder principles, as in the case of the Poor Laws. James Mill's son, however, John Stuart Mill, though he recognised the inadequacy of a purely rational social order in personal and social terms, could nevertheless pursue the Enlightenment tenets of his father's generation beyond its classic moment in the 1820s, to establish the basis of a profound liberal critique of paternalist social relations that would eventually lead him to feminism and a modified subscription to Socialism. More generally, the intellectual inheritance of Philosophical Radicalism, and the way it carried forward into the nineteenth century some of the intellectual and reforming zeal of the Enlightenment, would serve as a resource for many dissident intellectual groups throughout the century. What the social historian Harold Perkin has called differing 'class ideals'[18] – especially the ideals of the professional middle class – could consistently draw on this striking intellectual inheritance.

But let us turn to that other dissident fraction, which rejected contemporary social life not for its irrationality but for its heartlessness. I referred in Chapter 1 to a tradition of philosophical and social reflection opposed to industrial capitalism precisely because this was destructive of the affective ties which ought to bind people together in society – the so-called 'culture and society' tradition represented by Thomas Carlyle, John Ruskin and William Morris. The politics of this tradition are strikingly ambivalent. Carlyle's writings in the 1840s, for example, could appeal to Marx and Engels, especially in his diagnosis of the inhumanities of the contemporary world, and its substitution of the 'cash nexus' for the organic and affective relationships that might and perhaps once did bind the social organism together. But he was also and more famously authoritarian in his political attitudes, particularly in relation to the colonial world, where his writing is disfigured by the most unattractive racial attitudes. Similarly, Ruskin's hostility to Political Economy and to the spread of industrialism could lead him, in *Unto This Last* (1862), to a radical critique of the prevailing justification of the social order and to a potentially 'green' politics; but he too was attracted by some deeply paternalist social attitudes and described himself, in *Praeterita*, as 'a violent Tory of the old school; Walter Scott's school, that is to say, and Homer's'.[19] Finally, this same intellectual tradition, given an energetic transformation, could emerge in the revolutionary socialism of William Morris in the 1880s.

However, I also want to consider less exalted and more popular-radical versions of similar attitudes, as they were expressed earlier in the century, in some of the cultural productions of the 1830s and 1840s. A nexus of mostly short-lived journals, popular publishing ventures and popular theatre in these decades produced a number of comic and sentimental radicals, of whom the best known is Charles Dickens, but who also included Douglas Jerrold (1803–57), Henry Mayhew (1812–87) and Thomas Hood (1799–1845). The radicalism of this group was by no means systematic; it amounted to a rejection of the aridities and heartlessness of the social world, which it sought to soften with sentiment and to dissolve with laughter. The sentimental side: Dickens in *Dombey and Son* (1847–48) attacked the commercial firm of the title because 'Dombey and Son had often dealt in hides, but never in hearts' (ch. 1) – articulating an opposition between the world of commerce and of the heart, between the market and the affective realm, that underlies one aspect of the critique of the dominant social world articulated in this literature. The comic side: most famously the magazine *Punch* (founded 1841), which was only the most successful of a range of journals in the 1830s and 1840s which attacked bourgeois respectability and pretensions in a comic language. Though the Radicalism of *Punch* was short-lived, it is significant because it, and the other periodicals which it typified, drew upon popular-cultural forms and energies that we have seen expressed elsewhere – energies that were irreverent and anti-authoritarian. It was not only on the street that Punch and the preacher were 'hopposition parties'.

This is a significant cultural fraction, that could nourish a genuine and sustained radicalism on the part, for example, of Henry Mayhew, who made the transition from the world of *Punch* to the investigative journalism on the *Morning Chronicle* and then to his life-work *London Labour and the London Poor*. Other writers who emerged from this milieu include Thomas Hood, whose poem 'Song of the Shirt' was published in *Punch* in 1843, and which dramatised in sentimental fashion the plight of distressed needlewomen; and Douglas Jerrold, who in addition to his career in popular journalism had also written the melodramas *Black-ey'd Susan* (1829) and *The Bride of Ludgate* (1831) for the popular stage. The importance of this cultural moment is that it managed to make significant connections between popular cultural forms and a sometimes sentimental and sometimes compromised, but still real, radicalism.

Roughly contemporaneous with the moment of *Punch*, but producing a cultural politics of a very different kind, was the Pre-Raphaelite Brotherhood, which rejected the dominant modes in contemporary academic art, preferring instead an art which was at once more intensely detailed, and more hieratic in relying upon allegory and symbolism. The vivid, intense, mysterious art that the Pre-Raphaelites produced, both in painting and in poetry, worked as an implicit criticism of the drabness and ugliness of the contemporary world. This is especially clear in the medievalism of much of this work, where the medieval world is invoked as a measure of the impossibility of an aesthetically satisfying modernity. Clearly such a cultural politics can be inflected in several directions, towards the merely decorative, for example, or towards a kind of escapism; but combined with the explicit rejection of Political Economy to be found in the works of the group's champion, John Ruskin, Pre-Raphaelitism developed into a powerful critique of the aridity and inhuman destructiveness of the conditions of contemporary labour. Above all, through the life-work of William Morris,

the mid-century aesthetic predispositions of Pre-Raphaelitism became
the basis for a cultural politics that sought to mobilise craft production
and pleasure in labour against the ugliness and mechanism of capitalism.
In Morris's case, this developed, as we have seen, into active revolutionary socialist politics; but equally the aesthetic inheritance of Pre-Raphaelitism, via the work of Ruskin and Morris, informed some of the Arts and
Crafts experiments at the end of the century – experiments which
involved not only the rediscovery of traditional techniques of craft production, but also the establishment of workshops and rural settlements
to practise them. Though this may seem a long way from the paintings
of Millais or the poetry of Dante Gabriel Rossetti, Ruskinian and Morrisian notions about craft and labour did strike a chord, especially amongst
sections of the skilled working class, and the recruitment to these late-
century Craft experiments was by no means only middle-class.[20]

Turning finally to late nineteenth-century Socialism as it drew upon
elite cultural and intellectual resources, we can see that Morris, with
his Pre-Raphaelite and Ruskinian ideas, provided only one of the
many currents that fed into that broad stream. Quite apart from the contentious question of the influence of Marxism on Socialism in the last two
decades of the century, we can recognise an indigenous strain of progressive middle-class thought which made the transition to socialism
with relative ease – though the kind of socialism espoused, broadly evolutionary and even managerial, was very different from the revolutionary politics of Morris and the explicitly Marxist factions. Writers and
social critics as diverse as Sidney Webb (1859–1947), Beatrice Webb
(1858–1943), George Bernard Shaw (1856–1950) and J. A. Hobson
(1858–1940) made use of an eclectic range of social thought, from Herbert Spencer, Political Economy and John Ruskin, to fashion a varied
and authoritative critique of late nineteenth-century social relations – a
critique that would sustain its authority well into the twentieth century.

A very different figure is presented by Edward Carpenter (1844–
1929), sometimes described as the English Tolstoy, and like the Russian,
a prophet of the simple life. Carpenter's books and his poem, *Towards
Democracy*, were widely influential amongst sections of the Socialist
Movement in the late nineteenth century; coupled with his sexual politics (he was a feminist, and actively homosexual), his socialism represents a particular inflection of the tradition of Carlyle and Ruskin,
infused with a strong dose of mysticism and the poetry of the American,
Walt Whitman. This seems an unlikely combination to attract any
significant working-class support, but in fact in certain northern

towns, notably Blackburn and Bury, Carpenter did have a real following through such associations as the Whitman Club; he was also part of the intellectual world, for example, of the young miner's son D. H. Lawrence (1885–1930) at the end of the century. Carpenter's life encompassed a series of transitions through available cultural institutions. He was actually ordained in the Church of England (he was curate to F. D. Maurice, an Anglican priest sympathetic to Christian Socialism [see above, Chapter 2]); became a lecturer for University Extension, thus coming into contact with the industrial working class in Sheffield; and ended by becoming a kind of guru, living the simple life in a cottage near Sheffield with his working class homosexual partner. While his own life-history was clearly marked by a particular combination of sexual and class politics, his socialism, and the Utopian anticipations that characterise it, takes as its starting point the repudiation of the cluttered materialism and stultified sexuality of the middle class. His influence, both personal and in his writings, are an example of the way that certain elite cultural forms, with unlikely provenances, could nevertheless find a following amongst sections of the working class.

Finally, in addition to these explicitly socialist writers, late nineteenth-century writers testify to reading the works of Carlyle and Ruskin; it is clear that despite their authoritarianism, their anti-feminism and their racism, these canonical writers of the 'culture and society' tradition within English intellectual life could serve as an important cultural and intellectual resource for both middle-and working-class socialists. And this is perhaps the emphasis with which we should leave this chapter, an emphasis that points to the plasticity of cultural forms and cultural production. I have been stressing the connection between cultural forms and particular forms of life, but in the hopes of suggesting how the repertoire of cultural forms has its own diverse origins and history, and how different elements within that repertoire can speak with particular power at different moments and to different sections of the popular classes. In being made to speak, they can take on accents quite different from the ones in which they were first articulated. Socialism itself, I have suggested, had a limited but real following within the late nineteenth-century working class; Carlyle and Ruskin could be drawn on and refashioned to speak progressive and egalitarian meanings, to supplement the explicit Socialism of Morris, Carpenter or even Marx. There is little that is extraordinary in this; it is just the normal process whereby the meanings carried within and by the forms of culture are negotiated in the exigencies of individual and social life.

4

RURAL ENGLAND

In this chapter I consider one of the major faultlines that fissured the history of nineteenth-century England, the division between the urban and the rural. In particular, I will discuss the social and cultural life of rural England, and the continuing influence of this life throughout the century – this despite the fact that one of the most important transformations in the course of our period was from a predominantly rural to a predominantly urban and industrial country. The topic of this chapter, then, is both the culture *of* rural England, and the culture *about* rural England – much of which, it is important to note, is only to be understood as emerging not from the countryside but from the town.

The Cultural Forms of Rural England

We must begin the discussion by recognising that, while the visible signs of industrialisation and urbanisation were perhaps more dramatic, rural England at the beginning of the nineteenth century was undergoing changes every bit as profound as those which were boosting the populations of the manufacturing districts. The 'traditional' England of the countryside was not traditional at all, but was busy being transformed by the demands of profit-seeking and rationalising capital. Above all, in the arable areas of the South and East, the process of enclosures reached its climax in the early years of the century, transforming, where it occurred, even the physical appearance of the land – new field boundaries, patterns of settlement (isolated farmhouse rather than nuclear village), carefully placed coppice and covert. Other changes later in the century, especially the coming of the railways, were to change the countryside still further, allowing for unprecedented movements in population and goods: at the end of the century, milk on London breakfast tables could have been brought from the West Country or even Ireland.

The process of enclosure at the beginning of the century also transformed the social relations of the countryside. In part this was a process by which customary economic and social relations were replaced by more directly monetary ones – instead of receiving their wages in their keep, labourers would henceforth be paid a weekly wage; cottagers had their grazing and gathering rights bought out. But, more profoundly, this was a process of substantial dispossession, in the course of which a whole mass of the population were driven into the most direct and in places abject dependency on their farming employers, where previously they had had a variety of 'traditional' and customary supports – the patch of common land on which they could graze a cow, the bit of woodland in which they could gather fuel. By the beginning of the century, the typical English pattern of landlord, tenant farmer and landless labourer was established across large areas of the country.

This pattern was by no means universal, neither within the arable South-East where it predominated, nor in the pastoral and mixed economies of the North and West. Within the South-East, greater or lesser proportions of the country were owned by the aristocracy and the gentry, and the experience of village life could vary enormously between 'open' and 'closed' villages – that is, between villages dominated by a single landlord, and those with a number of small proprietors. In the former, relations of paternalism and deference could be especially marked, and the social and cultural power of the landlord, and his immediate ally the vicar, could be immense. In 'open' parishes, by contrast, more independent but also rougher and more unregulated social relations could prevail. A still more important contrast persisted throughout the nineteenth century between the South-East and the North and West. Though it was certainly possible, in the latter two areas, to find the same arrangement of landlord, tenant farmer and landless labourer, a number of conditions were very different. In the first place, competition from the industrial towns of the North meant that wage rates were usually higher there throughout the century. Secondly, older patterns of hiring persisted in the North long beyond their effective demise in the South, above all the practice of hiring by the year, with unmarried servants (and, in Northumberland especially, married servants) living with their farming employers and either eating at the same table or living in adjacent cottages. In the upland areas of the Pennines, Cumberland and Wales, independent peasant farming was the norm, and patterns of small proprietorship were common in other areas also, notably in south Lancashire. All these economic and social differences had profound implications for the cultures that both persisted and were reinvented in the course of the century.

The process of dispossession that I have described entailed a cultural realignment as much as a socio-economic one. One pattern of social relations, involving certain expectations of one's neighbours and of one's social superiors and inferiors, was rudely displaced in favour of another. This was a process that was bitterly resented and contested by its principal victims, namely the now landless labourers. In fact, the first forty years or so of the century was a period of sporadic and sometimes acute social tension in the countryside, seen very obviously in the Captain Swing riots and machine-breaking that swept the south-eastern counties in 1831, but also in the endemic rick-burning in these same counties, a form of embittered protest that persisted at least until the 1840s. The historians of Captain Swing have interpreted it as the last militant defence of a traditional 'moral economy' that had bound farmers and their servants in relations of at least partially mutual dependence (indeed 'labourers' is a term that registers, though not consistently, an employing situation that post-dates this moral economy).[1] But at just the same time as the Captain Swing riots, Parliament passed the new Poor Law (1834). This measure, which sought to abolish outdoor relief and to substitute for it the 'less eligible' option of familial separation and hard labour in the workhouse, should be seen as the culminating effort in a long-drawn out attempt to discipline the rural poor and to drive down their wages. The patterns of rural deference and paternalism that emerged in the middle years of the century can be described as a kind of new model paternalism, at once intent on exacting deference in sometimes minutely degrading ways, and at the same time intent on securing the 'independence' of the rural poor – i.e. their willingness to survive on diminished and, in places, near-starvation wages.

Culture, I have been suggesting, is the way in which people make sense of the lives they lead, the manner in which they attribute meaning to the world they inhabit and the people they encounter in it. What sort of sense did people make of the changes, realignments and dispossessions that I have been describing? Let us start with one power-ful voice from the beginning of the century, that of William Cobbett, (mentioned also in Chapter 3 above) – former sergeant and Tory propa-gandist, turned Radical journalist and spokesman for the agricultural labourers. His *Rural Rides*, written during the 1820s, provide sharply polemical accounts of the state of rural England as he rode through and about it. In the following passage he describes a sale at a farm near Reigate in Surrey – the farmer is selling up:

> Every thing about this farm-house was formerly the scene of *plain manners* and *plentiful living*. Oak clothes- chests, oak bedsteads, oak chests of drawers, and oak table to eat on, long, strong, and well supplied with joint stools. Some of the things were many hundreds of years old. But all appeared to be in a state of decay and nearly of *disuse*. There appeared to have been hardly any *family* in that house, where formerly there were, in all probability, from ten to fifteen men, boys, and maids: and, which was the worst of all, there was a *parlour!* Aye, and a *carpet* and *bell- pull* too! One end of the front of this once plain and substantial house had been moulded into a *'parlour;'* and there was the mahogany table, and the fine chairs, and the fine glass, and all as bare-faced upstart as any stock-jobber in the kingdom can boast of. . . . And, there were the decanters, the glasses, the 'dinner-set' of crockery ware, and all just in the true stock-jobber style. And I dare say it has been *'Squire* Charington and the *Miss* Charingtons; and not plain Master Charington, and his son Hodge, and his daughter Betty Charington, all of whom this accursed system has, in all like-lihood, transmuted into a species of mock gentlefolks, while it has ground the labourers down into real slaves. Why do not farmers now *feed* and *lodge* their work-people as they did formerly? Because they cannot keep them *upon so little* as they give them in wages.[2]

I am reluctant to describe this simply as nostalgia for the old days, though doubtless there is something of this in it. It is more important to see it as adopting a specific evaluative stance towards the changes it is describing, of scorn of course towards the modish and expensive new ways, and of praise, yes, for the departed system; but this is praise set in a specific set of social relationships, where the old and discarded items of furniture are redolent of the form of life to which they testify. That oak table, with its joint stools, testify, to Cobbett, of a way of organ-ising both familial and economic life that has been broken by the 'stock-

jobbing' system. Cobbett thus articulates a sense of a social and cultural
system, where such matters as household objects, first names and forms
of address are indicative of a whole way of life; in this instance, of one
way of life that has been supplanted by another. In doing so, he is himself being creatively and imaginatively inventive, making meaning out of
the bare facts of a farm sale. This *is* culture, expressed with a peculiar
directness and intimate knowledge on behalf of those people about
whom he writes.

Cobbett was certainly not alone in testifying to a sense of loss and
betrayal in the agricultural 'improvements' that overtook England
from the late eighteenth century onwards. Here is another voice, this
time emerging from amongst the ranks of the labourers, but inflected
through the accents of an elite cultural form, that of poetic satire. It is
the voice of John Clare, the 'Peasant Poet' (to give him the label by
which he was known and patronised). This quotation comes from his
poem *The Parish*, written at almost exactly the same time as Cobbett's
Rural Rides, expressing in some ways the same sentiments, but expressing them from a different position in the social hierarchy, and with
quite different accent and address:

> That good old fame the farmers earnd of yore
> That made as equals not as slaves the poor
> That good old fame did in two sparks expire
> A shooting coxcomb and a hunting Squire
> And their old mansions that was dignified
> With things far better then the pomp of pride
> At whose oak table that was plainly spread
> Each guest was welcomed and the poor was fed
> Were master son and serving man and clown
> Without distinction daily sat them down
> Were the bright rows of pewter by the wall
> Se[r]ved all the pomp of kitchen or of hall
> These all have vanished like a dream of good
> And the slim things that rises were they stood
> Are built by those whose clownish taste aspires
> To hate their farms and ape their country squires....[3]

These are remarkable lines, articulating so exactly the writer's sense of
the vanished 'dream of good', realised in just the same objects as Cobbett – the old-fashioned oak and pewter. But Clare's use of the heroic

couplets of elite culture give this quite a different force from the impatient vernacular of Cobbett, as indeed perhaps does the use of the derogatory 'clown' for agricultural labourer, where the 'peasant poet' has internalised, it seems, rather too much of the downward glance of his betters. Nevertheless, Clare finds just the appropriate combination of backward-looking righteousness and scorn for the crassly contemporary in the elite form of eighteenth-century satire where this combination is very familiar. As many later, urban, working- class poets found, the relatively archaic forms of the eighteenth century lay better to Clare's hand than the accents of the great Romantic poets, his contemporaries. So here is a case of a working-class rural poet powerfully articulating his sense of social and economic displacement, and drawing on the idiom of the elite to do so.

We can add to these accounts the following broadside ballad of the 'new-fashioned farmer', an attack on the 'pride' of the new farmers:

In former times, both plain and neat, they'd go to church on Sunday,
Then to harrow, plough or sow they'd go upon a Monday.
But now, instead of the plough tail, o'er hedges they are jumping;
Instead of sowing of their corn their delight is in fox-hunting.

The farmers' daughters used to work all at the spinning wheel, sir;
Now such furniture as that is thought quite ungenteel, sir.
Their fingers they're afraid to spoil with all such kind of sport, sir,
And sooner than a mop or broom they'd handle a piano-forte, sir.[4]

This is rough and ready, to be sure, but it too articulates a sense of a way of life being disrupted, not by anonymous economic forces, but by particular individuals acting in certain, blameable and culturally specific ways. A culture in which following the hounds is preferable to following the plough, and playing the piano is preferable to turning the spinning-wheel, is seen, from below, as a culture where 'improvement' is paid for by those at the bottom of the social hierarchy.

But how does all this look when seen from above? We need seek no further than the novels of Jane Austen for the answer. Making all due allowances for her sharpness of judgement, and admitting that her perspective is not quite that of the very highest members of the landowning class but of its subalterns, her novels take for granted the broad facts of social hierarchy and of the place of the great house at the top of it. This is especially true of *Mansfield Park*, published in 1814, and thus only a few years before Cobbett and Clare were viewing rural England with very different eyes. Seen from the great house, the farmers and the poor scarcely enter the landscape; they are there mostly to provide the servants to service the life that goes on in and between the great houses in which the novel is set – unless, indeed, they are there to scare Fanny, the novel's heroine, as the relatively impoverished life at Portsmouth is brought before her to remind her of what she risks losing. For all that, Austen is very aware of the agricultural landscape as a working one; Mary Crawford appears to her disadvantage when she expects a cart to be available to carry her trunk at harvest time. But even this example suggests the appropriate responsibility of the social leaders towards their social inferiors. This is not to criticise the novel, and certainly not to suggest that Austen herself is not critical of the life she is describing. *Mansfield Park* is in some respects sharply disapproving of the failures of the inhabitants of the great house to behave as they ought to – indeed they are seen as frivolously and recklessly superficial and immoral. But the novel is a call to arms: to the right-thinking members of the gentry to resume their appropriate responsibilities in the world, and to reassert the values (ultimately religious) which qualify them for rule.

'Improvement' in this novel therefore means something related to, but finally different from the 'improvements' wrought by capital on an unenclosed agriculture. Improvement concerns the transformations to be made to Sotherton, a neighbouring great house to Mansfield Park, where money is to be spent in turning the 'unimproved' house into something more like a tasteful mansion. This is a countryside that is changing, but seen from above, the changes are of a rather different and less painful kind than those felt so deeply, though in such different ways, by Clare and Cobbett.

The country-house novel, following *Mansfield Park*, will be one important form of fiction throughout the century, though of course the valuations being articulated through it, with respect to the paternalist social order represented by the country house, will vary greatly. Disraeli, Trollope, George Eliot, George Meredith, Dickens, Henry James, Thomas Hardy, H. G. Wells – all will take the social order of the countryside as the subject of their writing, and try to assess it through a study of its most visible and powerful symbol. The country house, in this sense, becomes a kind of imaginary place, an organising trope for the novelistic imagination, just as it had been for the poets and landscape painters of the seventeenth and eighteenth centuries. Moreover, since the great houses of the landowning aristocracy and gentry were effectively the houses of the British ruling class – those people dominating the offices of state throughout our period – in confronting the country house, these novelists were in effect confronting the people who ruled them. When Dickens writes about Chesney Wold in *Bleak House*, he is taking on not only Sir Leicester Dedlock, its owner, but the whole conservative ruling class which he represents. This means that though Dickens certainly recognises the specificity of the *rural* social order, he sees it also as part of a wider system of government and social domination that is not confined to the countryside. One of the great achievements of nineteenth-century culture was to recognise a whole system of rule beyond even that evident, and experientially crucial, division marking off the country from the city.

Early nineteenth-century rural society, then, was in a process of transformation, especially in those areas of rural England in which the transition to a fully capitalised economy was being effected – in those areas, especially, where 'King Corn' was to establish his dominion until the great rural depression in the last quarter of the century. What cultural understandings and resources could the inhabitants of nineteenth- century rural England make use of? I have already suggested that their resources were at the very least diverse. The rural elite, for instance, could participate to a greater or lesser extent in both the life of their immediate social surroundings and in the life and culture of the 'nation'. For the aristocracy, this meant an easy transition from country to town and back again; theirs was not a distinct rural culture but a sense of authority both in the immediate vicinity and in the country at large. Their male children were either educated at home, or, increasingly as the century progressed, in the great public schools which prepared them for rule. Their daughters were educated at home and trained, with obviously varying emphases, to take social and cultural leadership locally, and look to marriage with other similar families. The cultural resources of these people were, at least in principle, considerable; in the 1860s, however, Matthew Arnold chose to characterise them as 'Barbarians' in view of their apparent preference for military and sporting pursuits over the delights of the traditional classical culture in which they were nominally educated. Even given this hostile assessment, it is hard to underestimate the enormous social prestige wielded by the aristocratic elite throughout the nineteenth century.

The gentry equally could deploy considerable cultural resources, and though they might look to the 'county' and the nearest county town (rather than the nation and London) they too could move comfortably in and out of rural society. As we move down the social scale, participation in elite culture obviously diminishes, and reliance on traditional, oral cultural forms becomes more evident. But this too is a matter of great variety and change. Literacy rates among agricultural labourers, for example, improved greatly during the century, especially following the imposition of compulsory elementary education after 1870; but such labourers were by no means devoid of literate cultural resources earlier in the century. Joseph Arch, already mentioned in Chapter 2 for his hostility to the rural Church of England, and the leader of the National Agricultural Labourers' Union in the 1870s, could look back to a childhood in the 1820s and 1830s in which 'Shakespeare and the Bible were the books I was brought up on';[5] clearly, for many highly skilled rural workers like Arch there was access, not without great struggle and difficulty, to very considerable literate culture. Moreover, we should not assume that access to such culture was simply improved by the process of formal schooling, either in the patchy private and church-dominated schooling before 1870, or in the still church-dominated but state supported system after that date. These schools for labourers' children were not intended to do anything more than to fit them for a life of deference and labour; they scarcely took the children beyond the most basic levels, and right up to the very end of the century their priorities can be measured by the widespread practice of children being taken out of school by the requirements of local agricultural labour. The real education that people like Arch achieved for themselves they got by virtue of their own efforts and by the presence of dissenting cultural and social institutions – in Arch's case, by his membership of the Primitive Methodist Church.

The period from 1850 to 1875, sometimes known as the 'Golden Age' of English agriculture, can also be seen as the age of reinvented paternalist social relations, in which deferential attitudes were enforced in combination with benevolence and vigilant moral surveillance. This is as much an imaginative or cultural state of affairs as it is a matter of material history or sociology. We need to recognise the extent to which the imposition of such social relations in the countryside required prolonged imaginative preparation, in countless novels, paintings, poems, and extracts of political economy; and how it also required constant renegotiation as the rural elites acted out their sense of themselves and their social dependants in the actualities of their lives. In addition, we need to recognise how the rural poor were not simply consumed by their sense of deference or dependence, despite the comparative absence of overt forms of contestation (such as riots or rick-burning) after mid-century. Agricultural unionism from the 1870s onwards is only one piece of testimony in this vein. In the later years of the century, the countryside was increasingly penetrated by commercial cultural forms which proposed wholly other ways of relating to one's betters than those proposed by landlord or Vicar. It is also impossible to calculate how widespread were private areas of dissent or resistance, like the one recollected by a farmworker called Arthur Tweedy when he asked his father why he should address the landlord as 'Sir'. ' "Sir", my boy,' his father replied, 'is only the nickname for a fool.'[6] In short, despite the great prestige of the English landed gentry and aristocracy, despite the extraordinary expressions of that wealth and prestige found in the great country houses with their armies of servants, landscaped parks and protected shooting, the English countryside was never simply in their thrall but was inhabited by people with at least some cultural resources beyond their control.

The culture of rural England in the nineteenth century was therefore a complex matter in a number of ways. We have seen that we need to recognise both geographical diversity and change over time. But we also need to remember one of the themes of this book: that no culture, even of one single time and place, is simply homogeneous, but is much more raggedly diverse and self-contradictory, made up of cultural forms with different social origins, and permitting widely divergent attitudes and responses, sometimes in the same person and at the same time. Fred Kitchen draws a vivid picture of his youth on a Yorkshire farm at the end of the century, and of his fellow unmarried workers meeting in the stable in the evening to tell stories and sing songs. They told stories with which their grandfathers would doubtless have been familiar, of boggarts and witches; sang songs, some traditional, some from the music-hall, and some sentimental parlour ballads; and played traditional games like fox-and-geese. Kitchen himself was doubtless exceptional in reading his way through George Eliot and Dickens; but he also noticed that when his purely agricultural village was invaded by railways and then companies of miners, the range of songs extended to include more of the current commercial music. The farm lads used to gather for their social evenings on bicycles, exemplary product of late nineteenth-century industrialism. This is a recognisable and compelling account of a particular cultural moment, but the culture here is certainly not all of a piece, and Kitchen was at the crossroads of a rich diversity of cultural forms. To a greater or lesser degree, this is the story of the nineteenth-century countryside, though the potential conflicts between different aspects of this cultural mix were undoubtedly much more evident and stressful in other parts of the country, and at other times, in comparison with Kitchen's benignly remembered childhood.[7]

The day-to-day lived culture of the rural working class, then, was by no means one solely made up of the shreds and tatters of traditional culture, as more sentimental and backward- looking accounts have sometimes suggested. While it would be equally foolish to overestimate the cultural range and diversity of some areas of rural England, there was a real if limited diversity of institutions which encouraged some diversity of culture, and permitted varying degrees of resistance to or abdication from dominant and imposed cultural forms.

English Pastoral

In turning from the cultural resources *within* rural England to the culture *about* rural England, it is striking how the English countryside becomes the object of a great mass and variety of cultural constructions in the nineteenth century. The paradox has frequently been noted that just as England was becoming a predominantly urban country, its apparent sense of itself became increasingly fixated upon rurality. But I do not wish to suggest that all this variety of cultural material, from poems and novels to paintings and music and indeed the design, location and landscaping of domestic buildings, can simply be written off as a mistake, as some kind of collective delusion about the realities of nineteenth-century life. On the contrary, I shall seek to show how this multiplicity of cultural forms can carry important meanings, as much about urban and industrial life as about the rural life it takes as its predominant subject. There may indeed be an element of mystification in pastoral, but that is not the whole truth of the matter, for pastoral is a mobile form which can be deployed in very different ways and for very different purposes.

Pastoral, in all its varieties, provides a convenient way in to many of the cultural constructions of rural England throughout the nineteenth century. It has always been a sophisticated form, self-consciously offering the 'simplicities' of rural life as an antidote to the complexities of the court or the city. Precisely because it is a form which is conscious of other social possibilities, it can be used as an implicit or explicit critique of the urban or court milieu from which it typically springs. We shall see how these possibilities are realised in what follows. Principally, though, it should be noted how widespread are versions of pastoral in many different media throughout the nineteenth century. In poetry, painting, the novel, music and domestic architecture, it makes sense to talk of pastoral as a central form; at the end of the century, a range of writing came to be gathered together as 'country writing', and this too is a version of pastoral.

If evidence were required of the intimacy with which cultural forms can be lived, domestic architecture surely provides it. Not only the exterior shapes, but the organisation of interior space, the relation of work (domestic and non-domestic) to leisure, gender relations, and the boundaries of private space, are all mapped with greater or lesser degrees of fit on to the layout and design of domestic buildings. The historians Davidoff and Hall have provided an account of the way pastoral entered intimately into the self-perceptions of the Birmingham middle class at the beginning of the century, as they sought to leave the centre of Birmingham for the more secluded, less urban and more pastoral environment of Edgbaston, creating as they did so a new suburb for the city.[8] This involved, in addition to the genuine and personally felt pleasures of 'rural' life, a reorganisation of both social and gender relations, with families moving away from their place of work or business, the removal of women from working in or managing their concerns, the redesignation of the domestic home as predominantly feminine, and the creation of a sense of retreat from the difficulties and competition of the market-place. This is a movement that can doubtless be mirrored in most of the major cities of England in the course of the nineteenth century. It is quite a different phenomenon from the later aping of the landowning class by industrial manufacturers who had made their fortune. On the contrary, this is not a retreat from manufacturing or commerce, but a reorganisation of the social, cultural and gendered space in which they are conducted; at the heart of this profound reorganisation is the idea of pastoral.

I start with this particular use of pastoral to remind us of the intimacy and profundity of cultural forms – that they enter into and shape human lives, and are not merely added on after the fact to a social or economic history which is going on, essentially, elsewhere. In the case of domestic architecture, that is easy to see. But I think it is true in the other cultural forms that I shall be discussing now, where representations of rural England have real consequences for their readers' and spectators' sense of themselves, of who, and what sort of people, they are. When the Romantic poets, at the very beginning of the period, found the truth of themselves as human beings only to be realised in the natural world, not 'in the great city, pent 'mid cloisters dim', but 'By lakes and sandy shores, beneath the crags/Of ancient mountains, and beneath the clouds;'[9] or when Yeats, at the very end of our period, says that he feels the call of rural Ireland: 'While I stand on the roadway, or on the pavements grey,/I hear it in the deep heart's core;'[10] then these writers are situating themselves, and their most intimate sense of themselves, in relation to the social and cultural dividing-line between country and city that runs through nineteenth-century English (and Irish) society.

Romantic poetry, however, immediately complicates the idea of the 'pastoral', for though some Romantic poems are indeed 'pastorals' (or at least they describe themselves as such), much Romantic poetry invokes an idea of the natural world which goes beyond the possibilities of that form. While the characteristic landscapes of romanticism are certainly not urban, they are not simply pastoral either; at their most ambitious or sublime, poets like Wordsworth, Coleridge and Shelley find in the forms of the natural world – mountains, cataracts, sunsets, wind, bleak moors – profound challenges or antitheses to all merely human understandings or constructions. To read parts of Wordsworth's *The Prelude* (not published until 1850, but written much earlier in the century and much revised), or Shelley's *Mont Blanc* (1816) is not, however, to be removed from the actualities of social life, but to find a rebuke to them – Romanticism in this vein is the effort to find some ground or basis for a life beyond the inadequacies currently available (though recognising always the impossibility of such a search). Unlike pastoral, poetry of the sublime opposes to the degraded world of the city not a version of rural social life but a version of the natural world offered as beyond the social. Nevertheless, the poetry must return to the social world, and in doing so it offers to its readers a refreshed and reinvigorated sense of themselves.

The Romantic 'sublime', which I am offering here in contrast to pastoral poetry, provides a powerful model for poetry throughout the century. But pastoral persists as a form also, in innumerable poems expressing pleasure in the details of the countryside and in the so-called simplicities of rural life. I do not wish to deride this; we have already seen how John Clare could use the traditions of eighteenth-century satire for his own purposes in writing *The Parish*, and it is equally true that he could put the conventions of pastoral to use in his poetry. In other words, pastoral is not simply a form imposed upon the landscape and the rural poor as a kind of middle-or upper-class mystification – it could be taken and reused by the labouring poor themselves. Indeed, as we have seen, the idiom of pastoral, largely established in the eighteenth century, proved in some respects more amenable to self-taught writers than the idiom of the romantic sublime – Chartist poets in the 1840s found the idiom of pastoral a very congenial one for expressing their politics. And the language of pastoral also proved congenial to many women poets in the nineteenth century, offering them a surprisingly subtle vocabulary for the emotions. Laetitia Landon, Felicia Hemans, Elizabeth Barrett Browning, Christina Rossetti, to name only the most famous, could all in their different ways exploit the idiom of pastoral for complex and sometimes disturbing effects.

Questions of the 'truth' of pastoral, counter-pastoral, and the associated questions of the 'picturesque' were perhaps most intensely debated with respect to painting. When George Eliot, in the 1850s, wanted to find aesthetic models for the kind of writing she was producing (for example in *Adam Bede* [1859]), she turned first to examples from painting. A range of painters in the first thirty or forty years of the century produced a series of landscapes and genre paintings (exemplary situations of popular life) in which the possibilities of pastoral and its associated forms were exhaustively explored. Such painting (especially genre painting, which came quite low down in the hierarchy of genres) was not the most prestigious kind of painting in the early nineteenth century; nevertheless, in it we can trace a whole series of ideas about rural England and its social relations.

Different generic models were of course available to the painters in the first part of the century, ranging from 'classical' landscape-painting, through a more specifically 'Englished' version of pastoral, to genre painting taking Dutch scenes of peasant and domestic life as its model. Each of these forms had its own possibilities and limitations. In the classical tradition, as for example in some of the early work of J. M. W. Turner (1775–1851), the English (or Welsh or Scottish) landscape is reimagined in the light of the landscape tradition of the French painters Claude or Poussin. This is a very frank kind of idealisation, soon to be replaced in Turner by his own painterly version of the Romantic sublime. In the paintings of George Morland (1763–1804) and John Constable (1776–1837) we see very different solutions to the problems of representing the rural landscape and the people who inhabit and

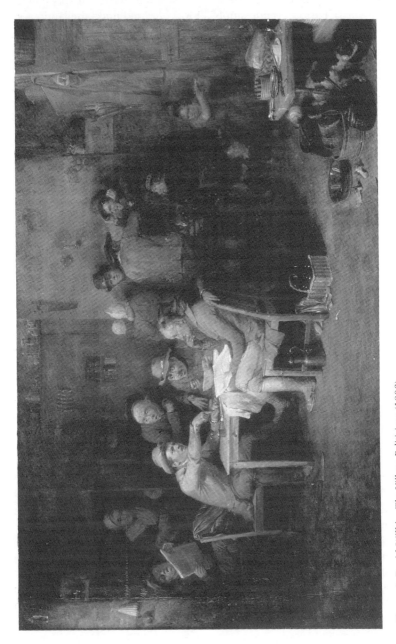

Figure 1   David Wilkie, *The Village Politicians* (1806)

work in it. Morland's painting, though often dismissed as a sentimenta-lising form of genre pictures, in fact is often much more equivocal in its treatment of the rural poor, in some cases refusing to represent them in groups of idealised labour or in equally idealised deference to their social superiors. Similarly, Constable certainly does not simply paint out rural labour from his landscapes, although that labour is suffic-iently distanced to be at once acknowledged and rendered unthrea-tening.[11]

In genre painting, which takes the domestic interior as its typical sub-ject, there is an equivalent range of possibilities.[12] One tradition looks directly back to Dutch painters such as Ostade or Teniers, and does not balk at the ugliness and comic degradation of the people it paints. So, in a painting like *The Village Politicians* (1806) by David Wilkie (1785–1841), the occupants of a rural inn are shown in unprepossessing attitudes: opinionated, stupidly agape, or just plain fuddled (Figure 1). No 'village Hampdens' here. But Wilkie could also paint *Rent Day* and *Distraining for Rent*, in which the rural poor are more sympathetically, if also more patronisingly, represented in attitudes of appropriate defer-ence as they pay their rent to the landlord in one instance and as their homes are threatened in another. And though Wilkie was the best known of the genre painters of peasant life at the beginning of the nine-teenth century, his work was accompanied by a great number of other paintings of the poor in domestic rural scenes, executed with more or less sentimentality and wishful thinking.

In all these cases, the painters are seeking to represent the rural poor, not to the poor themselves, but to their social superiors; the varieties of painterly arrangement, the decisions about attitude, perspective, figures in near, middle or far distance, all these matters are formal resolutions of this particular set of social relations. 'Sympathy', though of course preferable to the caricaturing hostility which represents the poor as stu-pid, degraded or ferocious, is equally a function of this downward glance, of this arrangement of people from above. It is not simply, then, that some of these paintings falsify the realities of rural life, though some of them undoubtedly do so. It is much more a question of the gen-res that were available to painters as they approached their subject mat-ter. Genres speak the social relations that produce them; and given the social relations that governed the production of art, it is hard to see how any painter could have single-handedly invented another mode. At all events, the alternative to the widely acknowledged sentimentalisation of rural labour in the pictures of the early nineteenth century was not simply an insistence upon its degradation – that too had its own ideological implications. In practical terms, this presented itself to painters (and to writers who shared many of the same aesthetic starting points and dilemmas) as the extent to which they should 'idealise' the rural landscape and its inhabitants. In negotiating this practical formal difficulty, the painters were inevitably positioning themselves in different ways in the set of social relationships constituted by the painting itself, in its calling into being of the differentially socially positioned subject and spectator.

Painters like Morland and Constable were essentially working within an older tradition of landscape painting, 'Englishing' it as necessary. Pre-Raphaelite painters at the middle of the century (discussed in the previous chapter as a dissident cultural fraction) set themselves against that tradition, finding in a still older medieval art examples that served their purposes much more productively. Though not usually landscape artists, the Pre-Raphaelites did observe the landscape minutely, often using it as a highly detailed and coloured element in their symbolic or didactic pictures. This moralised landscape – as in paintings by Holman Hunt such as *The Hireling Shepherd* (1851) or *Our English Coasts* (1852) – perceives the landscape quite differently from classicism, insisting on its vivid presentness rather than its shaped and aestheticised distance. But Pre-Raphaelitism, like the academic art which it sought to replace, can be inflected in very different directions. It produced paintings in which the injunction to 'realism' – understood as the exact observation of nature – was realised as unsentimental social concern, as in Henry Wallis's *The Stonebreaker* (1857) (Figure 2). It could also produce its own kind of decorativeness. But even here, the familiar plants and animals of the English countryside could be extensively used (in, for example, the decorative work of William Morris and later the Arts and Crafts Movement) as a protest against the neoclassical pomposities of high Victorian society – the direct traditions of the 'Great Exhibition of international vulgarity', as Oscar Wilde put it.[13] Furthermore, the insistence upon natural form could act as a protest against the perceived ugliness of industrialism. Once again, formal decisions, such as the colour and detail used to represent a landscape, have real ideological implications, but ones which are only realised in the changing contexts of the works' use and consumption.

In the later nineteenth century, the English rural landscape became the focus of ever more intense nostalgia, so that a painting like Benjamin Leader's *February Fill Dyke* (1881), with its remarkable sense of longing in a scene of a cottage at sunset in a partially flooded landscape, could become one of the most widely reproduced and famous images of its period. But this picture comes from the last two decades of the century, by which time the predominantly urban character of England was no longer in doubt, and when concerns about the degeneration of the towns were becoming widespread. In this situation, the countryside began to take a variety of meanings which emerge above all from its contrast to the town. *February Fill Dyke*'s appeal, then and now, comes in part from its capacity to envisage a landscape filled with the promise of significance, even spiritual significance, in a world apparently losing its capacity to speak in such ways.

English landscape painting in the nineteenth century, then, draws on several traditions, and inflects those traditions in different ways, re-presenting the landscape and its inhabitants, and positioning the spectator in different ways in relation to that landscape. All these are specific formal resolutions to differential social relations, some of them carried

Figure 2 Henry Wallis, *The Stonebreaker* (1857)

at deep generic levels (like the conventions of landscape painting and the positioning of the spectator with respect to natural features, figures and buildings); others to be found in the specific social and ideological address of the painter, as with Wallis's social concern in *The Stonebreaker*. Painting, no less than other cultural forms, draws upon conventions that are at once social and aesthetic.

I have suggested already that when George Eliot approached some of the aesthetic problems raised by representing rural life in the 1850s, both as a writer on social subjects and as a beginning novelist, she looked to painting to provide her with some of her models. What she wished to avoid above all was a version of the picturesque, pastoral labourers who would falsely excite the sympathies of middle-and upper-class readers, only to have those sympathies disgusted when confronted by peasants 'in all their coarse apathy'. As we have seen, it is not sufficient simply to confront the sentimentalities of pastoral with the brutalities of counter-pastoral; that has its own distortions, as when, in the same essay that she protests at picturesque distortion, Eliot writes as follows: 'That delicious effervescence of the mind which we call fun, has no equivalent for the northern peasant, except tipsy revelry; the only realm of fancy and imagination for the English clown exists at the bottom of the third quart pot.'[14] Eliot here has moved from a rejection of sentimentality to a scarcely more attractive reductiveness. She does not write like this in her novels, but this passage does alert us to a real social fissure in them. George Eliot's novelistic project, in the early novels which are most concerned with rural life (*Scenes of Clerical Life* [1857], *Adam Bede* [1859], *The Mill on the Floss* [1860] and *Silas Marner* [1861]), can be described in a phrase of her own that we have already encountered in Chapter 2 above – 'the extension of our sympathies'. Her project was to write about the inhabitants of rural England in such a way as to represent their lives truthfully (so avoiding the sentimental or the picturesque), but also to represent them in a way that would brace the ties of sympathy and charity between the classes; her readers would be led to recognise that they shared the same fundamental joys and tragedies underneath the superficial barriers of class, dialect and locality. This ambitious humanist project – which even claims some of the great aesthetic categories like tragedy for the lives of the rural lower middle class – yet finds it difficult to sustain the same interest in the labouring poor. Eliot certainly refrains from writing with the same brutal frankness that we saw in the quotation above, but she sometimes reverts to her own version of the picturesque when agricultural labourers are in question. The 'extension of our sympathies', in its full aesthetic and social richness, only goes so far down the social scale.

Nevertheless, George Eliot's novels represent one important voice at mid-century which struggled to find an appropriate way of writing about rural England and its inhabitants, rejecting the simplicities of pastoral or the picturesque, though finding it difficult to sustain the fully sympathetic and yet realist combination across the whole social range. Some of her aesthetic difficulties were, of course, created by the complexities of her own position as a writer, both in and out of the social groups she was writing about – the daughter of an agent of the landowning elite, with multiple family connections to the small farmers and provincial middle class of Warwickshire; yet also a metropolitan intellectual in an anomalous personal situation because she lived with a married man. But her difficulties, as I have been emphasising, were also difficulties of genre and form, of the available repertoire of ways of writing, and the inflections she could give to those forms.

Similar points can be made about the nineteenth-century novel more generally. This was a flexible and open form, apparently available to all. But in fact it was made up of a repertoire of sub-genres and more local cultural forms, which entered into the novel not just at the wholesale level ('historical romance', 'silver fork' novel, 'romance', etc.), but also at a lower level, in which writers could avail themselves of different genres or conventions for particular topics. Pastoral, understood as one of these more local forms, thus entered the novel much more frequently than might at first appear, even in novels predominantly about urban England. Thus Dickens, in *Bleak House* (1852–53), draws upon a form of pastoral in talking about the landscape around Chesney Wold, the home of Sir Leicester Dedlock. In general Dickens is hostile to Chesney Wold, seeing it as the centre of a system of paternalist social relations to which he is opposed, and seeing the countryside, indeed, as typically dominated by such relations. But he can also write in a more insipidly pastoral vein, and the novel concludes with a flight to the countryside (or at least the pastoral outskirts of a small rural town) for its heroine. Pastoral has entered even this great novel of nineteenth-century London. It need not be insipid, however. Elizabeth Gaskell, in her Manchester novel *Mary Barton* (1848), adopts a more Wordsworthian pastoral in giving a sense of the early life of Alice, who came to Manchester as a child and dreams of returning to her home in rural north Lancashire. In this way a characteristic nineteenth-century experience, that of the migration from country to town, is managed by means of a literary form which allows Elizabeth Gaskell to suggest the full affective force of such movements.

Dickens and George Eliot were predominantly hostile to the landowning elite, and their view of the great house and its allies was mostly from outside looking in. This was not the case for the majority of nineteenth-century novelists, who, while sometimes critical of the inhabitants of those great houses, mostly shared their perspective and looked from the inside out. As we have seen in the case of Jane Austen, this perspective on the rural landscape is one which generally occludes the majority of its inhabitants, as indeed in literal terms it was designed to do (what else is the function of those parks with their uninterrupted prospects?). The novels of Bulwer Lytton (1803–73), Charles Lever (1806–72), Benjamin Disraeli (1804–81), Anthony Trollope (1815–82) and Catherine Sinclair (1800–64), all in their different ways, take the rural social order for granted and see the great houses of the rural elite, or at least some of them, as the benign centre of that order.

The later nineteenth-century novelist who took rural England as his predominant topic was of course Thomas Hardy. Hardy too draws on a range of forms for making sense of the life he writes about, from the idyll of an early novel like *Under the Greenwood Tree* (1872), to the conscious reference to Greek tragedy in the late novels *Tess of the d'Urbervilles* (1891) and *Jude the Obscure* (1896). Though his work has certainly been assimilated to a nostalgic ruralism, he does not simply show an idyllic rural world threatened by urban modernity; indeed, some of his work is marked by a deliberate counter-pastoral. Moreover, the forces of change and conflict are internal to the rural worlds he writes about, such that destructive social ambitions cause tragedy in *The Woodlanders* (1887), Tess is a victim (among other things) of exploitative economic relations on the farm at Flintcomb Ash, and Jude's tragic itinerary takes him across a southern England which is recognisably that of the late nineteenth century – an England in which rural and urban economies are fully integrated, and where Jude is at home in neither. His tragedy, in one possible Darwinian perspective, is that of modernity itself; he is a man too fine to survive in a coarsely built world – though his is also a common story of a man brought low by his appetites. Rural England evinces Darwinian truths just as much as the world of the city. Which is not to say that Hardy does not give an account of a rural world in transition – he certainly does do this. But the real complexity of his novels is best understood by seeing them as cut across by a variety of forms and ideological commitments, all of them with their own particular history; nostalgic rur-alism is certainly present, but it is definitely not predominant.

Hardy wrote no more novels after *Jude the Obscure*, claiming that the controversy over that novel, and over *Tess of the d'Urbervilles*, had per-manently disgusted him with producing fiction. His decision to stop provides a convenient place to conclude an account of the novel and rural life in the nineteenth century. Such a stopping-point is of course arbitrary; the themes that we have been considering did not cease to be widely interesting in 1900. Thus, two early twentieth-century novels, H. G. Wells's *Tono-Bungay* (1909) and E. M. Forster's *Howard's End* (1910), are both in part 'country-house' novels, seeking to assess the place of that traditional-seeming institution in the ongoing life of a pre-dominantly urban nation. Likewise, the novels of D. H. Lawrence look back in powerful and sometimes underground ways to the novels of Hardy, and are certainly strongly anti-urban. Many of the questions that preoccupied Hardy and other nineteenth-century novelists contin-ued to preoccupy novelists in the twentieth century also.

Late-century Ruralism

'Ruralism' is essentially an urban phenomenon; that is, it arises when there is some perceived threat to rural life from an urban social order that appears in some sense inadequate or even degenerate. In the remainder of this chapter I wish to examine ruralism in late nine-teenth-century England, when anxiety about urban England was acute, and when many people, across a whole range of political posi-tions, sought the antidote to this anxiety in some version of a revived country life. It appeared across a number of cultural forms, from poetry through music, painting, dance, 'arts and crafts', popular iconography and advertising, through to domestic architecture and town planning.

This whole movement should be seen as part of a crisis in the self-understanding of English society in the late nineteenth century, a crisis in turn caused by irreversible changes in that society, which meant that by the 1880s there could no longer be any doubt that this was an urban nation. Moreover, this was an urban nation that had begun to realise what urbanism meant – squalor and misery for many of its inhabitants. The 1880s were no more miserable than the 1860s or the 1870s; simply, more middle-class people began to realise that many others lived in a

permanent state of misery. As we shall see in the next chapter, if Manchester was the shock city of the 1840s, London was the shock city of
the 1880s, a London that was now the metropolis of a great empire.
Many sought a remedy for urban degradations in some kind of return
to rural life, either for themselves, for labouring people more generally,
or for the 'residuum' of the cities degraded beyond help by the urban
circumstances of their lives and dragging others down with them.

A further element contributed both to a sense of crisis, and to particular ruralist resolutions to it. A crisis in English agriculture itself, known
as the Great Depression, set in from the mid-1870s onwards. Beginning
with a series of bad harvests caused by persistent wet weather, by the
1880s the crisis became more widespread as the long-term effects of
American and Canadian imports of wheat began to be felt. The depression was especially severe for arable farmers; it meant, in effect, the end
of 'King Corn'. It entailed widespread rent-reductions for landlords;
impoverishment and often bankruptcy for tenant farmers; further
casualisation or unemployment for rural labourers. Some parts of the
land, most famously in Essex, simply went out of production; many
other areas were forced to switch from arable to mixed farming, still
further increasing their dependency on the towns by producing milk
for the urban market. The countryside which many sought to offer as
a refuge from the problems of the city was itself in manifest difficulties.

A combined sense of urban squalor and rural depression meant that
nothing less than the future of England seemed at risk. This was in part
the result of a specific theory, that of urban degeneration – the belief
that over a matter of three generations, healthy rural immigrant stock
(fine strapping peasants) degenerated to become the miserable physical
specimens that swarmed on the London streets (underbred Cock-
neys).[15] Such a theory could only take widespread hold because it contributed to other anxieties of the period, such as Social Darwinian fears
about breeding a race of moral and physical degenerates who were
nevertheless better adapted to urban conditions (for a brief account of
Social Darwinism, see Chapter 2, above). These fears seemed to get
some confirmation when a very high proportion of recruits for the
Boer War had to be rejected because they were inadequate physically
in one way or another. But more generally, the late nineteenth century
was the period in which a renewed sense of 'Englishness' was created, in
which Englishness came to be overwhelmingly associated with rural
England, especially of the South, with its thatched cottages, half-tim-
bered houses, winding lanes and straggling hedgerows. This was in

part an imaginary place; nevertheless it appealed strongly even to those with little apparent stake in it, that is to the large majority of the population who now lived in towns, and whose experience of England was indeed quite unlike that version of it. One historian, Martin Wiener, has gone so far as to suggest that the power of this metaphor of England was such as to deflect the entrepreneurial and technologically innovative ethos of the early part of the century and to replace it with misplaced social goals that contributed to England's industrial decline at the end of the century and beyond.[16]

This cultural construction did not mean the same thing to all the people who espoused it; it was expressed in a variety of cultural forms, it could have very different political connotations, and it is not simply to be thought of as false. Many people lived a version of ruralism, taking seriously the slogan 'Back to the Land', and living out their version of the simple life in Tolstoyan colonies, Arts and Crafts settlements, or rural cottages. For many more it meant an interest in the countryside expressed in weekend rambling or cycling, both of which came to be widespread recreations in the late nineteenth century. For others again it meant no more perhaps than a sentimental print on the wall. But the range and possible seriousness of this late nineteenth-century ruralism can be seen, for example, in the work of William Morris and his influence on the Arts and Crafts Movement of the 1880s and 1890s.

William Morris was a complex and accomplished figure, who certainly cannot simply be thought of as a ruralist. He lived most of his life in London. But he was driven, in part, by an abiding hatred of what he saw as the ugliness of nineteenth- century urban life, and in seeking to remedy this ugliness, both social and aesthetic, he drew upon versions of rural life. This was true as much in his remarkably diverse design work, as in his socialist vision – given expression, for example, in the Utopian romance *News from Nowhere* (1891). The design work, in tapestries, furniture, carpets and wallpapers, makes use of vernacular English rural traditions and the familiar trees, flowers and animals of the countryside – honeysuckle, willow, chaffinch, and so on. More importantly, perhaps, Morris's ideas on crafts and design, partly inherited from Ruskin, espoused an ideal of work which saw skilled work as the highest expression of human faculties; this notion was mobilised against the deadening routines of mechanised factory labour. Aspirations of this kind were widely acted upon in the last two decades of the century and later; the Arts and Craft Movement drew heavily upon Morris's ideals, and several craft-based settlements, especially in the Cotswolds, attempted to live out broadly Morrisian ideals – with the inevitable mixed success.

News from Nowhere, a propagandist socialist work which imagines a happy future for mankind, is profoundly imbued with a ruralist spirit. But it is not simply that Morris envisages a future for people in the countryside rather than the town. In effect the opposition between the town and the country has been overcome in 'Nowhere', so that London's slums have been cleared away and the old city is recognised now by no more than a slightly greater density of housing. There is no doubt, however, that the affective centre of the book is in the countryside, culminating in a trip up the Thames to Kelmscott House, Morris's rural retreat which has survived into the Utopian future. Certainly the future for Morris, and for one submerged strand of the subsequent socialist movement which carried forward his ideas, was a rural one. But his influence was by no means confined to the socialist movement; both Ebenezer Howard and Raymond Unwin, the architects and planners of the early twentieth-century garden cities, were deeply affected by the Utopian projection of a future which had done away with the ugliness and misery of the late nineteenth-century city.[17] Morris's attempt to overcome the opposition of town and country in the imagination was partly to be realised in bricks and mortar.

Morris and the Arts and Craft Movement represent one strand of late nineteenth-century ruralism; Cecil Sharp (1859–1924) and the folksong and folk-dance revival represent another, though this is an effort that really flourished in the first decade of the twentieth century. What was at stake for Sharp was no less than the soul of England, to be found in traditional songs where they had not been replaced by commercialism; Sharp and fellow enthusiasts such as Rev. Sabine Baring-Gould (1834–1924) and Ralph Vaughan Williams (1872–1958) collected many thousands of 'folk' songs as evidence of the persistence of both a regional and national musical spirit, now disappearing into oblivion with the rural way of life that supported it. To revive such traditional songs and dances was to be in touch with the genius of the race expressed through the collective authorship of these forms over many generations. Though there may be some absurdity in this (and some bowdlerisation), there is also a real attempt to find some cultural resources outside simple commercialism.

In literary terms, the late nineteenth century also saw the growth of what is almost a specific genre of writing, 'country writing', which took the countryside for its topic. In the work of Richard Jefferies, Edward Thomas, W. H. Hudson, and many more local writers like Alf Williams around the upper Thames Valley, the country, its inhabitants, its local history, its flora and fauna, served as a topic of absorbing interest for readers in the great cities. At times, this writing could take on apocalyptic overtones, as when Richard Jefferies anticipated the destruction of London and its reversion to a giant forest inhabited by warring peoples, in *After London* (1886). But more usually it verges towards sociological survey on the one hand and guidebook on the other. It is directly contemporary with the success of the magazine *Country Life*, founded in 1897, which served a cognate but rather different interest in the lives and lifestyles of the landed elite. It was mostly read by the members of the urban middle and professional classes.

Late nineteenth-century ruralism thus took a variety of cultural forms, in addition to a variety of directly social and economic schemes for reviving agriculture, land reform, small proprietorship and farm colonies. It was linked up, on one side, with some regressive and mystificatory ideas about 'Englishness', and about national and even racial degeneration. But on the other side, it could become the vehicle for imagining radically different alternatives to the ugly and squalid world of the late nineteenth-century city, and the industrial capitalism that had produced it. It could be used to articulate genuine notions of land reform, which went some way to challenge landlord power. And, to strike a note that I have not yet touched upon, it could articulate ideas about a human scale of living, and appropriate technological forms, which have been taken up in a more urgent key in the contemporary ecological movement.

England began the century a predominantly rural country, and ended it a predominantly urban one. In this respect, it was the pioneering country for much of Europe in the later part of the nineteenth century, and for much of the world in the twentieth. The division between the urban and the rural was a material fact for millions of people, one that they crossed as they migrated to the city in one direction, or perhaps as they made their escape from it in the other. But it was also an imaginative or cultural reality, which entered intimately into people's sense of themselves and of the communities in which they lived. For many people at the end of the century and beyond, the imagined community of 'England' was rural. This cultural and imaginative construction, however, could be inflected in multiple directions and could articulate quite different senses both of the past and the future. Nevertheless, for most people in England at the end of the century, their actual future was bound to be in the cities. The next chapter will examine how this unprecedented state of affairs came to be.

5

UNDERSTANDING THE CITY

Cultural forms, I have been insisting, have a history, and work to historical rhythms, which are not simply congruent with the forms of life they represent and address. Certainly, the city has been the site of conflicting representations since classical antiquity; London in the nineteenth century was the inheritor of these conflicting representations, and could be celebrated both as the imperial metropolis and as a sink of iniquity in ways that have ancient precedents. But London was not the typical nineteenth-century city in England; at least, though it grew enormously in the course of the century and reproduced many of the features of other nineteenth-century cities, it is not to London that we should look for the most spectacular rates of growth or the most distinctively nineteenth-century patterns of urban settlement and industrial use. For these we should look to the industrialising cities of the Midlands and the North, which grew at prodigious rates in the nineteenth century, and which were in fact practically unprecedented in human history. For these cities – and for the reality of an enormous and socially segregated London – the old paradigms simply did not fit. Nineteenth-century cultural forms, to a very considerable degree, emerge from the novel realities of the nineteenth-century city.

The distinction between London and the industrialising cities of provincial England suggests one facet of the city in the nineteenth century – the diversity of its types, and within broadly similar types, the diversity of social and cultural life. Birmingham, a city of small industrial producers, contrasts with Manchester and its large factories, which contrasts again with Liverpool, a commercial city and major port, all three cities having distinctive recruitment from surrounding districts and from Ireland, very different class compositions and class relations, and equally distinctive patterns of urban settlement and housing-types. Not surprisingly, the three cities produced very different local politics, and distinctive social and cultural institutions, with different groups, at different moments, providing leadership. Other industrial cities were equally various, affected by such matters as the rate of growth, the type of industrial production on which they relied, the presence of the railway, the antiquity and prestige of the ruling elite, the presence or otherwise of an influential landowning magnate, and distinctive civic and religious traditions. Diversity of urban experience extends more profoundly than this: two of the fastest growing cities in the nineteenth century were Brighton and Cheltenham. Resort towns such as these were products of the nineteenth century also.

The most striking single aspect of nineteenth-century social history is the transformation of England into a predominantly urban country. At the beginning of the century, a third of the population of England and Wales were urban dwellers; by the end of the century nearly four-fifths of the population lived in towns.[1] Rates of urban growth were highest in the 1820s and 1830s, when the urban population was growing at nearly 30 per cent per decade; by the 1890s this had decreased to a more modest but still remarkable 17.5 per cent. London itself grew throughout the century: it contained 12 per cent of the population of England and Wales in 1801, but by 1901 this figure had grown to 20 per cent.[2] But the whole country was transformed by the extraordinarily rapid growth in the industrial towns of the Midlands and the North; at the beginning of the century London was the only city in the country with more than a million people, and was over eleven times bigger than the next biggest, Liverpool. By the end of the century, many others, such as Manchester, Birmingham and Liverpool, had themselves become large and recognisably modern cities. England had become a majority urban country by the middle of the nineteenth century, and saw spectacular rates of urban growth throughout our period, with places like Liverpool and Preston multiplying their population by a factor of five between 1811 and 1861, and Blackpool growing to seventeen times its 1861 size by 1911.[3]

This transformation was effected, of course, by industrialisation, gathering pace throughout the eighteenth century, but having its greatest impact upon urban growth in the first decades of the nineteenth century. Industrialisation itself is a diverse phenomenon; in all cases, however, and despite differing patterns of employment and settlement, and differing moments and rates of growth, similar broad transformations can be traced: towns and cities absorbed increasing numbers of people, and were themselves transformed from relatively intimate and knowable places into large, socially zoned spaces with culturally and socially segregated populations.

Geographers sometimes characterise this latter transformation as one from a 'walking city' to a 'tracked city'; that is, that the early nineteenth-century city was a place in which, by force of the absence of cheap and technologically appropriate transport, all distances had to be negotiable by foot, notably the distance between home and work. While it is important not to romanticise the eighteenth-century city, it was a place where the middle classes habitually lived on the premises in which business was conducted, and where the urban poor perforce lived in close proximity to them. Even that most notorious early and mid-nineteenth-century London slum, the 'rookery' of St Giles, was a small, concentrated patch of poverty in the heart of Westminster. By the end of the century, thanks above all to the horse-drawn and then the electric tram, and thanks also to the growth of suburban railways and omnibuses, the city could expand its space enormously. This 'tracked' city was a place of suburbs and social zoning, in which the distances between the social classes were a matter of literal distance, the classes living in extreme social and cultural isolation from each other. The 'slums' of London now meant above all the East End, square miles of urban areas into which the upper classes had no normal cause to venture. The cultural life of the nineteenth-century city, the forms of self and mutual understanding forged in and about it, were largely created out of the processes of social zoning – out of suburban growth, the acts of mutual ignorance and discovery and the cultural isolation that accompanied the dispersed and socially marked spaces of the city.[4]

Social life, of course, has its paradoxes. It is possible to represent this transition as a fall from the relatively intimate and even face-to-face character of the eighteenth-century city (though this could hardly be said about eighteenth-century London), to the 'anonymity' often ascribed to its modern counterpart. But it is also the case that the nineteenth-century city, in all the heartbreaking misery of its unplanned growth and the repellent social isolation of its class-specific districts and suburbs, was the site of a striking and unprecedented density and range of civil society. We can get some sense of this from the range of social and cultural institutions which either continued to flourish in

the nineteenth-century city, or were first invented there. In the introduction, I discussed some of these sites or locations of culture: the
churches and chapels, publishing houses, libraries and circulating
libraries, museums, art galleries, concert halls, theatres, athenaeums,
clubs, institutes and music-halls that abounded in the nineteenth-century city. Here, I wish to insist upon the urban nature of these cultural
sites, since it was, of course, due to the size and density of population,
characteristic of the city, that this range of institutions became possible.
Whether or not these institutions were provided by the operations of
the commercial market, active benevolence, state and municipal action
or self-sustaining forms of sociability, they were all conditional upon,
and a response to, the sheer density of people gathered together in
such unprecedented numbers.

Numbers

We should start with 'numbers', in considering the nineteenth century's
efforts to apprehend the city. This was the century of statistics; the historian Asa Briggs has suggested that their collection issued necessarily
from the social division and heterogeneity of the urban world: 'It was
far more difficult, in socially and geographically segregated cities with
unequal spatial densities and manifestly unequal conditions of "class",
segregated district by district, to grasp the idea of the city as a whole
and to identify its "problems" except through the collection and deployment of statistics.'[5] The great decennial censuses, starting in 1801, were
only the most prominent of a series of efforts at statistical collection, provincial as much as metropolitan; Manchester and Liverpool had their
own Statistical Societies in the 1830s, through which the local progressive middle class hoped to survey and thus address the incidence of poverty and improvidence in their areas. But this was an ambivalent effort,
as perhaps all efforts to map the social space of the city, to grasp it 'as a
whole', were bound to be. Something of their ambivalence can be
caught in illustrations of the activity of the census enumerators provided
in the *Illustrated Times* in 1861[6] (Figure 3). They are shown entering a
poverty-stricken tenement, counting the homeless on a bench in St
James's Park, penetrating the dark arches of the Adelphi with torch
and clipboard to count the destitute. It is easy to see them as agents of

Figure 3 *Talking the Census in the Dark Arches of the Adelphi, Illustrated Times,* xii (1861), p. 264

light, bringing the disparate, unfortunate and neglected multitudes of the city into order and dispassionate system. So they are. But they are also agents of a less politically benign order, their resemblance to the police not only strongly suggested visually, but also by their use of the 'bull's-eye', or policeman's lantern, to illuminate the destitute. The two aspects of their task, in fact, are inextricable; grasping the city as a whole via statistics at once involves an effort of social solidarity and an effort of system and control.

The same can be said of many of the other efforts to chart the city in the nineteenth century, to comprehend it as an object of cultural representation. As I remarked above, the city has been the object of cultural representations from at least classical times. If what was new about the nineteenth-century city was its unprecedented social segregation, then the effort to map the city was also an effort to bring the segregated classes into order and mutual relation. The old paradigms of city life, the historic cultural forms that carried the meanings of the word 'city', were no longer adequate, or had to be stretched, redefined, reinvented. Novelists, painters, illustrators, journalists, writers of government reports, sociologists, district visitors and city missionaries, settlement workers – all were acting in effect as 'explorers', to use a typical nineteenth-century metaphor. They were bringing back reports of uncharted territory to periodically startled readers, presenting the results of their expeditions in sometimes old and sometimes reinvented cultural forms.

The mid-nineteenth-century debate about 'numbers' illustrates this diversity, since both the protagonists of statistics and their attackers sprang from and addressed the same social and cultural reality, namely the socially segregated space of the city. Hostility to statistics, and enthusiasm for them, divides the intellectual classes in mid-century England in perhaps predictable ways. Enthusiasm in their use is to be found amongst utilitarians and political economists, amongst incipient social scientists anxious to quantify the changes in contemporary life that surrounded them, and to map the city in ways that I have suggested. Hostility to them came from writers like Carlyle and Dickens, whose intellectual affiliations were to the romantic critique of capitalism, and who understood the bonds of society to exist at profounder, organic, and essentially unquantifiable levels. 'Tables', wrote Carlyle in 1839, 'are like cobwebs, like the sieve of the Danaides; beautifully reticulated, orderly to look upon, but which will hold no conclusion. Tables are abstractions, and the object a most concrete one, so difficult to read the essence of.'[7] Dickens, famously in *Hard Times* (1854), voiced a profound suspicion of statistics as a way of understanding social life; for Sissy Jupe, and through her Dickens, statistics were inherently incapable of capturing the actual lived specificity of social and individual experience. For both writers, a mode of writing that had recourse to the symbolic, that drew sharp oppositions and connections via metaphor and caricature, seemed a more appropriate way of grasping the totality of social life. A more nuanced sense of the inadequacy of statistics can be found in George Eliot's work, when she wrote in 1856 that 'appeals founded on generalisations and statistics require a sympathy ready-made, a moral sentiment already in activity'; it was just the function of art, in this account, to bring that sympathy into existence.[8] Her own novels, though not characteristically having an urban setting, are nevertheless typically directed to overcoming social divisions.

We cannot assume, however, that antipathy to statistics meant disentanglement from the project of ordering and systematising urban life which the gathering of statistics partly represented. Dickens, too, relied on the policeman's bull's-eye to guide him through the more unknown parts of London, notably in an article in *Household Words* that fed into *Bleak House*. What that bull's-eye revealed, in a controversial passage in the novel, was the destitute of London crawling 'in maggot numbers'. The harshness of the phrase, the authoritarian attitude it reveals (present elsewhere in Dickens's writing, but not consistently), certainly suggests that while the numbers gathered by statistical methods were not necessarily innocent, nor were the numbers perceived by those who refused to count them.

'Oh For a Good Spirit...'

The debate about the value of statistics was in part, then, a debate about *form* – a debate about the appropriate cultural form in which to seek to capture the realities of the contemporary city. Many such forms were developed in the course of the nineteenth century to address the city, each with its own specific ways of construing the realities it confronted, and with its particular construction of the relationship between author, topic and audience. If I have quoted Dickens adversely, let me now contrast that moment in *Bleak House* with another from *Dombey and Son* (1847–48), where he expresses a powerful wish:

> Oh for a good spirit who would take the house-tops off, with a more potent and benignant hand than the lame demon in the tale, and show a Christian people what dark shapes issue from amidst their homes, to swell the retinue of the Destroying Angel as he moves forth among them! For only one night's view of the pale phantoms rising from the scenes of our too long neglect; and, from the thick and sullen air where Vice and Fever propagate together, raining the tremendous social retributions which are ever pouring down, and ever coming thicker! Bright and blest the morning that should rise on such a night: for men, delayed no more by stumbling-blocks, of their own making, which are but specks of dust upon the path between them and eternity, would apply themselves, like creatures of one common origin, owing one duty to the father of one family, and tending to one common end, to make the world a better place![9]

Here Dickens is imagining a moment of revelation – literally an apocalypse – in which the secrets hidden in those massed urban houses will be made manifest, and the common humanity of all will become apparent. The good spirit, of course, is Dickens himself, offering his own activity as a novelist as a locus in which the divisions of the city can be healed, for it is precisely in the novel that the house-tops are removed, and as readers we can come to know of the lives that are lived beneath them. This seems to me a moment when Dickens is articulating an urban version of that aesthetic which George Eliot described as 'the extension of our sympathies', and which we have encountered before in relation to rural social relations. It informs Elizabeth Gaskell's writing as much as parts of Dickens's and George Eliot's, and it arranges the objects of social sympathy into revealing and affecting attitudes. In Gaskell's Manchester novel *Mary Barton* (1848), for example, the barriers of mutual ignorance are to breached by an often painful – indeed ultimately tragic – recognition of a shared humanity between employers and employed. So here I wish to explore this humanist aesthetic of extended sympathy, proposing that it can be seen as a way of negotiating the class-divided space of the nineteenth- century city.

The moment of revelation is crucial in that passage from *Dombey and Son*. This is what distinguishes this nineteenth- century aesthetic from previous cultural forms directed to the life of the poor, since it takes upon itself to reveal to readers or spectators realities of city life of which they are presumed ignorant. Where Dickens imagines a good spirit taking the house- tops off, and thus revealing myriad private stories to sympathetic gaze, Elizabeth Gaskell takes her readers on a voyage of discovery to the working-class districts of Manchester, and reveals the lives lived in court and cellar. A number of other novelists, at mid-century in particular, similarly penetrate to working-class districts of the city, and bring back compassionate (and at times terrifying) reports of the lives they find there.[10] Characteristically in this writing, the poor are revealed in legible symbolic attitudes, in affective groupings whose affect is organised to include the reader. The realities of city life are at once revealed, and, in the same gesture, readers are invited to reach feelingly across the gulf that divides them from the topic of the writing. The revelation of distance, and the act of redeeming sympathy, are enacted in the same moment. A set of social relations – of mutual social isolation – are presumed by this aesthetic of sympathy, and these relationships are inflected in a particular direction by reading the novel, which brings into being a way of negotiating the relationship between (predominantly) middle-class writer and (predominantly) middle-class reader with respect to the working- class topic of the writing.

This aesthetic has its roots in a number of eighteenth- and early nineteenth-century forms of writing and painting.[11] Genre painting is one such form, which I have discussed with relation to rural life. When genre painting is infused with this aesthetic of sympathy the result is such a painting as Sir Luke Fildes's *Applicants for Admission to a Casual Ward*, painted in 1874[12] (Figure 4). Here, the queue outside the casual ward (in which the destitute could get a night's lodging) is made up of a representative selection of the urban poor, disposed to reveal their situations in readable and touching 'attitudes'. Thus a family is grouped together with father holding a young child, the mother in tears, and older children huddled around them. There are two mothers, without male partners, clutching children. A variety of single men are displayed in various positions of patience, listlessness, cold or despair. The 'realism' of the painting is not in dispute, but the painting construes the realities of urban poverty in ways that are analogous to the work of the novelists I have discussed, calling into being a comparable set of aesthetic and thus social relationships.

This aesthetic of sympathy is most widespread in the mid- nineteenth century novel; by the end of the century it was largely displaced by other aesthetic strategies and ways of mapping the divided social space of the city. Indeed, in the work of a novelist like George Gissing, the aesthetic of sympathy is systematically undercut, to be replaced by a far bleaker sense of the intractability of urban alienation and division. Social Darwinist fears of evolutionary degeneration, models of 'naturalist' writing in which the writer subjects the people about whom he writes to a series of experiments like a natural scientist, doctrines of aesthetic detachment – all these entailed hostility to the humanist gesture of an aesthetic of sympathy. Earlier, it could still seem possible that the revelation of urban misery would render it tractable to awakened middle-class concern. In the words of Elizabeth Gaskell in *Mary Barton* (1848),

> It is so impossible to describe, or even faintly to picture, the state of distress which prevailed in the town at that time, that I will not attempt it; and yet I think again that surely, in a Christian land, it was not known even so feebly as words could tell it, or the more happy and fortunate would have thronged with their sympathy and their aid.[13]

Writing or painting which worked in the ways I have described did not thus passively reflect the social realities it addressed – rather, it constituted in itself a social relationship with respect to those realities, *was the locus in which the possibility of redeemed social relationships could*

Figure 4 Sir Luke Fildes, *Applicants for Admission to a Casual Ward* (1874)

be enacted. Thus the sympathetic activity of the writers and painters provided a model for the affective bonds which they diagnose as absent from the realities they depict. Indeed, in being moved in the right places, in crying or laughing in appropriate ways, readers too are constituted in a transformed relationship to the unknown social zones through which they are being led. As ever, cultural forms are condensed and active forms of social relationships.

I conclude this section by contrasting two different views of late nineteenth-century urban experience. One powerful and widespread response to the vastness and seeming anonymity of the urban world was to understand it in terms of the 'masses' – a word that was to be taken up in the twentieth century with very different emphases. It may be that to see other people in this way is a gesture of despair. Consider, for example, this passage from George Gissing's 1889 novel, *The Nether World*:

Presently [Clara] was standing at her window, the blind partly raised. On a clear day the view from this room was of wide extent, embracing a great part of the City; seen under a low, blurred, dripping sky, through the ragged patches of smoke from chimneys innumerable, it had a gloomy impressiveness well in keeping with the mind of her who brooded over it. Directly in front, rising mist-detached from the lower masses of building, stood in black majesty the dome of St. Paul's; its vastness suffered no diminution from this high outlook, rather was exaggerated by the flying scraps of mirky vapour which softened its outline and at times gave it the appearance of floating on a vague troubled sea. Somewhat nearer, amid many spires and steeples, lay the surly bulk of Newgate, the lines of its construction shown plan-wise; its little windows multiplied for points of torment to the vision. Nearer again, the markets of Smithfield, Bartholomew's Hospital, the tract of modern deformity, cleft by a gulf of railway, which spreads between Clerkenwell Road and Charterhouse Street. Down in Farringdon Street the carts, waggons, vans, cabs, omnibuses, crossed and intermingled in a steaming splash-bath of mud; human beings, reduced to their due paltriness, seemed to toil in exasperation along the strips of pavement, bound on errands, which were a mockery, driven automaton-like by forces they neither understood nor could resist.[14]

This passage captures the full ambiguity of the attempt to get above the city and see it as a whole. The very act of climbing above it all seems to

entail alienation from the lives of those left behind, though the particular circumstances of the character here allows one to see this as a
moment which exposes such alienation rather than simply partakes of
it. There is a very strong sense, in this passage, of the city 'as a whole';
the forces which are driving the inhabitants can be clearly perceived as
the patterns of their activity become visible from above. But this is definitely not a 'good spirit' that has revealed the ant-like behaviour of these
people; rather, it appears as futile, unselfconscious, and 'paltry'.

This moment can be contrasted with Charles Booth's *Life and Labour
of the People in London*, whose volumes are dense with statistical tables,
but which are also enlivened by sympathetic vignettes of London life,
however distorted by condescension.[15] The irony of the contrast
between the two writers is in part an irony of mode. Gissing is writing
a novel, the form that ought to permit him to enter into the details of
people's lives; instead, he almost systematically refuses the opportunities
for sympathy that the form offers him. Booth, by contrast, is writing
something that aspires to social science; but he eschews at times the
false objectivity of numbers and descends instead to sympathy.

Melodrama

Melodrama is a diverse artistic mode, and plainly was not solely or even
primarily directed to urban life. But it was certainly drawn on heavily by
artists and writers, as a way of mediating the social divisions of the city. I
distinguish it from that aesthetic of sympathy which I have just
described, for writers like George Eliot and Mrs Gaskell, though they
certainly use melodrama at times in their writing, characteristically
work in a more sober and less heightened mode. Drawing on the
work of the critics Peter Brooks and Martin Meisel, I suggest that it is
best to think of melodrama as a way of imagining the relations between
people in which otherwise suppressed realities of relationship – social,
moral, sexual, even spiritual – are made manifest in an overt language
of gesture and attitude.[16] Though we may think of the heartland of
melodrama as the theatre, in fact it is a mode that can be found also in
writing and painting. In exploiting the melodramatic mode to construe
the nineteenth- century city, artists necessarily established a different set
of aesthetic and social relationships than those to be found in the aesthetic of sympathy.

Crime, in fact, became the typical way by which the explosive social tensions of city life were both suggested and imaginatively solved, in a variety of texts using melodramatic means to establish oppositions and connections. Dickens's *Oliver Twist* (1837–38), for example, places the innocent child in the power of a criminal gang, whose threat to Oliver vividly dramatises the threat posed by a hidden criminal underworld to the good order of the city. A few years later, G. W. M. Reynolds was writing *The Mysteries of London* (1844–56) in imitation of Eugène Sue's *Les Mystères de Paris*; this too used melodrama to dramatise the suppressed connections of a socially and geographically divided city, as in the following passage, where a heightened vocabulary, and striking contrasts, suggest the melodramatic mode:

There are but two words known in the moral alphabet of this great city; for all virtues are summed up in the one, and all vices in the other: and those words are
WEALTH. | POVERTY.
Crime is abundant in this city: the lazarhouse, the prison, the brothel, and the dark alley, are rife with all kinds of enormity; in the same way as the palace, the mansion, the clubhouse, the parliament, and the parsonage, are each and all characterised by their different degrees and shades of vice. But wherefore specify crime and vice by their real names, since in this city of which we speak they are absorbed in the multi- significant words – WEALTH and POVERTY.

Crimes borrow their comparative shade of enormity from the people who perpetrate them: thus it is that the wealthy may commit all social offences with impunity; while the poor are cast into dungeons and coerced with chains, for only following at a humble distance in the pathway of their lordly precedents.

From this city of strange contrasts branch off two roads, leading to two points totally distinct the one from the other.

One winds its tortuous way through all the noisome dens of crime, chicanery, dissipation, and voluptuousness: the other meanders amidst rugged rocks and wearisome acclivities, it is true, but on the wayside are the resting-places of rectitude and virtue.

Along these roads two youths are journeying.

They have started from the same point; but one pursues the former path, and the other the latter.

Both come from the city of fearful contrasts; and both follow the wheels of fortune in different directions.

Where is that city of fearful contrasts?

Who are those youths that have thus entered upon paths so opposite the one to the other?

And to what destinies do those separate roads conduct them?[17]

While this is not wholly clear or consistent, it does provide a vivid and melodramatic way of seeking to comprehend mid-century London, in which the 'fearful contrasts' are at once economic, geographic and moral – though the ways in which these different contrasts are mapped on to each other are rather different from the comparable contrasts in *Oliver Twist*. Working with a powerful suggestion of 'mystery' – this is indeed the title of the book – Reynolds undertakes to make manifest the realities of the city understood as a series of striking moral and social contrasts.

The pictures of Gustave Doré, and the accompanying text of *London: A Pilgrimage* (1872), can also be seen as drawing on melodramatic modes to construe the urban landscape. In this volume the work of the French artist Doré is accompanied by text written by the journalist Blanchard Jerrold (1826–84); the book depicts a tour through various districts of London, with some startling, dramatically drawn, and crowded pictures. Interestingly using the category of the *picturesque*, which we have earlier encountered in a rural context (see above, p. 89), Jerrold's text seeks to justify his own and Doré's effort to capture the busy urban scene, even the crowded streets of the City and the East End:

Who says that all this movement is ugly? At every turn there is a sketch. Every twisting or backing of a cart; every shifting of the busy groups suggests a happy combination of line and light and shade. About the Tower there are picturesque studies by the score. The Jewish quarter is at hand; and therein may be found in plenty such dark alleys and bye-ways for such venerable or striking figures as would have warmed the genius of Rembrandt to enthusiasm. Or take the line of marine-store dealers facing the brown, unbroken walks of the docks! Their shows abound in the delightful accidents of form and colour. The hard-visaged dealers, and the slouching customers form themselves into well-contrasted groups.[18]

What is at stake here is precisely the question of the appropriate cultural form with which to mediate the realities of urban life; Jerrold is claiming it for a version of the picturesque, in which the figures who inhabit the urban landscape 'form themselves into well-contrasted groups'. Doré's accompanying pictures exploit to the full these 'combinations of lines', these 'striking figures' and these 'well-contrasted groups', disposing them in equally striking and dramatic configurations of urban architecture. In a picture like *Bluegate Fields*, for example, a single lamp fitfully

Figure 5 Gustave Doré, *Bluegate Fields*, from Gustave Doré and Blanchard Jerrold, *London:* A Pilgrimage (London, 1872), between pp. 138 and 139.

illuminates a street of towering houses, in every doorway of which are gathered groups of lowering and threatening figures[19] (Figure 5). The eye is drawn down the perspective of the street to suggest still further mysteries and terrors beyond what can be seen. This is a powerful and melodramatic picture, in which the extremes of poverty and crime are exposed to partial view; but the gaze is not so much a sympathetic one, as one which perceives the urban poor as threatening, and, in the crowds of them who mass in Doré's pictures, dangerously prolific. We are back here to Dickens's 'maggot numbers'.

Finally, the urban detective novel is a form whose roots are clearly in the melodramatic mode, and which, while evoking the dangers of city life, offers at least some imaginary solution to them. From Inspector Bucket in *Bleak House,* through to Sherlock Holmes in the 1890s, the detective offered a figure whose specialist vision could penetrate the social and criminal mysteries of the city, who could walk its most dangerous streets with impunity, and who could expose the truths which would otherwise remain hidden. To this extent, the detective is a surrogate social explorer, enabling the readers to confront the 'fearful contrasts' of London but with the reassurance of authority and specialist knowledge.

Comedy

Persisting alongside these forms, and indeed at times informing them also, were various comic traditions of urban life, traditions, that is, of characterisation and situation. Once again, Dickens's writing provides the readiest example, in *Sketches by Boz* (1837). But these sketches draw on situations, types and attitudes that together can be said to constitute a distinctive cultural attitude – that of the knowing urban expert, able to direct his comic attention into all the nooks and crannies of city life. This is not the initiation into destitution provided by the sympathetic guide, but rather the guide to 'low life', to an urban world inhabited by a collection of knowable types.

Like all widely available attitudes, this is capable of very different emphases and political inflections. It is an attitude that can be found, early in the century, in Pierce Egan's *Life in London* (1821), which takes the reader on an expert's tour of London's taverns and sporting locations. Egan's stance derives from the rakish traditions of the Regency;

it can be traced back to longer traditions of underworld writing.[20] At mid-century, different inflections of the wider attitude can be found in the proliferation of popular comic journals, of which only the most famous and long-lasting was *Punch*. I have discussed the world of comic and popular journalism as a distinct cultural formation in Chapter 3 above. The accounts of the city in these publications are much less brutal than Pierce Egan, and at times indeed can modulate into campaigning journalism or the aesthetic of sympathy. But in general they rely upon a repertoire of comic types and caricatures, and upon a comic manner, which makes the city available to their readers in a relatively relaxed manner. This is not to say that the tensions and class-conflicts of the nineteenth-century city are absent from these various texts, rather that such tensions appear in them in a wholly different guise; the positions they offer the reader, and the class and gendered intensities with which the spectacle of low-life London is presented can, naturally, vary greatly. The social location of these journals, especially in the 1830s and 1840s when so many of them were founded, was the mildly Bohemian world of small publishers and journalists, a world which Dickens partly inhabited, and which included such figures as Thackeray, Douglas Jerrold and Henry Mayhew. [21]

Such popular journalism is especially sensitive to changes in taste, technical conditions of production, and changes in the constitution of the reading public. By the end of the century, responding in part to such things as the advent of universal primary education and the Saturday half-holiday, a range of other comic publications were available. From the 1870s onwards, for example, one of the most successful was *Ally Sloper's Half- Holiday*, which inflected the comic guide to urban life in an altogether more riotous direction. Ally Sloper, 'the most frequently kicked out man in Europe', provides access to the various sights and festivals of London, but in a carnival spirit which undoes their class pretensions and exclusiveness in an atmosphere of booze and bonhomie.[22]

Journalism and the Social Survey

I have been suggesting different modes in which, across a variety of cultural forms, the nineteenth-century city was made available to its inhabitants. In discussing journalism, especially in its close relation to the social survey, we have to recognise that we are encountering a mixed mode, which can draw upon a variety of different ways to mediate the realities of the city. But of course that is true of many kinds of writing, which can move in and out of different generic attitudes, attempt to direct and redirect readers' responses in very different ways, and make use of widely varying traditions of writing – all within the space of a few pages. So in discussing a recognisable tradition of nineteenth-century writing, from mid-century onwards, I wish to emphasise that the generic resources of this writing are especially varied, both in terms of the relationships it seeks to establish with its readers, and the ways in which it goes about collecting information and establishing its own authenticity. Nevertheless, it is possible to recognise here a distinctive cultural form.

I have already mentioned Henry Mayhew, as a journalist who inhabited the world of mid-century journalism (see p. 72 above). His moment came in 1848, when he began a series of articles for the *Morning Chronicle* about the London trades, which involved him, with some colleagues, in investigating the rates of wages and living conditions of London, and then other parts of the country. These articles became the starting point for *London Labour and the London Poor* (1861-62), a massive survey of London labour and poverty. Mayhew used a number of different investigative techniques, some statistical, some more obviously humanistic. Most importantly, he sought to represent the speech of the people he interviewed; in the days before the tape recorder, this involved using a shorthand writer, and then transcribing the interviews later. The majority of the text, both of the *Morning Chronicle* journalism and *London Labour and the London Poor,* thus consists of transcripts of people talking about their own lives, though these have been considerably edited, their speech and grammatical forms shifted towards standard written English, and Mayhew's own leading questions omitted.

There is no doubting the strong impression created by Mayhew's writing, especially the *Morning Chronicle* articles when they were first published in 1848–49. Their impact was doubtless heightened by their publication coinciding with a recent crisis over Chartism, suddenly reappearing as a political force in 1848, the cholera scare of that year, and the general political excitements of the Year of Revolutions. But the specific revelations about the sweated trades, especially the tailoring trades, which traumatised a figure like Charles Kingsley, are not my immediate point. Rather I wish to focus on the peculiar power of Mayhew's reporting, in the manner in which it mediates working-class experience to its readership. It is in effect a type of oral history; while the speech of Mayhew's respondents has doubtless been edited and somewhat sanitised, it is nevertheless possible to hear some of the original cadences of that speech, and to hear the accents of a particular class and culture in those cadences. But this is to give the writing too sociological an inflection; it is possible to hear, very directly, the voices of distinctive individuals as they speak to Mayhew, but to hear in those individual voices the manner in which they have made sense of their sometimes desperate life-histories in the collective idioms and cultural forms available to them.

Mayhew's writing has no successors in the nineteenth century, in the sense that no other writer can find ways of mediating the social divisions of the city which give as full and detailed a sense of the self-understanding of the people whom they delineate. Mayhew himself alludes to specific cultural and aesthetic ways of framing his material, of course, so that his respondents are variously presented as objects of pathos, of humour, or as figures in a tragic and affecting tableau. But the text of his writings, as much that published in newspapers as in volume form, necessarily exceeds these framings, allowing readers to engage with his respondents in ways other than those that Mayhew himself suggests. If at times subsequent editors of Mayhew have shifted him into adjacent modes, from which he in part emerges, then this is not Mayhew's fault. But he is certainly other than a sociologist, or an investigative journalist, or a purveyor of Cockney types, or a novelist *manqué*, even if his writing at times has recourse to all these modes.

Mayhew's mid-century moment, I have suggested, is the moment of 1848, a moment of especially overt class-conflict and political upheaval. Though there was a considerable amount of journalistic reporting of working-class London, in particular, in the third quarter of the century, it is not really until the 1880s that there was a comparably sustained and serious effort to investigate the realities of the city. In the 1880s, indeed, that city *had* to be London. Mayhew's emphasis on the capital was almost untypical in the 1840s, when the shock city was Manchester; by the 1880s, the shock city was undoubtedly London, whose sheer size, and the extent of its social segregation, made it the locus for all kinds of investigation. The writings of Andrew Mearns, W. T. Stead (1849–1912), William Booth (1829–1912) and Charles Booth (1840–1916) all sought both to chart the city in the 1880s, and to suggest, in the process, the possibility of its redemption. Something of the variety of their projects, and the varying modes on which they drew, can be suggested simply by their titles: *The Bitter Cry of Outcast London* (1883), 'The Maiden Tribute of Modern Babylon' (1885), *In Darkest England and the Way Out* (1888) and *Life and Labour of the People in London* (1892–97). London here has become a densely mapped place, whose social segregation requires widely varying modes in order to be made visible.

Charles Booth's survey of the city, in *Life and Labour of the People in London*, is the most evident of these mappings – the books contain a number of maps of districts of London, their incidence of poverty carefully indicated by an intricate system of colour-coding. In fact Booth's whole project is an elaborate enterprise of classification, in which not only are the densities of poverty in London systematically calculated, but also the various grades of poverty are classified, and their proportions and relative effects determined. His method was quite different from Mayhew's, however; he accumulated his material by using information from the School Board officials appointed to enforce the 1870 Education Act. The writing thus situates the reader quite differently to its subject; we are invited to share in an objective-seeming act of social classification, and to draw policy conclusions from the information with which we are presented. This is not to say that Booth treats the London poor unsympathetically; on the contrary, as we have seen, his writing includes sharply realised vignettes of working-class life. But these only serve to give colour to an enterprise whose dominant mode of understanding and address is that of the 'objective' social-scientific survey.

The journalism of Andrew Mearns and W. T. Stead works very differently. *The Bitter Cry of Outcast London*, a pamphlet published anonymously in 1883 but since ascribed to the Congregationalist minister Mearns, situates itself as presenting the agony of London destitution and misery in a vocabulary at once religious and melodramatic:

> ...seething in the very centre of our great cities, concealed by the thinnest crust of civilization and decency, is a vast mass of moral corruption, of heart-breaking misery and absolute godlessness, and ...scarcely anything has been done to take into this awful slough the only influences that can purify or remove it.[23]

The redemption of this suffering is thus at once a matter of religious duty, and of common prudence; the poor are not only housed in misery, they are also dangerous. Stead's campaigning journalism – 'The Maiden Tribute of Modern Babylon' is an exposé of child-prostitution in

London – similarly used the language of religion to present a reality so shocking that any more sober mode would have seemed inadequate.

Finally, William Booth – the 'General' Booth of the Salvation Army – presents another kind of map altogether in *In Darkest England and the Way Out*. Once again there is a literal map, one of England in which the escape from the misery of the urban slums is Utopianly realised via a helping hand and an escape to rural labour colonies. The metaphor of Booth's title is itself significant. It draws on perhaps the dominant metaphor for travel into working-class districts – that of exploration – but makes that metaphor especially pointed by alluding to the phrase becoming widespread in the 1880s, 'In Darkest Africa'. The poor of metropolitan London, in an irony often noted of the world's largest city and the capital of the world's largest and most powerful empire, are themselves as benighted as the inhabitants of the continent just then in the process of colonial subjugation. Booth's book is of course a missionary tract, its aim to encourage the evangelisation of the poor. But in disposing the social map of London in the way it does, it too renders the poor the object of a particular kind of pathos and offers them up to dramatic social intervention.

My emphasis upon mode and form is a way of highlighting the social relations that are built into the writing itself, or, in other ways, into visual and oral cultural forms. It can appear to pass over their substantive content; I am especially conscious of this in discussing the attempts to map London in the 1880s, the complexities and density of which are particularly remarkable.[24] But if the moment of Mayhew was the social and political crisis of the late 1840s, then a perceived crisis in social relations was equally the moment of this 1880s writing – 'perceived', because there is little evidence to suggest that matters were actually much worse in the 1880s than they had been in previous decades.[25] Unlike the crisis of the 1840s, however, which was national and even international in character, the crisis of the 1880s was perceived essentially as a crisis of the cities, and especially of London. The journalism that I have discussed both contributes to this sense of crisis, and addresses it in specific ways.

The City as Gendered Cultural Space

I have emphasised how the social zoning of the nineteenth-century city meant that to write about the city was necessarily to write about class; it was, of course, also a gendered space, though its gendering must be mapped more subtly on to its geography. Indeed, part of the very complexity is created by the profound and multifaceted interrelationship of the divisions of class and gender in the public and private spaces, the suburban and central zones, and the commercial, marketing, professional and industrial differentiations of the city.

The cultural forms that I have discussed up to this point can be thought of as to some extent external to the city, seeking a vantage-point outside or above it from which to get a sense of its totality, or exploring the city's nether regions from the standpoint of a middle-class visitor. I wish now to suggest how certain social and cultural understandings are built into the very fabric of the city. The layout of public spaces, the building, arrangement and interior organisation of working- and middle-class housing, the design of public buildings such as churches, chapels, schools, banks, libraries and town halls, the very distinctions into 'public' and 'private' space, all these are cultural forms which involve intimate assumptions about social and gender position. Obviously a history of the public buildings and civic spaces of nineteenth-century cities is well beyond the scope of this chapter; large portions of these diverse spaces survive even at the end of the twentieth century, and their particular force can still be felt by walking around the great public buildings in the centre of Liverpool, by observing the monuments to civic self-confidence represented by the town halls of many a provincial city, or simply by standing in Trafalgar Square. But a more manageable sense of the social and cultural disposition of urban space can be obtained from considering the particular meanings that cluster around the urban and suburban home.

This is a matter that I return to in the next chapter, when considering the dividing-line of gender that runs through society and culture in our period. Davidoff and Hall trace, in fine and compelling detail, the process of suburbanisation in early nineteenth-century Birmingham, how this involved a separation of workplace and domestic home for the middle-class family, which was simultaneously a reorganisation of gender roles and of domestic space (see above, p. 87). The suburban home was henceforth to be much more exclusively a female space, while men could pass from the space of the home to the now exclusively masculine space of work. 'Home' thus becomes a place of refuge from the harsh and competitive world of the inner-city office or factory where work is conducted. But this is by no means an exclusively middle-class division. Consider the following passage from a working-class

Lancashire writer, Benjamin Brierley – a passage which could be readily multiplied from other working-class male writers:

> Bedlam, however, was not a social desert without its oasis. Stiffy's home glimmered out in the cloudy void like a green spot upon which a streak of refreshing sunlight had settled. It was a home that you would think ought to have had more genial companionship that [*sic*] could be found among squalid dens, where vice and unkindly feelings gendered and grew in festering loathsomeness. It was a home that ought to have had such associations as green meadows, blossoming hedgerows, gardens, the song of the wild bird, and the breadth [*sic*] of the sweet moorland breeze. But had it been placed among the wigwams of some savage tribe it would have been just the same, for woman had made it what it was; and she has the power to make such a place a Paradise or Pandemonium, whichever she wills.[26]

Here, the presence of the home as a refuge from the city, conceived in a thoroughly negative way ('squalid dens...'), could not be clearer. The connection of the home to a version of pastoral is also evident here, recalling the prevalence of pastoral as we discussed it in Chapter 4 above. It is equally clear that this refuge is dependent for its particular quality on the rule of the woman who runs it – we are witnessing a way of understanding the city which is intrinsically gendered. The particular way in which the city is experienced, then, involves a kind of internal or imaginative map whose contours are drawn in the inextricable colours of class and gender, and whose different regions have deep emotional valencies.

It is possible to trace a further collaborating process which bears upon the meanings attached to 'home' in the nineteenth century, insofar as this home is counterposed to the urban world which surrounds it. In one sense Davidoff and Hall describe a process of *privatisation*, in which the combined domestic and workspace of the eighteenth-century middle-class home is divided into quite separate and geographically distinct areas. Henceforth the domestic home will be exclusively private, no longer a place of economic activity. The bank, for example, especially with the rise of joint-stock banking in the 1830s and 1840s, will no longer mean a banking 'house', in the rooms of which clients are met and business transacted, but rather the imposing city-centre building – the domestic homes of its managers now exclusively private places. This too does not occur solely among the commercial and industrial middle class, though it is perhaps especially visible there. The gradual but by no means universal predominance of factory production in the course of the century meant that many working-class homes also ceased to be sites of economic activity and became more exclusively private. The spectacular demise of hand-loom weaving in the cotton districts is only the most evident example of this process, though domestic production and outwork did persist in many areas. The very layout of working-class housing in most nineteenth-century towns testifies to the advance of privatisation. The characteristic early nineteenth-century housing layouts of enclosed 'courts' (difficult to penetrate for the visitor, but constituting a semi-public housing space for the inhabitants) were mostly either replaced or opened up in the course of the century in the name of improvement and better sewage-disposal. The improvements were real enough, but the housing patterns that they created typically reproduced that absolute distinction between the public and the private.[27] Within these improved and private spaces, people could live their lives, as far as their means allowed, according to notions of respectability that permitted certain kinds of work for women, and that reserved certain areas for domestic labour and certain others, notably the parlour, for 'best'.

If I have emphasised the similarities of middle- and working-class experience, we ought nevertheless to recognise some profound differences also in the ways that people experienced their relation to their urban environment. With respect to the shock city of the 1840s, Manchester, Friedrich Engels (1820–95) has given us a vivid portrait of the bourgeois paterfamilias, making his way from the outer suburbs to his place of work in the city centre through working-class districts whose reality is shielded from him by a screen of shops on the highway on which he travels.[28] Manchester in the 1840s was still a relatively small city, certainly a 'walking city' for its working-class inhabitants, whose sense of place, and whose relationship to the city as a whole, would certainly have been very different from that of their employers. London at the end of the century, a vastly greater place, naturally offered still more varied contrasts. This was a tracked city par excellence, with vast armies of clerks and minor functionaries making their way to work from their suburban homes to a place of work in the City; their wives perhaps making a different trip to the West End for shopping, but having to negotiate their place on pavement and in shops with more uncertainty.[29] Manual workers, travelling earlier to their place of work, might well have no cause to visit the city centre at all, but might have a much stronger sense of immediate locality. Again, male members of the City elite and the governing class, able to travel comfortably, and at a later time, between their urban centres of power and a house in the outer suburbs or the country, with an all-male club in the West End as a place for recruitment and participation in the networks of power, naturally had a very different sense of the city they ruled – and different once more from that of their wives and daughters, largely though not completely excluded from these networks of influence. The urban space was geographically distinct, and experienced at different times of day, for all these groups of people. I deal here, perhaps, in stereotypes. But I do so to emphasise that the differing cultural forms that speak of urban life emerged from particular and distinct ways of living that life, and entered into those lives in profound ways.

6

GENDER AND CULTURAL FORMS

Negotiating Domestic Ideology

I have described gender as one of the great faultlines of nineteenth-century cultural history. In this the history of the period is no different from
that of any other century or culture, for social and cultural differentiation along the line of gender is one of the universals of human history.
What is special to the nineteenth century, however, is the prominence of
that differentiation, and the prominence of the explicit efforts to alter its
terms. Appropriate and inappropriate behaviour for women and men
was the subject of intense and prolonged debate, with constant redraw-
ings and redefinitions of the gender line, and increasingly confident
challenges to the proscriptions and limitations placed upon women.
Feminism, after all, is the invention of the nineteenth century, though
conflict between the sexes, of course, is not. However, this chapter will
not be centrally concerned with feminism, even in its cultural manifesta-
tions. Rather, it will seek to suggest the ways in which cultural forms
themselves encode assumptions about gender. But this is to put the matter too neutrally. For gender differentiation is in large part a matter of
culture – that is, the very ways in which people understand their own
and others' sexuality and its implications for behaviour are partly determined in the sphere of culture. So the gender assumptions that are
encoded in cultural forms of all kinds are not the reflections of realities
of gender differentiation that exist elsewhere, but are themselves those
realities. Gender is lived through culture, be it forms of dress, the organisation of domestic space, or identification with the representations

of women and men offered by the novel, poetry or painting. Each and every cultural artefact, therefore, negotiates and renegotiates the terms within which people live their gendered selves.

This is an important point to remember, because the temptation is great to see nineteenth-century women as victims of monolithic entities called 'domestic ideology' or 'the doctrine of separate spheres'. These entities were real, but they did not exist outside the particular cultural forms in which they manifested themselves; as such they could be negotiated, acquiesced in, resisted, put to differing uses and taken advantage of by women and men with widely varying results. There is a danger that even in explicating some general account of the notion of 'separate spheres', it acquires a solidity or reality beyond its existence in these actual and negotiated forms. Nevertheless, it is possible to recognise a widespread and fundamental set of assumptions about gender divisions in the nineteenth century, which can be summarised as follows. Men and women have different aptitudes and capacities, which fit them for different spheres of activity. Men are best suited to the active, public world, whether this be the world of work or the market, political institutions, or the various institutions of civil society. Women, by contrast, are better suited for the domestic sphere, where their talents for loving care and self-sacrificing management especially qualify them to act as the guardians of the home. The broad terms of this summary, of course, appeared with very different emphases, and lent themselves to very different formulations, superimposing distinctions of gender on to quite disparate fields: the male public sphere and the female domestic sphere, the male world of means and the female world of ends, masculine activity and female passivity, masculine intellect and feminine emotionalism. Finally, the apparent complementarity of these terms does not obscure the fact that the masculine is the dominant term, and that men were the privileged sex, not only because of their presumed authority over women, but because they could move between both the public and the private spheres. Women's confinement to the domestic sphere was both an ideal and a reality.

But this 'domestic ideology' nowhere appears in a pure form; it always appears in particular realisations, and thus in complex and negotiated cultural artefacts. This process of cultural negotiation occurs both *within* cultural artefacts and *in relation to* cultural artefacts. Take the case, for example, of Jane Austen's *Pride and Prejudice*, published in 1813. This is precisely concerned with the terms that middle-class young women can exact for themselves in the marriage market – a complex process of bargaining which involves estimations of their own beauty and its worth, the dowry which can be provided by their father, their class position, not to mention such matters as their personality, its vivacity or otherwise, their emotional resilience and their ability to show themselves sexually attractive while staying within the bounds of decorum. There is no question here of any scope for these women beyond the domestic sphere, and thus the whole novel might be said to exemplify a version of the doctrine of separate spheres, in which the public world of action, work and politics remains firmly the domain of men, while that of the domestic space remains the domain of women. Yet the different young women in the novel *do* negotiate within their relatively narrow confines and with differing degrees of success, so that one character, Charlotte Lucas, is shown making the best of a very bad job in marrying the foolish sycophant, Collins, while Elizabeth Bennet does very much better in capturing (and partially re-educating) the fabulously wealthy Darcy. The novel thus shows a world in which a real space of freedom is available to its characters, within which they can make real choices, and the terms of which they can partly turn to their own advantage. And the novel itself thus becomes part of the very struggles it depicts, for in representing the triumph of Elizabeth Bennet's intelligence and vivacity, it recommends those qualities as suitable and attractive for its readers.

But *Pride and Prejudice*, and the case of Jane Austen more generally, points us in other directions as well. For clearly the questions of gender that are raised by her books are inextricably linked to questions of class also, so that the renegotiated models of decorum that the book offers are as much class ideals as gender ideals. In one of the most satisfying scenes in the novel, Elizabeth Bennet sees off Lady Catherine de Burgh when the latter tries to veto her attachment to Darcy on the grounds that she is of unsuitably low birth. Thus in staking out a claim for the appropriateness of Elizabeth Bennet's code of manners, the novel is simultaneously rejecting more narrowly conceived aristocratic notions of worth. More strongly still: the novel is offering a female-regulated domestic space as a site of power for middle-class women, and thus inevitably entering into the contest of competing representations that surround that space. In this sense, Jane Austen was one novelist – among many others – who was using the form to define and redefine the relative positions of women and men, without in any way being a conscious feminist.

Thinking of *Pride and Prejudice* in these terms enables us to see, then, that such large cultural and ideological entities as 'domestic ideology' do not exist outside the cultural forms in which they occur; this has important implications for the ways in which we conceive of people living and living through these larger entities. Yet the question remains: is it possible to give a more synoptic picture of gender roles and positions, and their transformation over time? The difficulties in the way of such a task are certainly formidable. We have already noted that questions of gender are inextricably imbricated with questions of class, so that the cultural forms in which these matters are decided vary widely from class to class. Most dramatically in this context, the prohibition upon manual work for respectable middle-class women could only be sustained by the massive employment of working-class women as servants. Similarly, these matters varied from region to region and from place to place. Notions of femininity and masculinity varied widely between town and country, and between one kind of industrial labour and another. The working factory women of the cotton towns of Lancashire, for example, represent a very different tradition even from the pit-brow lasses of Wigan in the same county; differences among the cultural forms of gender between the metropolis and provincial England were still more marked.

There are thus very real difficulties confronting any attempt to construct a general history of gender-divisions and their cultural forms in the nineteenth century. These are in part empirical; they concern the problems of organising a mass of material of an extremely diverse kind. These empirical difficulties are compounded by one of principle: in seeking to give a history of cultural forms as they press upon the question of gender, one is in effect proposing a history of subjectivity, of the ways in which individuals have assimilated, appropriated and rejected the cultural forms offered to them and in doing so formed themselves and have been formed as subjects. This is *in principle* an almost impossible task, not merely because every individual's life-story is different but also because such a history would of necessity be speculative, relying heavily on the insights of a novelist or a psychoanalyst. Nevertheless, there are models of a kind of history-writing which does attempt an overarching or synoptic history of such matters as gender roles, and yet can ground that wider account in the most minute portrayal of individuals' lives in all the density of their social and cultural history. For our period, as I have frequently suggested, the work of Leonore Davidoff and Catherine Hall is exemplary. Their book, *Family Fortunes: Men and Women of the English Middle Class 1780–1850*, traces the history of a range of middle-class families in two provincial centres, Birmingham and Essex, from

LIVERPOOL JOHN MOORES UNIVERSITY
LEARNING SERVICES

the late eighteenth century to the mid-nineteenth century. In particular, it traces a process in which family-run enterprises, based on the place of work, were gradually transformed into exclusively male-run concerns, with a separate place of residence for a female-run family home. This is how Davidoff and Hall describe one aspect of this process:

> As the spatial and temporal quarantine between the public and private grew, they were ever more identified with gender. A masculine penumbra surrounded that which was defined as public, while women were increasingly engulfed by the private realm, bounded by physical, social and psychic partitions. Men, in their privileged position, moved between both sectors. These dichotomies and their association with gender identity, inevitably emphasized hierarchy, the fixing of individual and social place.
>
> Such massive reordering necessitated leaps in imagination interspersed with painstaking, minute, even trivial changes . . . .[1]

In this perspective, cultural forms emerge from and feed into a particular social history, in which relative understandings of gender are transformed along with transformations in the economy (including the domestic economy). These transformations, for the provincial middle class at least, involve changing notions both of masculinity and femininity, as the public world of work, controlled by the market, is increasingly gendered as male, and separated from the feminine domestic sphere, seen now as a haven for men from the rough world in which they have to contend.

It should be possible to extend this powerful and densely realised account in thinking about other sectors of society. For the domestic ideal pioneered by the provincial and perhaps the metropolitan middle class offered a seductive model for other classes to follow, with obvious compromises made necessary by reduced circumstances. William Booth, at the end of the century in London, could provide carefully graded accounts of its population, in which lines of respectability were drawn and redrawn, at different levels of society, about such matters as the presence of a servant (and of which kind), the necessity of the woman of the house having to work, and the respectability or otherwise with which the woman managed her domestic resources. I would not wish to suggest that the ideal of separate spheres was simply imposed upon deluded people; on the contrary, working people could have a tremendous investment in such ideals, and their successful realisation (in however reduced a form) could mean the difference between misery and modest comfort. But the general point is this: pervasive and related changes in the organisation of work and the home accompanied powerful and widespread notions of separate spheres for men and women, which spread from the middle class in the course of the century to many sections of the population by its close.

It is in this context that the nineteenth-century preoccupation with questions of gender should be understood. On the one hand people living their lives within relatively stable patterns of gender differentiation, with separate spheres marked out for men and women; on the other hand, gradual and occasionally dramatic alterations in those gender differentiations, as the lines between the spheres get either more firmly drawn and redrawn, or are challenged and crossed. Culture is the space in which these differences are imagined and secured, or occasionally reimagined and undermined. This is a constant and never-ending process, in which the contours of people's lives are perpetually being confirmed or reshaped. And this is a material history, in which the actual forms of life provide the ultimate context in which those cultural forms make sense.

Gender and Cultural Forms

This process, of the confirmation and disconfirmation of the contours of gender, was true for both men and women, though the fixation on the Woman Question – the explicit consideration on the role and mission of women – might lead you to forget this. Cultural forms imagine and reimagine the roles of men equally with women. Why, then, the preoccupation with the latter, as though masculinity were an unproblematic term? Principally, because these terms are not simply equivalent, but hierarchical; masculinity is the assumed stable centre against which the unstable term of femininity has constantly to be measured. Given the unequal access to the means of cultural production between men and women in the nineteenth century, it is scarcely surprising both that 'woman' should appear problematic for men, and that woman's place should become so problematic for women when they gained access to the means of production themselves.

However, if all cultural forms are engaged in the process of gender definition and redefinition, then all such forms, from the cut of a pair

of trousers to the most elaborate poem, should be grist to the mill of a
chapter such as this. Both class and gender notions are clearly present,
for example, in the transformations of women's and men's upper-class
fashion in the nineteenth century: the 'Empire line' at the beginning
of the century, the crinoline at mid-century, and the bustle of the
1870s and 1880s all speak different versions of women's sexuality,
while the Regency dandy and the mid-century paterfamilias equally
project very different versions of male sexuality. But gender divisions
are obviously relevant across all cultural forms: in the theatre, in painting, in ballet, in ballads and chapbooks and in emerging popular-cultural forms such as the music-hall and popular journalism. I offer the
following accounts as examples only, as demonstrations of the ways in
which cultural forms, with greater or less explicitness, address and
assume questions of gender. The presumed social ground of all these
is the sexually divided social space, characterised by the male public
sphere and the female private sphere. This of course was not monolithic
during the nineteenth century; it required constant reinforcement and
policing, appeared in very different ways in the different classes in
society, and was under substantial and partially successful challenge
from mid-century onwards.

I start with a brief account of the novel in the nineteenth century as it
relates to these issues. In the first place, we can recognise that the nineteenth-century novel is overwhelmingly concerned with the private
rather than the public sphere, with the domestic sphere gendered as
'feminine'. When, towards the end of the century, there was a more general turn in British culture towards Imperialism, this was accompanied
by the reinvention or rediscovery of the 'masculine romance', adven-
ture-stories for boys that formed an escape from the more domestic
and sober realism that characterises much of the nineteenth-century
novel (though of course there was a tradition of adventure novels
throughout the nineteenth century, from Walter Scott onwards, which
provided a fertile source for this reinvention).[2] As a form, then, the
novel addressed the cultural and social construction of gender in the
most fundamental ways. It both established and policed the boundaries
of gender, and challenged them also.

Second, the novel was the form which provided the most obvious
scope for women writers, from the now canonical names of Jane Austen,
Charlotte Brontë, Emily Brontë, Elizabeth Gaskell and George Eliot, to
a host of less well-known novelists who used the form for a multiplicity
of purposes. Whether or not there was a specifically female tradition

within the history of the nineteenth-century novel, the form certainly lent itself to be used by women writers to voice the particular insights made available to women by their place in society – though the manner in which these insights were articulated, and the kinds of authority claimed by women novelists for them in their novels, varied greatly.

Third, the great variety of modes of writing within the novel permitted varied ways of framing questions of gender. Sober domestic realism, the melodrama of the 'sensation novel', the novel of manners, the silver-fork novel (addressed admiringly to aristocratic life), religious novels, romance: all these modes of writing permitted very different ways of understanding gender, and of shaping and reshaping gender roles and relations. We have already seen how such a process could occur within a novel of manners like *Pride and Prejudice*. We have only to think of such well-known novels as *Jane Eyre* (1847), *Dombey and Son* (1847–48), *Middlemarch* (1871–72), or *Far from the Madding Crowd* (1874), to see how differing modes such as romance, humour, melodrama, realism and pastoral could be used to articulate differing shapings of gender and gender differences. Thus Charlotte Brontë in *Jane Eyre* could use what is fundamentally the mode of romance to give voice to a feminine subjectivity that becomes explicitly feminist in its challenge to artificial limitations of female desire and aspiration. In the exactly contemporary *Dombey and Son*, Dickens drew upon the melodramatic mode in the characterisation of Edith Dombey; perhaps only in this way could he imagine a female challenge to the power of the patriarch Dombey. George Eliot wrote *Middlemarch* in part as an explicit contribution to the 'Woman Question'; the meticulously detailed realism of the characterisation of Dorothea permits Eliot to trace, as carefully as she is able, what she takes to be the conditions and limits for a meaningful and worthwhile life, as they act upon a woman's life in the early years of the nineteenth century. Finally, Hardy, in *Far from the Madding Crowd*, drew upon a version of pastoral to explore the operations of desire, and different codes of manliness. It would be no exaggeration to say that *every* novel explores, in its own particular accents, some aspect of gender relations and gendered difference.

My principal examples, however, come from mid-century, above all from the notable series of poems published at this period in which questions of gender appear in especially salient and at times problematic forms. I choose this sequence of poems because of their close temporal range (the earliest was published in 1847, the latest in 1862); because of the diversity of poetic forms which are employed in them; and because they can be seen as a set of permutations among the various possibilities for the understanding and re-presentation of gender at mid-century.

The poems that I discuss are as follows: Alfred Tennyson, *The Princess* (1847); Elizabeth Barrett Browning, *Aurora Leigh* (1857); Arthur Clough, *The Bothie of Tober-na Vuolich* (1848); Robert Browning, *Men and Women* (1855); Coventry Patmore, *The Angel in the House* (1854–56); Christina Rossetti, *Goblin Market* (1862); William Morris, *The Defence of Guinevere and Other Poems* (1858); George Meredith, *Modern Love* (1862). All of these poems circle around questions of gender with more or less self-consciousness, some, like Tennyson's *The Princess*, explicitly addressing the 'Woman Question', others, like Rossetti's *Goblin Market,* considering questions of sexuality in highly coded and oblique ways. The range of forms is striking, from ballads, through long narrative poems, to dramatic monologues and a 'medley', which is how Tennyson subtitles *The Princess*. Each of these forms carries its own construction of meaning, positioning the reader in different ways with respect to the women and men of which the poems speak.

The Princess is an apparently anti-feminist poem, which tells an exemplary tale of the re-education of a woman who sets up an all-female academy to establish the equality of her sex. Her scheme is defeated, mostly by the softness of her woman's heart. The academy is infiltrated by three men disguised as women, one of whom is her princely suitor; they are discovered, and after a battle, the princess agrees to nurse the wounded, who include her suitor; she agrees to marry him. Judging from this crude synopsis alone, the drift of the poem appears clear enough, towards the re-education of women away from hard, false ideals of equality towards truer, softer and more appropriately feminine notions. The poem, in this light, is exactly one which speaks the doctrine of separate spheres. Nevertheless, this is also a poem which arrives at its conclusion with difficulty – whose conclusions have to be worked for and managed, and in the course of which many fixities about gender have to be at least temporarily set aside. For example, the most brutally masculine attitudes of the martial father of the Princess's suitor are repudiated:

> 'Look you , Sir!
> Man is the hunter; woman is his game:
> The sleek and shining creatures of the chase,
> We hunt them for the beauty of their skins;
> They love us for it, and we ride them down.'[3]

And similarly, it is this martial father who speaks those lines of the poem which most famously articulate the doctrine of separate spheres:

> 'Man for the field and woman for the hearth:
> Man for the sword and for the needle she:
> Man with the head and woman with the heart:
> Man to command and woman to obey;
> All else confusion.'[4]

While these lines retain some of their force in the poem (and are certainly the most widely quoted from it), in their immediate context they are softened by a doctrine of separate spheres which recognises equality and not command as the basis of the relationship between men and women in their different roles.

Furthermore, despite the way in which the poem sets up women as the object of inquiry – as the problem, as it were, to be solved – it is actually the male subjects who tell it in the first person and who undergo the most radical questionings of their gendered identity. It is the men who must dress up as women to test the strength of the women's resolve; the poem often treads the skirts of bathos as its heroes traipse about in women's clothes. On several occasions the men are ridiculed for their attire; there is undoubtedly some question as to their manliness, and the poem can be considered to be as much concerned with renegotiating the terms of masculinity as it is with its more ostensible project of reasserting, in however modified a way, dominant ideas about *women's* role.

Finally, the way in which this elaborate narrative is framed needs to be considered, as affecting the force and seriousness with which it might be received. The story of the princess is told as a summer's-day entertainment, by a group of undergraduate friends as they meet on the occasion of an open day, when the lord of the manor, and the father of one of the friends, throws open his grounds to the local populace. The daughter of the house has aspirations of just the kind held by the princess of the poem – it is to her re-education, that of the heiress of the English manor (by extension, of England more generally), that the poem is addressed. But actually this is left open at the end of the poem. While the young men and women argue about the genre of the tale they have just heard – the women claiming the seriousness of epic for this story of woman's rights, while the men are happy to rest in the 'mock-heroic gigantesque' – the heiress remains thoughtfully undecided, and then refers the whole question to her learned maiden aunt...who never delivers a final verdict. So while this framing device seeks to point the relevance of this elaborate fable to the contemporary world, it also undermines that relevance with the same gesture, and leaves the conclusion arrived at within the narrative significantly open. In short, the poem offers its readers multiple perspectives, which, while Tennyson himself clearly seeks to give a particular rhetorical shaping to the poem, nevertheless offer its readers diverse points of entry.

Shortly after writing *The Princess*, Tennyson was made Poet Laureate – this is the work of a male poet, aware of his stature, and self-consciously addressing one of the important topics of the day. While something similar could be said of Elizabeth Barrett Browning's *Aurora Leigh* – she too was a well-known poet, who announced in the Dedication that it contains her 'highest convictions upon Life and Art' – the differences are also crucial. Foremost among these, in the context of this chapter, is of course that the writer is a woman, who writes, in the first person, in the persona of a woman poet, Aurora Leigh. The poem, in short, starts from the subjectivity of a woman, and does not pose the 'Woman Question' as a problem to be solved by male consideration on it. This radically alters the ways in which the poem offers subject-positions to its readers, even if the conclusions which it draws – of the centrality of heterosexual love – might seem to make it not dissimilar to Tennyson's poem in its explicit address to gender politics.

Aurora Leigh is a long narrative poem which revolves around the three topics of the relative position of men and women, the social question (Romney, the male hero of the poem, is a Fourierian – a Utopian socialist), and the role of Art in relation to those important matters. At times it draws upon an aesthetic of heightened or melodramatic speech to articulate its moments of especial poignancy or significance. The inseparability of questions of gender from the other social questions with which they are caught is again evident from the poem, which deals with the defeat of Romney's Fourierian schemes and his recognition that the world of poetry, previously patronised, indeed deals with the highest aims of life, while schemes of mere social reform deal only with the means. But because the protagonist of the poem is a woman poet, this recognition inevitably identifies the realm of ends as feminine. In this respect, the poem can be read as a female reworking of some of the themes of the ideology of separate spheres.

Nevertheless, Elizabeth Barrett Browning expresses some powerful critiques of both of conventional middle-class female education and of a certain style of essentially upper-class femininity. To that extent, the poem avails itself of a tradition of feminist thinking which goes back at least to Mary Wollstonecraft (1759–97) at the end of the eighteenth century, a tradition in part carried by circles of progressive liberal thought of which Elizabeth Barrett Browning was the inheritor. Thus the poem's strong critique of girls' education and of the conduct books that justified it, is based upon a liberal view that each individual should be allowed to discover their own fullest potential regardless of artificial constraints:

> I read a score of books on womanhood
> To prove, if women do not think at all,
> They may teach thinking, (to a maiden-aunt
> Or else the author) – books that boldly assert
> Their right of comprehending husband's talk
> When not too deep, and even of answering
> With pretty 'may it please you,' or 'so it is,'-
> Their rapid insight and fine aptitude,
> Particular worth and general missionariness,
> As long as they keep quiet by the fire
> And never say 'no' when the world says 'ay,'
> For that is fatal, – their angelic reach
> Of virtue, chiefly used to sit and darn,
> And fatten household sinners.[5]

The poet's sardonic tone here sharply underlines the critique of the narrowness of women's education, a critique that forms a substantial part of the feminist case throughout the century. This is accompanied by a still sharper distaste for the kind of woman produced by this education. The poem is hardest, not upon men, but upon the character of Lady Waldemar, who is manipulative, dishonest and sexually immodest in her nineteenth-century aristocratic women's flaunting evening-dress: 'How they told, / Those alabaster shoulders and bare breasts....'[6] In articulating one high ideal of educated womanhood, Elizabeth Barrett Browning is simultaneously repudiating what she sees as an unworthy class and sexual ideal.

Her way of doing so can be illuminatingly compared with a male poet's treatment of related themes, Arthur Hugh Clough's mock-heroic narrative of undergraduate life, *The Bothie of Tober-na-Vuolich*, published in 1848. This is a story which concerns the repudiation, by an Oxford undergraduate, of the social and political ideals of his class. Crucial in his process of discovery and emancipation is his courtship of a Highland peasant woman, and his temporary infatuation with an aristocratic beauty. The authenticity of the hero's rejection of the false ideals of his class is thus measured by his willingness to commit himself to a sexual relationship across the classes, and thus to commit himself to an ideal of femininity very different to that represented in the poem by the 'lovely' Lady Maria. In one persistent theme of nineteenth-century writing, social problems are to be solved by cross-class marriage – a solution rejected by Elizabeth Barrett Browning in *Aurora Leigh*, though the narrative of the poem turns on one.

Yet such an outcome – the male hero of a narrative demonstrating the authenticity of his commitment to class reconciliation, or indeed his own repudiation of his class-situation, by marrying across the classes – is not without its problems in gender terms. This is a story which comes dangerously close to the exploitative narratives, in which lower-class female sexuality is seen as available by predatory upper-class men. This danger is anticipated to some extent by Clough in *The Bothie of Tober-na-Vuolich*; the hero is mocked for his idealisation of working women:

> Ay, doing household work, as many sweet girls I have looked at,
> Needful household work, which some one, after all, must do,
> Needful, graceful therefore, as washing, cooking, and scouring,
> Or, if you please, with the fork in the garden uprooting potatoes.[7]

This is laughed at as a form of prurience, the predatory masculine gaze masquerading as chivalry. But this mockery is not the final word of the poem, which allows its hero to persist in a marriage to a peasant woman, and to articulate a critique of middle-class notions of femininity which deny women the possibility of useful work – at one point such women are addressed in the following terms:

> – Ye unhappy statuettes, and miserable trinkets,
> Poor alabaster chimney-piece ornaments under glass cases.[8]

It may be that the notions of useful work for women that the poem suggests in passing remain locked within the ideology of separate spheres, so that the questions raised by the poem about gender and class are thus finally resolved in ways which involve a decisive break with the constrictions of class – but a very much less decisive break with the constrictions of gender. Nevertheless, the poem does seek to rethink gender relations and possibilities, and partially articulates its radicalism through such rethinking.

The Bothie of Tober-na-Vuolich is very much an Oxford University poem, almost a coterie poem in its ostentatious experimenting with English verse forms and its display of learning. The 'generosity' of the poem's hero – his willingness to lose caste in marrying a lower-class woman and thus to demonstrate his commitment to his political views – anticipates the real-life actions of another Oxford poet of the middle of the century, William Morris. In 1859 he married Jane Burden, the daughter of an Oxford ostler; by so doing he sealed his emotional rejection of the ideals of the commercial bourgeois class into which he was born. He too was in part motivated by notions of chivalry, which might have surprisingly radical implications for social relations but were highly ambivalent when taken seriously as a guide to gender relations. Some of these ambivalences can be seen in the historical figure of Jane Morris, whom hostile observers have persistently seen as part of the decor of the Morris household. They can also be pursued in Morris's own early poetry, which was published as a collection ten years after Clough's poem: *The Defence of Guinevere* (1858).

The poems that make up this collection – some Arthurian, some set in late medieval times – come at their various topics in very unusual ways. Some are vivid, dreamlike fragments, intense but also obscure. Others are longer narrative poems, such as the title poem itself, 'The Defence of Guinevere', which interestingly reworks its familiar Arthurian material. An obvious starting point for our purposes would be to see the poems as 'Pre-Raphaelite' (see above, Chapters 3 and 4); the notions of masculinity and femininity that they carry are cognate with the well-known images of chivalry and brooding beauty to be found in the paintings of Burne-Jones and Dante Gabriel Rossetti. This Pre-Raphaelite art is one of intense idealisation, of both men and women; its protest against the commercial drabness and squalor of mid-nineteenth-century England involves a still more extreme separation of the roles of men and women, so that women's faces and bodies in particular become the focus for all the longings for beauty and fulfilment that the present age cannot satisfy. But while this is certainly true of much of Pre-Raphaelite visual art, some of these themes appear very differently in Morris's poetry, which is as much a critique of chivalry as it is a celebration of it. The masculine world can certainly demonstrate an unworldly chivalry, but it also, more typically, evinces a violence of a grotesque kind. The women in the poem are often shown as victims of this male violence, and are themselves capable of an intense erotic consciousness, frequently impeded or blocked. Far from being merely escapist art, in which the gender contradictions of the nineteenth century can be resolved in the simplifications of an imagined chivalric world, Morris's poetry indeed re-imagines gender relations in the sharply realised figures of another time and place, but this place also turns out to be the site of frustration and violence.

This leads me to Meredith's *Modern Love* (1862), which bears some resemblance to Pre-Raphaelite poetry by its suffusion with intense but frustrated erotic feeling. But the contrast with Morris's medievalism is most apparent from the very title of the collection, *Modern Love*; the poems are explicitly offered as in some sense symptomatic of a more widespread contemporary situation. The volume is made up of a sequence of fifty sixteen-line sonnets; they are examples of what Isobel Armstrong has described as 'double poems': that is, while written from an intensely subjective standpoint, they also subject that standpoint to irony, allowing the reader to recognise it as in some sense inadequate or exemplary. In the past the poems have suffered from a too exclusively biographical reading; since the sequence concerns the failure of a marriage, and because Meredith's marriage with his first wife had just recently failed, the temptation has always been to read them as a personal confession. But in the context of this chapter we can see the sequence as a complex exploration of various, gendered subject positions. The 'narrative' of the sonnet-sequence is that of a married woman who is being unfaithful to her husband; he, in turn, is unfaithful to her. The poems are remarkably frank in their account of the sexual feelings and frustrations of the male poet, and are indeed explicit about when and with what feelings sexual relations have ended. The sonnet-sequence is well suited to the role of 'double' poem, since each individual sonnet can be used to articulate the complexities of one particular idea, moment or feeling; the reader can at once feel the force of this moment in the sequence, and see how it fits into an overall pattern. The form thus lends itself to the full exploration of a subject-position; Meredith's distinction in *Modern Love* is that he simultaneously explores an emotionally charged subjectivity in terms of wider expectations of what should constitute marriage and love between men and women. The following poem provides an example:

> We three are on the cedar-shadowed lawn;
> My friend being third. He who at love once laughed,

Is in the weak rib by a fatal shaft
Struck through, and tells his passion's bashful dawn
And radiant culmination, glorious crown,
When 'this' she said: went 'thus': most wondrous she.
Our eyes grow white, encountering: that we are three,
Forgetful; then together we look down.
But he demands our blessing; is convinced
That words of wedded lovers must bring good.
We question; if we dare! or if we should!
And pat him, with light laugh. We have not winced.
Next, she has fallen. Fainting points the sign
To happy things in wedlock. When she wakes,
She looks the star that thro' the cedar shakes:
Her lost moist hand clings mortally to mine. (Sonnet XXI)[9]

This is a simple incident: a secretly estranged couple are called upon by a friend to give him advice and bless his love; they are appalled but keep up the pretence; she faints. The poem both draws on and undermines the poetic vocabulary of feeling; there is a strong air of irony surrounding the new lover's 'bashful dawn / And radiant culmination'. Indeed, the tense situation is exactly created by the friend's expectation that this pair of wedded lovers can share in his feelings and pronounce a blessing upon them. This expectation is compounded by the wife's fainting; the 'happy things' of which this is supposed to be the sign are not just pregnancy but the sexual happiness of which pregnancy is the presumed fruit. Since we know from earlier poems in the sequence that sexual relations between the couple have been suspended, we must attribute her reaction to the strain of keeping up appearances. But the poem does not only undermine these conventional expectations; it still inhabits a world of feeling in which such language is appropriate. This is seen most clearly at its end, when the wife wakes from her faint. The sonnet resumes the heightened poetic diction without embarrassment ('She looks the star that thro' the cedar shakes'), and ends with an image of the wife's vulnerability in her 'lost moist hand' clinging to the male poet's. Yet it clings 'mortally', in partial contrast to the ethereal vision of her as a star; her frailty and vulnerability are in part a product of her 'mortal' – i.e. physical – inability to sustain a pretence. The poem thus inhabits, with some intensity, the contradictory pulls of socially established gendered subjectivities, which at the same time it also partially exposes.

Robert Browning's volume, *Men and Women* (1855) similarly consists of 'double poems'; indeed, the form for which Browning is most famous, the 'dramatic monologue', is the canonical version of the double poem. As we have seen in Meredith's *Modern Love*, what the double form permits is the capacity both to inhabit available languages and to stand outside them, to expose them as at least contingent upon particular subject-positions. The range of love poems in *Men and Women* act in this way, with varying intensity. The collection includes, among a variety of other poems, the following poems which take 'love' as a central preoccupation: 'Love among the Ruins', 'A Lovers' Quarrel', 'Evelyn Hope', 'A Woman's Last Word', 'By the Fire-side', 'Any Wife to Any Husband', 'A Serenade at the Villa', 'A Pretty Woman', 'Respectability', 'A Light Woman', 'Love in a Life, Life in a Love', 'In a Year', 'Women and Roses', 'One Way of Love, 'Another Way of Love' and 'Two in the Campagna'. All these are permutations upon central themes of love, desire and sexual idealism; they present both an ideal of heterosexual love, and its inevitable entanglement in a material and conflictual world. To the extent that the poems present an ideal, they are drawing upon an aspect of the ideology of sexual spheres; insofar as they recognise its entanglement in other, often conflictual considerations, the poems represent an acting-out of a set of imaginary experiential possibilities in which that ideology is inevitably inflected and challenged in different ways.

This imaginary acting-out can be seen in 'A Woman's Last Word', which must serve as only a single example of the set of possibilities which the whole collection represents:

I

Let's contend no more, Love
  Strive nor weep:
All be as before, Love,
  – Only sleep!

II

What so wild as words are?
  I and thou
In debate, as birds are
  Hawk on bough!

III

See the creature stalking
    While we speak!
Hush and hide the talking,
    Cheek on cheek!

IV

What so false as truth is,
    False to thee?
Where the serpent's tooth is
    Shun the tree –

V

Where the apple reddens
    Never pry –
Lest we lose our Edens,
    Eve and I.

VI

Be a god and hold me
    With a charm!
Be a man and fold me
    With thine arm!

VII

Teach me, only teach Love!
    As I ought
I will speak thy speech, Love,
    Think thy thought –

VIII

Meet, if thou require it,
    Both demands,
Laying flesh and spirit
    In thy hands.

IX

That shall be to-morrow
    Not to-night:
I must bury sorrow
    Out of sight:

X

– Must a little weep, Love,
    (Foolish me!)
And so fall asleep, Love,
    Loved by thee.[10]

This poem, spoken from the (imagined) subject position of a woman having the last word in a lovers' quarrel, should be read as putting into play, or 'acting out', the notions of feminine submission which it ostensibly concedes. It mimics the accents, intonations and grammatical forms of actual speech; this is why it is a dramatic monologue. As it does so, it necessarily places the ideas with which it deals into this imagined discursive situation, making them a matter for contention between the lovers. 'Truth' is thus not neutral, but can only ever be invoked as part of the battle between them – so much so that to insist on the truth is to risk the destruction of the relationship, as suggested by the metaphor of Eve and the apple of the Tree of Knowledge. When the woman does concede (in stanzas VII and VIII), she does so apparently in deference to due ideas about feminine submission, but her concession too, while real enough, is also part of the continuing discursive contention between the pair. This is true even of her sexual acquiescence; that is duly promised ('Laying flesh and spirit / In thy hands'), but is post-poned. So while the poem certainly does contain accents of tenderness, they are mixed with sadder tones also. The notions of female deference which the poem dramatises, then, are caught up in the subjective emo-tional values which it suggests, and the never-to-be-completed discurs-ive contention in which such notions appear.

The dramatic monologue is perhaps especially well-suited to demon-strating ideology in action. 'A Woman's Last Word' is just one of many of the poems in *Men and Women* which do so; others in the same collection are equally concerned with ideas concerning the relationship of men and women, though they manage those ideas in different ways. They are not therefore reducible to ideology, even where it is not explicitly challenged in the course of the poem itself. Rather this particular cultural form, the dramatic monologue, dramatises an aspect of the ideology of separate spheres in especially complex ways, giving the reader a sometimes unnerving sense of the imbrication of all ideology in particular interpersonal relationships, and of the differing ways it enters into and forms a particular subjectivity.

Christina Rossetti also wrote a number of powerful and disturbing lyrics, such as 'Remember' and 'At Home', which adopt a feminine subject position, and which, taking the pieties of female deference and subjection, turn them towards resentment and bitterness. But in order to extend the range of forms which are present in the poetry of mid-century, and which dramatise in different ways the profound dividing-line of gender which runs through nineteenth-century culture and society, I want to consider, not these lyrics, but the extraordinary poetic fairy-story 'Goblin Market'. This is the story of two sisters, Laura and Lizzie, who are tempted to buy the fruit sold by goblins. Laura succumbs; sickens almost to death; and is rescued by Lizzie who obtains the antidote when the goblins, unable to tempt her to try their fruit, crush it on her body until the juice runs. The poem has been variously interpreted as an allegory of heterosexual temptation, or of Christian redemption, or of lesbian sexuality. While it is an imponderable question to ask whether Christina Rossetti knew of these meanings, it is undeniable that the poem is suffused with an acute erotic sensibility, which makes the whole poem a coded account of sexual relations. The desires, longings and violence of the poem, together with its more general delight in sharp sensuous intensities, make it an especially unpredictable acting-out of nineteenth-century gender relations.

The following quotation concerns the moment when the goblins turn on Lizzie after her refusal to eat the fruit whose juice she seeks for Laura:

> Lashing their tails
> They trod and hustled her,
> Elbowed and jostled her,
> Clawed with their nails,
> Barking, mewing, hissing, mocking,
> Tore her gown and soiled her stocking,
> Twitched her hair out by the roots,
> Stamped upon her tender feet,
> Held her hands and squeezed their fruits

> Against her mouth to make her eat.
> White and golden Lizzie stood,
> Like a lily in a flood, –
> Like a rock of blue-veined stone
> Lashed by tides obstreperously, –
> Like a beacon left alone
> In a hoary roaring sea,
> Sending up a golden fire, –
> Like a fruit-crowned orange-tree
> White with blossoms honey-sweet
> Sore beset by wasp and bee, –
> Like a royal virgin town
> Topped with gilded dome and spire
> Close beleaguered by a fleet
> Mad to tug her standard down.[11]

It is not difficult to decode this as a woman defending herself against masculine sexual violence – indeed, the lines hint at this possibility in the final simile of Lizzie as 'Like a royal virgin town'. However, it is important once again not simply to reduce the poem to its decoded ideological kernel. Rather, we need to recognise that it is not simply an allegory, but a self-sufficient story – even a children's poem, as it has appeared in many anthologies – which is shot through with disturbed erotic intensities. The sexual conflicts and tensions of the mid-century thus appear here in displaced ways. Masculine sexual power and authority appear in the guise of intensely imagined but diminished and ultimately defeated goblins – who nevertheless offer fruit which is piercingly attractive ('Bloom-down-cheeked peaches / Swart-headed mulberries / Wild free-born cranberries...'). Female solidarity in the face of masculine sexual violence, by contrast, is imagined with perhaps the most intense erotic charge of the poem ('Hug me, kiss me, suck my juices...Eat me, drink me, love me, / Laura, make much of me...'). Altogether, the poem's form, the children's imaginary story, permits it to act out and subvert prevailing sexual ideology in deeply unstable ways.

Finally, to complete this survey of mid-nineteenth-century poetry especially concerned with gender relations, we can turn to Coventry Patmore's *The Angel in the House* (1854–56). This poem, though widely popular in the nineteenth century, would almost certainly have been forgotten in the twentieth, were it not for the currency given to it by a tradition of feminist criticism, starting with Virginia Woolf, which has seen in the poem's title a convenient shorthand for 'Victorian' ideas about femininity and the doctrine of separate spheres. The poem concerns the courtship and marriage of Felix and Honoria; it consists of a series of first-person accounts of the turning-points of the courtship, prefaced by wider reflections on the meaning of love, marriage and kindred topics. The poem is high-minded, serious and vapid. It has in fact little to say about domesticity, since it ends with the wedding; but it does propose women as moral guardians for men, and as the aim and purpose of male activity.

The Angel in the House is perhaps most interesting in proposing 'Love' as a topic for poetry 'In these last days, the dregs of time',[12] explicitly repudiating more epic or martial themes. Patmore thus offers his work as one which deals with the most appropriate topic for poetry in the modernity of the nineteenth century, so that marriage and courtship become the only valued space in a world otherwise drained of affect. Consequently, the relationship between Felix and Honoria has to carry the burden of providing all the focus and significance in the male protagonist's life. The following passage from the 'The Prologue' to Book II suggests the almost solipsistic circularity of heterosexual relations as they are imagined in such a version of marriage:

> Her sons pursue the butterflies,
> Her baby daughter mocks the doves
> With throbbing coo; in his fond eyes
> She's Venus with her little Loves;
> Her foot-fall dignifies the earth,
> Her form's the native-land of grace,
> And, lo, his coming lights with mirth
> Its court and capital her face!
> Full proud her favour makes her lord,
> And that her flatter'd bosom knows.
> She takes his arm without a word,
> In lines of laurel and of rose.[13]

Here, marriage appears as a wordless sanctification of human relationships, effortlessly conflict-free, and characterised by a tacit exchange of deference and affection. It is also strangely devoid of erotic charge, the possibility of which is suggested by the reference to Venus in the lines above, but immediately deflected into coyness by her accompanying cupids ('her little loves'). Indeed, modesty and chastity are central values for the poem which awards women almost metaphysical moral prestige. This is all sustained by a completely unquestioning social conservatism, which takes quite for granted the social order in which this fantasy is enacted (Felix is a landowner and Honoria the daughter of a cathedral Dean).

It is tempting to see *The Angel in the House* as the norm from which the other poems that I have discussed are deviations. But while it is certainly true that the poem offers, in an especially idealistic vein, many of the mid-century commonplaces concerning gender relations, they too need to be worked for, produced by an effort of intense artistic labour. In this sense, the poem is one more version, amidst a range of others, of the possible ways of understanding the relations between men and women at mid-century.

Gender and Social Change

I have invoked the work of Davidoff and Hall, for the beginning of the nineteenth century, as exemplary in the way it maps differing narratives of gender identity on to the changing social and economic contours of the provincial middle class. I wish to conclude this chapter by considering national and metropolitan social and cultural changes in the last two decades of the century. Following the work of Judith Walkowitz in *City of Dreadful Delight: Narratives of Sexual Danger in Late-Victorian London*, I take the complex and differentially negotiable space of the city – London, above all – as the social ground on which the proliferation of discourses about gender and sexuality at the end of the century could occur.[14]

There can be no doubt about the proliferation of these discourses – indeed, this is to state the matter too moderately. The 1880s and 1890s saw an explosion of interest in, and anxiety about, matters of sexuality and gender, articulated in an array of elite and popular cultural forms. These were the decades of the 'New Woman', a partly journalistic invention which proposed the prevalence of emancipated young women; of a significant popular audience for feminism; of explicit discussions of homosexuality, culminating in the trial of Oscar Wilde (1895); of the lurid disclosures by the popular journalist W. T. Stead, about child-prostitution, known as 'The Maiden Tribute of Modern

Babylon', published in the *Pall Mall Gazette* in 1885, and already mentioned as one of the late-century constructions of London; of the Jack the Ripper murders (1888); of the study and publication of numerous sexological studies, such as Richard Krafft-Ebbing's *Psychopathalia Sexualis* (1886) and Havelock Ellis's *Studies in the Psychology of Sex* (1897); of numerous purity campaigns (attempts to clear the bookshops of pornography and the streets of prostitution). Indeed, one book about these matters in the 1890s has the title *Sexual Anarchy*.[15] While we must not assume too readily that all these discursive excitements translated themselves into actual changes in the lives that people lived, outside very particular (especially metropolitan) groups, we can nevertheless see that profound imaginative renegotiations of the certainties and boundaries of gender were under way at the end of the century. These renegotiations were managed in a variety of cultural forms, in the theatre, in dress codes, in the novel, in popular journalism, in academic discourse and in poetry.

Cognate with this ferment was the more widespread social and political ferment of the 1880s and 1890s, decades which saw, according to Beatrice Webb's retrospect in the 1920s, a 'new consciousness of sin among men of intellect and men of property', connecting to various movements elsewhere in society.[16] The 1880s saw the take-off of socialist movements in Britain, as we have already seen in Chapter 3; and of proliferating feminist and other movements, such as anti-vivisectionism and spiritualism, which interconnected with each other in many complex ways. A number of groups in London (and elsewhere), then, provided the cultural and intellectual personnel which permitted these explicit renegotiations of the sexual settlement to occur. Figures as diverse as Havelock Ellis, Karl Pearson, George Bernard Shaw, Eleanor Marx Aveling, William Morris, Olive Schreiner, Edward Carpenter and Oscar Wilde criss-crossed around numerous socialist and feminist groups, arguing and debating. These debates can be traced in Ellis's *Studies in the Psychology of Sex* (first volume, 1897); Shaw's plays such as *Widowers' Houses* (1892) and *Mrs Warren's Profession* (1893); Morris's *News from Nowhere* (1891); Olive Schreiner's *Story of an African Farm* (1883) and *Woman and Labour* (1911); Edward Carpenter's *Towards Democracy* (1883–88) and *Love's Coming of Age* (1896); Oscar Wilde's plays, poetry and essays. Furthermore, beyond this immediate social and cultural milieu, we can trace some wider patterns of social change in the latter half of the nineteenth century which gave these re-imaginings of gender divisions their particular resonance. I want to discuss briefly three such changes – in demography, education and employment – which are all closely related, the issues raised in discussing them being discussed prominently both within feminism and in relation to it.

First, it was known from at least the 1850s that there was a broad demographic imbalance in England in favour of women. Whatever the causes (e.g. differential emigration rates between the sexes, late marriage ages amongst men), this meant that there was a substantial number of women of marriageable age who simply could not, statistically, expect to marry. This posed an obvious 'problem' to those who assumed that the natural destiny of womankind was to serve as helpmeets to their husbands. The problem of 'surplus women' was capable of several solutions, including proposals for emigration; but it fed directly into feminism from the 1850s onwards; early feminism laid a special emphasis upon education and the finding of employment for women who simply did not fit the traditional gender categories. Of course, the inevitable imbrication of gender with class is apparent here as elsewhere; the employment of 'surplus' women is only problematic for middle-class women, since paid employment was a normal phase in the life-cycle of most working-class women. Nevertheless, the fact of this demographic imbalance impelled many men to consider feminist arguments, as George Gissing did in *The Odd Women* (1893); the very title of this novel suggests both 'surplus' women and their 'oddness' in the conventional scheme of things. However, we should not simply assume (as Gissing partly does), that a surplus of women over men at once produced a pool of women to whom feminism spoke directly – demography does not translate that immediately into ideology. Rather, the fact of demographic imbalance challenged rigid versions of domestic ideology, and impelled people to consider alternative destinies for women than marriage and childbearing.

The second large social change underlying these ferments was the increased availability of education, including higher education, to women from the 1860s onwards. This increased access was limited but real, and it produced a cadre of highly educated and dedicated women who had very different social ideals from the generations that preceded them. Some important dates in this gradual opening-out of education and higher education for women were the following: the foundation of Queen's College and Bedford College, connected to London University, in the late 1840s; the opening of Cheltenham Ladies' College in 1854; and the establishment of Girton College in 1869 and Newnham College in 1875, both of which were related, contentiously, to the University of Cambridge. The content of this education remained controversial – should it simply take over the traditional male syllabus, or should it be designed to suit women's particular needs? This debate, parallel to some basic divisions within feminism, fed into wider debates about femininity and womanhood.

The third large-scale social change that needs to be considered is the return of middle-class and lower middle-class women to employment at the end of the century. But this was a return with a difference, since the exclusion of such women at the beginning of the century had involved the restructuring of the place of work and its separation from the 'family home'. At the end of the century, work for middle-class women typically meant going out of the home to work. Women gained employment not only in visible and contentious professional areas like medicine and journalism, but also in the growing ranks of clerical workers. In addition, they continued to work in the small number of jobs traditionally coded as feminine, such as nursing and teaching, though such jobs began to alter their status as the education and training that they required became more fully regularised, and their numbers increased after the establishment of compulsory state education in 1870.

Taken together, then, these three larger-scale factors underlay many of the cultural re-imaginings of gender in the 1880s and 1890s. But as I have also indicated, such social transformations do not translate themselves into cultural or discursive terms directly; they are always mediated by existing cultural forms. One crucial mediating term in the latter half of the nineteenth century was 'feminism' itself, a term that condenses a nexus of individual and collective efforts with social and philosophical thought, and which was articulated in a range of cultural forms. There is perhaps space here to extract two main and partially opposed emphases from feminism, which underlie many of its cultural articulations. These two emphases represent differing responses to the ideology of separate spheres which we have been following as a dominant discourse in the nineteenth century.

The first emphasis was broadly liberal, and made a direct challenge to the premises of domestic ideology. In a line of argument going back at least to Mary Wollstonecraft, one tradition of feminist thought disputed the constraints and artificial restrictions placed upon women by an upbringing and expectations which fitted them only for amorous or domestic life. This is the tradition of thought most powerfully expressed by John Stuart Mill and his wife Harriet Taylor, in the single most important English feminist book of the nineteenth century, *The Subjection of Women* (1869). In an argument that is consonant with a more general liberalism, false educational and social expectations and restrictions are here taken to be the problem for women; freed from these, individual women would be enabled to develop their own particular bents as their capacities determined. As can be readily seen, this is a line of argument – or indeed a whole personal and social programme – which especially appealed to middle-class women who felt that their education was constricted and that their opportunities for work and a career were limited. One substantial tradition within English feminism, from Barbara Leigh Smith (1827–91) and Bessie Parkes (1829–1925) in the 1850s, through to Millicent Fawcett (1847–1929) at the end of the century and beyond, made arguments of this kind central.

It can be contrasted with another emphasis, still broadly feminist, which developed one aspect of the doctrine of separate spheres, and turned it on its head. This took seriously the notion of the essential moral superiority of women, and redirected it towards a critique of male immorality and violence. This emphasis within feminism tended to stress the 'sacredness' of woman; it was both conservative and radical at the same time – conservative insofar as it stressed the moral fixity of women, and insisted on their essentially superior moral nature; radical in the political attitudes that this could inspire, especially in the areas of male sexual violence. Perhaps the most charismatic figure to draw upon this nexus of attitudes was Josephine Butler (1828–1906), who led the campaign against the Contagious Diseases Act in the 1860s and 1870s. These Acts permitted the compulsory medical examination of prostitutes in garrison towns; in a series of highly charged meetings and equally powerful writings, Butler attacked the Acts as state-sanctioned vice, which led to the victimisation and medical invasion of women while ignoring the real instigators of prostitution, men. More generally, this general emphasis on the moral superiority of women (seen as especially violated by Butler in her rhetoric) was present in much of the cultural production at the end of the century. Many purity campaigns of the 1880s and 1890s drew substantial support from feminists inspired with notions of this kind.

The pervasiveness of gender as a fundamental structuring opposition is unavoidable. As we have seen, it connects with other faultlines, especially divisions of class, to produce both contradictions and mutual reinforcements. In the next chapter, we shall be considering the related scissures of race and ethnicity, which, like gender, divide the space of culture in the nineteenth century, and which also reach into the intimate subjective space of individual identity.

7

ETHNICITY, RACE AND EMPIRE

Cultural forms have a double existence – they live both in the intimacies of self-understanding, forming individuals' very sense of themselves and who they are, and they arise out of material forms of life, the social relations that subsist between people. This duality is nowhere more apparent than in the history of those cultural forms in the nineteenth century which depended upon or were formed around notions of ethnicity and race. Such forms, and the wider discursive patterns on which they rely, spoke on the one hand to English people's very identity – formed it, indeed. On the other hand, they sprang from patterns of relationship between themselves and both the other inhabitants of the 'British Isles' and the inhabitants of the rest of the globe. This was true even when the contrasts and oppositions at the heart of culture – between the 'civilised' and the 'savage', or between the Englishman and the 'Oriental' – were apparently remote to the majority of English people who had never met a savage or an Oriental. The force of such oppositions was certainly not diminished by their being imaginary.

In this chapter I will be considering the broad faultline of material and cultural division that operated along the axis of race. The very notion of race was to some extent a nineteenth-century invention; at least, it was certainly then that explanations of history and society based on the category of race became widespread, so much so that by the end of the century they could form part of the common sense of a majority of English people. But the broad category 'race' hides within itself a number of other distinctions, for which the notion of 'ethnicity' is more appropriate. Certainly in the nineteenth century people were as

156

keen to distinguish *between* Europeans as they were to distinguish Europeans from other races. And within Britain, distinctions between the various peoples that inhabit these islands were drawn and redrawn in various ways in the course of the century. I have insisted that cultural forms spring from, and take on their force in, particular material situations. The material situation most relevant to the category of race in the nineteenth century was of course the Empire. I will conclude this chapter by a consideration of the profound impact of the Empire on English culture in the nineteenth century, both earlier when the Empire was less obviously visible, and later when Imperialism had taken on the dimensions of conscious policy and doctrine.

Ethnicity

First – an embarrassment that we have already encountered in Chapter 1. How do English people refer to themselves, and the country in which they live? 'English' seems exclusionary, falsely assimilating to itself the Welsh, the Scots and the Irish. But is 'British' any better? Far from being a neutrally inclusive term, 'British' was a term precisely coined and given currency as part of an imperial project, first within the British islands, and then made available for worldwide imperialism.[1] This was accomplished in the course of the eighteenth and early nineteenth centuries, and it was effected by a whole panoply of narratives, patriotic stories, historical paintings, songs and grandiose buildings. The term 'British' thus hides within itself centuries-long processes of cultural exclusion and suppression on the one hand, and of cultural production on the other. But this was a process that was only ever partially successful, as the survival of powerful national identities in Wales, Scotland and Ireland demonstrates, as does also the persistence of alternative meanings for the word 'English'. The struggle over these terms in the nineteenth century is an index of fundamental social and cultural dislocations and realignments.

The nineteenth century began with the Act of Union between England and Ireland (1802), itself modelled on the Act of Union between England and Scotland of a hundred years previously. In both instances, the effect was to eliminate the separate political identity of the two countries. As far as Wales was concerned, no such Act of Union was necessary because the elimination of a Welsh political identity was accomplished long before anyone felt the need for constitutional niceties. But in all cases, the elimination of a political identity did not bring with it any accompanying effacement of a cultural identity – though in all cases also, it is impossible to speak of a single identity, be it 'Welsh', 'Scottish', or 'Irish'. All three countries were internally divided, not least between the speakers and non-speakers of the different Celtic languages. One of the features of nineteenth-century 'modernisation', in fact, was to be the steady retreat of those languages, in some cases by deliberate suppression. However, in differing ways the three countries retained some autonomous cultural institutions, and in the case of Scotland at the beginning of the nineteenth century, very considerable independent cultural prestige – Edinburgh, for instance, remained an important publishing centre throughout the century. On the other hand, the spaces reserved for the specifically Celtic or traditional elements in these national cultures was at the very least ambiguous. Such elements as language, traditional dress and traditional music were to be sentimentally admired, but consigned to the past, the site for nostalgic retrospect in a utilitarian modern world. Such ambiguities could be profitably exploited at the end of the century by the writers of the 'Celtic revival', who sought to revive traditional Celtic (especially Irish) art in opposition to a dominant Englishness.

But just as crucial as these wider cultural shifts and transpositions, and to some extent underlying them, were the literal shifts of population between and within. the islands. Though only a small proportion of the Irish who left Ireland in the course of its nineteenth-century depopulation emigrated to Britain, the numbers were still substantial, both before and after the catastrophe of the famine in 1846. Substantial minorities of the populations of Liverpool, Manchester, other Lancashire towns, Scottish cities and London were of Irish descent – in 1851, 22 per cent of the Liverpool population was Irish-born, 13 per cent of Manchester and Salford, nearly 5 per cent of London.[2] Irish depopulation was matched by the depopulation of the Scottish Highlands, as the crofters were cleared to make way for the more profitable Cheviot sheep. Many of those dispossessed ended up in the cities of the Scottish Lowlands. South Wales, later in the century, witnessed an influx of immigrants, some from Ireland, as the coalmines were developed and the docks of Cardiff and Newport were built to ship the coal. In a variety of different ways, these massive displacements were part of the material underpinning of the cultural and discursive dispositions that we need to examine. On the part of the immigrants, or emigrants, themselves, their national cultures were carried with them to form significant enclaves in the cities they inhabited, often revolving around their religious affiliations. Thus, Catholic Irish emigrants could affirm their sense of their distinctive identity through their adherence to the local Catholic Church, while Welsh-speaking Baptists in Liverpool could maintain their cultural identity through membership of various Welsh-speaking chapels in that city. On the part of the indigenous inhabitants (many of them also recent internal migrants), the typical representations that they formed, of varying degrees of hostility, are in part to be attributed to the material relationships which pertained between the differing populations of the great cities.

At all events, the distinction between English and other inhabitants of these islands was an important fracture throughout the nineteenth century. It was understood in a variety of different ways. One way was already implicitly racial – seeing the distinction as one between Saxons and Celts. Another way was to distinguish between broad national stereotypes, drawing on long histories of mistrust and mutual contempt between, for example, the English and the Scots. Such distinctions relied upon the ability to think in types, to represent oneself and others in terms of particular combinations and hierarchies of characteristics. Popular stereotypes were only the most obvious example of such ways of thinking. However, they were not fixed and immutable, but subject to constant renegotiation, and from both sides. Indeed, the same set of characteristics could be redescribed to make them appear positive or negative. Thus Saxons were at once solid, honest, taciturn and energetic, while Celts were feckless, voluble and lazy; or, to say the same thing again, Saxons were stolid, stupid and unimaginative, while Celts were spiritual, imaginative and articulate.

Such typifications circulated in many and diverse cultural forms. This is not merely a question of the circulation of specific stereotypes, but of a profounder discursive practice which permitted people to understand themselves and others as typifying a certain ethnic and ultimately racial hierarchy. The novel was an important form for the circulation of these racial typologies, as indeed was the proliferation of magazines and journals from the early nineteenth century onwards. Equally, visual representations, be they the innumerable historical paintings which realised scenes from Walter Scott, or the *Punch* cartoons which depicted both the sufferings and the perceived brutality of the Irish, could be used to further *typical* representations of the differing ethnicities.

In considering representations of the Irish in the English nineteenth-century novel, for example, it is clear that there is far from being a fixed and stable stereotype, but rather a fluid set of characterisations that are prepared to ascribe a disparate and contradictory set of characteristics to the Irish. These are likely to vary in accordance, not only with writers' particular dispositions, but also in line with questions of class. The fiction of W. M. Thackeray is perhaps especially filled with characterisations of Irish people, as it is indeed with ethnically based characterisations of all kinds. Restricting our attention merely to Thackeray's military Irishmen (both Scots and Irish had a disproportionate presence in the British military throughout the nineteenth century, and one Irish writer, Charles Lever [1806–72], a frequently parodied butt of Thackeray's, made a speciality of the military romance), it is easy to find both the deeply hostile account of the Irish soldier-as-bravo in *The Memoirs of Barry Lyndon* (1844) and the sympathetic account of the loyal Irish officer in the figure of Major O'Dowd in *Vanity Fair* (1847–48). Thackeray's fiction can be thought of as drawing on residual modes in mid-century, in which Irish 'types' take their place alongside the whole gallery of class, gender and ethnic types who inhabit Vanity Fair. The variety and instability of these representations stems from Thackeray's unwillingness to let his readers rest in any fixed moral or political position – which is not to deny that ethnicity enters into his characterisations at a fundamental level. The same could be said of the fiction of George Meredith (1828–1909), though in a very different way. A novel like *Diana of the Crossways* (1885), for example, draws very heavily on the contrast between Celt and Saxon in understanding the career of the novel's Irish heroine – her wit, her intelligence, her spirit and her courage are all very positively counterposed to the stolidity of her various English suitors. The heroine's Irishness, in other words, is being deployed as part of a cultural argument about English culture, conducted in terms cognate to those of Matthew Arnold (discussed below; but see also Chapter 2 above). These various characterisations, of course, are only a few among hundreds of Irish men and women who appear in the novels of the century; they are sufficient to suggest not only the pervasiveness of ethnicity as a basis for understanding personality, but also how ethnicity was constructed in various ways according to differing aesthetic and ideological projects.

I wish to pursue one further strand of this diverse social and cultural history: the connection between nineteenth-century historical ideas and ideas about Saxon identity. One of the great intellectual advances of the nineteenth century was to understand human society in historical terms; to understand, that is, how human societies have changed and developed over time, and how these developments can be understood in rational ways. But the terms of this understanding obviously differed greatly; it was certainly possible to trace or explain the contemporary social world as a development of intrinsic racial characteristics that have been working themselves out over centuries. Such explanations appear in the course of the nineteenth century with varying degrees of seriousness, and in a variety of different cultural forms, from the novel, to essays, to history-writing both academic and popular. To some extent, the source of many of these ideas is to be found in Walter Scott's novel *Ivanhoe* (1819), which is based on the notion of continuing opposition between the Saxons and Normans as one of the driving forces of English history. But another important source for such ideas was the continuing presence, indeed revival, of the popular radical myth of the Norman Yoke, by which English history was to be understood as the imposition of oppressive feudal laws upon a Saxon folk who lived by a form of popular self-government. In this popular and radical form, the idea of Saxon descent has a strongly anti-aristocratic tinge; the idea of the Norman Yoke appealed strongly to some Chartists at mid-century, and indeed 'Saxon' came to connote not only strength, honesty, taciturnity and self-reliance, but some popular and democratic meanings as well. But the ambivalence of these meanings can be seen from their use in the popular histories of England by the liberal historians E. R. Freeman (1823–92) and J. R. Green (1837–83), or by their use in Benjamin Disraeli's novels of the 1840s, *Coningsby* (1844), *Sybil* (1845) and *Tancred* (1847). In these texts, the identity of the mass of the population as 'Saxon' becomes the basis for various projects of social and political regeneration. Equally, when one of Thomas Arnold's sons, Tom Arnold (1823–1900), emigrated to New Zealand in the 1840s, in part from a sense of Radical distaste at English society, he speculated in his letters to the poet Clough about the possibility of establishing a 'pan-Saxon' federation between all the white settler colonies of the British Empire. A racial story of England's past, in other words, is readily transformed into a racial story of Britain's imperial present and future.

The French historian Thierry also took up ideas about Saxons and Normans from Walter Scott, in ways which influenced the historical and racial ideas of Thomas Arnold (1795–1842). But perhaps the most important nineteenth-century historian to draw on fundamentally racial categories was Thomas Carlyle (1795–1882), who saw himself as engaged, in part, in writing a national epic whose protagonists were racial types. Even in his various writings, however strongly marked as they are by authoritarianism and racism, there can still be found traces of the radical roots of the notion of Saxondom. Another way to say this is that it was very difficult, in the nineteenth century, to conceive of a social history of the inhabitants of these islands which was not couched in fundamentally racial terms.

This is true even of the cultural criticism of Thomas Arnold's son Matthew Arnold, who had very little sympathy for the writings of Carlyle. In *Culture and Anarchy* (1869), there is in effect a racialised diagnosis of English culture, as being divided between the Hebraic and the Hellenic – the former stern, dutiful, single-minded, essentially moral; the latter open-minded, intellectually mobile, aesthetic. Arnold's diagnosis of the state of English society is that more of these Hellenic qualities are required to complement its predominant Hebraism. If these terms appear eccentric or indeed only metaphorical, they should be put alongside the same author's 'On the Study of Celtic Literature' (1867), where an analogous diagnosis of the limitations of English complacency and 'Philistinism' (a term that Arnold derived from Heine to denote the anti-intellectual solidity of bourgeois life) leads to the advocacy of the study of Celtic literature as an antidote. This essay displays a characteristic development in its use of racialised categories, which are absolutely formative in it, even to the extent of trying to assess the particular ethnic quality of individual lines of poetry. The development is this: given that one valorised term of an opposition (in this case 'Saxon' or 'English') generates a particular set of characteristics for the non-valorised term (in this case 'Celtic'), it is almost inevitable that dissatisfaction with, or critiques of, that valorised category should elevate and redescribe positively the qualities of the previously downgraded. Arnold mobilises the qualities of the Celt – his (*sic*) sensibility, the 'nervous exaltation' of his nature, his affinity to the 'spell of the feminine idiosyncrasy' – against the stolidity and 'flat commonness' of the purely Saxon English.[3] In the course of his argument he contends for the notion that the English anyway have been leavened throughout their history by admixtures of Normans and Celts, so this is not an argument about racial purity. The point is, however, that it *is* an argument which thinks, at a fundamental constitutive level, in racial categories.

The contrast between Saxon and Celt, or between the English and the various other ethnicities within the islands, was not the only way of drawing ethnic lines in the nineteenth century. The century also witnessed a simultaneous flattening and reinvention of regional distinctions, which may be thought of as 'ethnic' insofar as self-conscious regionalism involves drawing lines of distinction and identity along classic markers of ethnicity such as language, dress and culinary traditions. The 'flattening' can be seen in the century-long assimilation of certain regional distinctions into a more homogeneous national culture, so that distinctions of dialect tended to become less marked, large urban demotics spread from a few strongly marked regional centres (Manchester, Newcastle, Birmingham, London), and regional styles of dress disappeared (agricultural workers, for example, ceased to wear smocks by the end of the century). But the reinvention of regional distinctions can be seen, *inter alia*, in the growth of dialect literatures, especially in Lancashire, Yorkshire and some of the southern agricultural counties, and, at the elite level, in the scholarly project of the English Dialect Dictionary, premised on the notion of the survival of an authentic Englishness in the distinctive and fugitive regional dialects uncontaminated by modernity and commercialism. This whole process was heavily overdetermined by considerations of class – to understand oneself as 'Lancashire', when the predominant marker of 'Lancashireness', the dialect, survived predominantly among working-class or lower middle-class people, was of course to align oneself in class terms as well.

It should not be assumed that because I have been discussing predominantly elite cultural products that none of these more ethnically based ways of understanding English and 'British' culture had no wider popular appeal. On the contrary, they both drew on particular popular notions, like the notion of the Norman Yoke, and made pervasive ways of understanding history and society that were to feed into what can be called the 'democratic imperialism' of the last quarter of the century. Before turning to this topic, however, I wish to discuss the influence of more exactly *racialist* ideas in the course of the nineteenth century.

Race

There were several related transitions in the explicit construction and understanding of race in the nineteenth century. In terms of the wide political and social climate, the beginning of the century was the period of the Anti-Slavery campaign, which successfully saw the abolition of the slave trade in 1807, and the abolition of slavery itself in the British Empire in 1833. While doubtless marked by paternalism, the various organisations of the Anti-Slavery Movement managed to make hostility to slavery, and with it hostility to the most obvious and brutal forms of racial domination, widespread attitudes among the Evangelical middle class, and among Radicals of all classes. The persistence of such attitudes can be seen from the extraordinary success of Harriet Beecher Stowe's anti-slavery novel, *Uncle Tom's Cabin*; when it was published in England in 1852, it had the biggest immediate sale of any work of fiction in the century. By contrast, as little as a decade later, this broadly benign consensus had been severely undermined, so that, in the words of the cultural historian Robert Young, 'full-blown assumptions and prejudices about race, and the cultural implications about racial differences, . . . became dominant in the general public domain by the 1860s'.[4] The social and political climate was one in which a more explicit Imperialism made these hardened attitudes to race both more legitimate and more widespread.

A parallel series of cultural and scientific transformations accompanied this general transformation. It is important first to recognise that the whole context of thought in which race was understood was transformed in the nineteenth century. It was indeed the area most affected by the decline of religion and the advance of science as dominant ways of understanding. At the beginning of the century race was understood in predominantly biblical terms, so that the various human racial groups could be explained as the offspring of the sons of Noah. While it was certainly possible to justify oppressive racial attitudes and racial slavery itself on the basis of the Bible, the undeniable centrality, in the biblical account of human origins, of common descent from Adam and Eve, tended to push Christian orthodoxy towards 'monogenetic' accounts of race (that is, towards accounts which stressed a single origin for the different races, rather than 'polygenetic' accounts which suggested multiple origins). So much was this the case, that there was a tradition of anti-religious Enlightenment iconoclasm, going back to the eighteenth century, which precisely emphasised racial differences as a way of discrediting the biblical account. As the authority of religion declined in the course of the century, the way was left more open for supposedly scientific accounts of race to gain authority. The new scientific disciplines of ethnography and anthropology provided descriptions and classifications of human beings which tended, with more or less insistence, to arrange them into hierarchies, with white Europeans at the top and other races in a descending scale beneath them. At the extreme were those who claimed that the races were in fact different species; since the test of specific difference is the fertility of hybrids, there was a sustained debate, especially in the latter half of the century, which turned on the question of the fertility of the offspring of interracial sex.[5] Some of these changes in thought were already under way before the publication of Darwin's *Origin of Species* (1859) and *The Descent of Man* (1871). While there is no necessary connection between evolutionary science and racism, it is certainly the case that it was possible to understand the relations between the races as subject to evolutionary competition and to use this to justify the displacement of one race by another under imperialism.

There is an important distinction to be drawn between much nineteenth-century scientific writing which is, as it were, inadvertently racist (drawing, that is, on racialised thought and categories, where 'race' is nevertheless not a central object of attention) and a body of writing which is explicitly directed to race theory – advancing the category of race as a central explanatory term in its understanding of society and human history. Racial theory in this sense is very much an invention of the nineteenth century, and of a group of writers active at mid-century: the Americans Nott and Gliddon, the Scotsman Robert Knox and the Frenchman Comte de Gobineau. Their books *Types of Mankind* (1854), *The Races of Men* (1850) and *Essai sur l'inégalité des races humaines* (1853–55) – themselves drawing on previous efforts in physical anthropology and ethnography – lent the apparent authority of science to simple race prejudice. The circulation of such pseudo-scientific theories was one factor in the transformation of racial attitudes in the course of the nineteenth century. Outside the bounds of the academic journals and the debates of the Anthropological Society of London (founded in 1863 as a breakaway from the more traditional Ethnological Society), such theories contributed to a general sense of the scientificity of racial ideas and of their applicability to contemporary social and political problems. Indeed, the progenitors and popularisers of these ideas were keen to emphasise their applicability: to such questions as slavery in America, the cause of the Confederacy in the American Civil War and the whole question of British rule over its racially diverse empire.

But an explicitly racial discourse can be found elsewhere in nineteenth-century culture, coming from traditions of thought other than those of these 'sciences', or of a self-consciously iconoclastic writer like

Knox. Perhaps more important for instituting the prestige of racial ideas than either ethnography or anthropology was the science of philology. The historical study of language, in fact, is one of the great achievements of nineteenth-century scholarship. Starting from the work of Sir William Jones (1746–94), who established the affinity of Sanskrit to European languages, and from the work of the brothers Grimm in Germany (Jakob Grimm [1785–1863] and Wilhelm Grimm [1786–1859]), who established the ways in which language mutations occur, scientific scholarship was able to demonstrate the histories and interconnections of the 'Indo-European' or 'Indo-Aryan' family of languages. However, this 'family' was understood in more than metaphorical ways. Linguistic descent – the common descent of all Indo-European languages from a presumed single originary language – appeared to provide the key to racial descent and kinship. Thus the genuine scholarly achievements of philology lent authority to a racialised view of human, and particularly European, history. More particularly in an English context, the unequivocal establishment of the Germanic roots of the English language supported a Germanicising strain in English culture, which can certainly be seen in the historical work of Thomas Carlyle, discussed above (pp. 161–2).

However, it is not Carlyle's Teutonism which prompted his most notorious intervention in the politics of race. His 'Occasional Discourse on the Negro Question' (1849) – later retitled 'Nigger Question' – lent the full force of his cultural authority to rebarbative racial attitudes of a frankly authoritarian kind. The essay can be thought of as a kind of rearguard action against the abolition of slavery in the colonies:

> no Black man who will not work according to what ability the gods have given him for working, has the smallest right to eat pumpkin . . . but has an indisputable and perpetual right to be compelled, by the real proprietors of said land, to do competent work for his living. This is the everlasting duty of all men, black or white, who are born into this world.[6]

Here, an opprobrious typification of black men is put to work to justify their direct coercion, in the name of an 'everlasting duty' which Carlyle himself is, it seems, best qualified to describe. While it is difficult to date precisely such things as shifts in opinion, Carlyle's essay does seem to be symptomatic, along with the other explicitly racialist texts that I have mentioned, of a wider discursive shift at mid-century towards more explicitly authoritarian and oppressive attitudes on the question of race.

Further specific events can be evinced as marking turning-points in attitudes to race in the latter half of the century, quite in addition to the continuous pressure of British imperial wars (British forces were engaged in one colonial war or another practically continuously throughout the period). One such event was the Indian Mutiny of 1857, which finally brought an end to the rule of the East India Company and saw its replacement by the Indian Empire. The Mutiny condensed and hardened racial attitudes – it was the Mutiny, for example, and the panic and hysteria which it provoked, which brought back into general usage the opprobrious term *nigger* for Indian, and which reinforced some otherwise latent racist tendencies in British culture.[7] In particular, concentration on the atrocities of the native Indians (and amnesia on the atrocities committed by the British) seemed to justify Imperialism and racism.[8] Dickens, for example, though he displaced his response to the Mutiny into a story about 'West India' called 'The Perils of Certain English Prisoners', was prepared to envisage the execution and extinction of the entire 'Oriental race'.[9] This genocidal strain in English racism resurfaced at moments of crisis throughout the nineteenth century – the Mutiny was one such moment of provocation.

Another such pivotal event, occurring in the following decade, was the bloody suppression of a riot in Jamaica by its Governor, Edward Eyre. The subsequent attempt to prosecute him for the illegal severity of his actions (which included the summary execution and flogging of several hundred people and the hanging of a member of the Jamaican House of Assembly), sharply divided the leading figures of English culture. On the one hand a Jamaica Committee was established to lead the attack on Eyre, containing among others such leading Radical and scientific figures as John Stuart Mill, Thomas Hughes, Thomas Huxley, Herbert Spencer, Charles Lyell, Charles Darwin, John Bright, Leslie Stephen and Frederick Harrison. On the other hand, an Eyre Defence Committee was set up in defence of him and of the draconian measures he had adopted. This latter committee included Thomas Carlyle, Charles Dickens, Charles Kingsley, John Ruskin and Alfred Tennyson.[10] The controversy provided a kind of litmus test of political and cultural loyalties, the dividing-lines between the committees reproducing the dividing-line between those two currents in English social and cultural thought which I referred to in my introduction (see above, p. 9) – that is, between the liberal, individualist, anti-paternalist and

anti-authoritarian tradition strongly represented in Mill's Jamaica Committee, and the broadly conservative, organicist, paternalist and authoritarian one represented on the Eyre Defence Committee by Carlyle,
Ruskin and Tennyson. It is very significant that these two currents of
social thought should divide so strongly over a political issue where
questions of colonial authority and race are so prominent. The case
exposes very sharply the limits of the popular sympathies of Ruskin
and Dickens – the latter, both in this instance and in the case of the
Indian Mutiny, being dragged from his English Radicalism into strongly
authoritarian attitudes by the issue of race.

Finally, we should recognise that such attitudes are not unnerving
exceptions to the generally benign writings of these great men, nor
are the pseudo-scientific inanities of such writers as Knox and Nott
just an unfortunate and unimportant byway in the progress of science.
In the cases of Carlyle and Dickens (and, one might add, Ruskin also),
there is an intimate and necessary connection between the organicist
ideas which give such power to their writings about English society,
and the authoritarian and racist ideas which disfigure their writings
about the colonial world. Moreover, though I have adduced examples
from the 'minor' works of these men, they share a more fundamental
discursive feature across all their writing, which is the willingness to
understand human diversity in terms of racial types. Above all, however,
we should recognise the insistent pressure exerted by Imperial history
in the nineteenth century, and its capacity to deform and distort understanding of race.

Culture and Empire

The context for all these ideas about ethnicity and race was of course the
constant presence and expansion of the British Empire. The scale of the
Empire was remarkable, its growth during the century was extraordinary, and the social and cultural penetration of its conquered and colo-
nised peoples had no precedents in the history of empires. In 1815,
Britain possessed various West Indian colonies, ruled, through the
East India Company, parts of the Indian subcontinent, and governed
parts of Canada, the Cape and Australia. By the end of the century
the Empire included the Indian subcontinent in its entirety, Burma,
the most substantial of the European possessions in Africa (including

Egypt, the Sudan, Nigeria, South Africa, Kenya and Uganda), Canada, Australia, New Zealand, the West Indies and innumerable islands, way-stations and other important colonies such as Singapore and Hong Kong. In addition, Britain's informal empire, or region of economic and political influence, included Latin America and China. The constant presence of this empire in the century provided one pressure on cultural production, for this empire had to be sustained imaginatively, its officials and military officers prepared for their posts, and a set of cultural dispositions had to be naturalised to carry its operations forward. Culture, in short, though obviously not the 'cause' of empire, was a principal site on which the success and legitimacy of empire was secured.

We need to draw a distinction between imperialism and Imperialism – the capital letter indicating the conscious and explicit doctrine that began to become prominent from about 1870 onwards in Britain. By contrast, *imperialism* can be used to refer to the practice of imperial conquest and rule, which can be dated much further back, certainly to the sixteenth century, and indeed earlier if the case of Ireland is included. This is not to suggest that there was no conscious and explicit justification advanced before about 1870, but rather that after that date various ideologues of Imperialism made the doctrine appear central to Britain's sense of itself and its position in the world. In the late nineteenth century, empire was everywhere, from the school curriculum to children's reading, in novels, paintings and poetry. But before that also, culture had contributed to a mapping of the world, and an imaginative ordering of its peoples, which both permitted and consolidated Britain's imperial role. Edward Said, for instance, in *Culture and Imperialism*, has insisted upon this 'consolidating' role for culture in the period *before* 1870.[11] In particular, he discusses the role of the novel as providing a mapping of the world, a certain set of assumptions about Britain and its place in relation to its various colonies and imperial dependencies, even when the novels do not afford an apparently central place to narratives of empire. His central discussion, in this vein, is of Jane Austen's *Mansfield Park* (1814) – a novel we have already discussed in Chapter 4 above. The owner of Mansfield Park derives a portion of his income from a plantation in Antigua, which he has to visit, and from which he returns at a crucial moment in the narrative. But other instances abound where the narratives of novels are forwarded or resolved by departure to the colonies. Thackeray's fiction is especially full of references to the West Indies and to India in particular; the central character of *The Newcomes* (1853–55), Colonel Newcome, for example, is an officer

in the Indian Army, and the narrative turns on his investment in, and
the collapse of, an Indian bank, the Bundlecund Banking Corporation.
In the earlier *Vanity Fair* (1847–48) Colonel Rawdon Crawley is des-
patched to become a colonial governor, thus neatly removing him
from Becky Sharp's life. Dickens's novels, also, frequently manage
their narrative resolutions via colonial escapes, when the domestic English situation seems to offer no possibility of a positive resolution. In fact,
the frequency of these colonial resolutions to the 'Condition-of-England' fiction at mid-century (including novels by Elizabeth Gaskell and
Charles Kingsley as well as Dickens) has been remarked upon by Raymond Williams; he suggests that the impossibility of resolutions within
English social conditions thereby becomes apparent.[12] Here I wish
only to emphasise how the Empire and the different colonies within it
are part of the assumed and taken-for-granted backdrop in which the
narratives of the novel are played out.

The point is not that the English novel in the first two-thirds of the
century turns out to be centrally concerned with the Empire – for it is
not, though there are of course plenty of minor characters drawn
from it, and plenty of references to it also. It is rather that the great
canonical novels of Austen, Scott, Dickens, Thackeray, Trollope, Gaskell,
the Brontës, Collins and George Eliot need to be understood as framed
or permitted by an imperial dimension. To put it more strongly: the
kind of attention to the English domestic world that these novels can
manage is only possible given the non-attention to England's empire –
about which other kinds of writing, other cultural forms, are more
appropriate. The case of Trollope is instructive in this context. Framing
his novels of English provincial life are a series of travel books, describing journeys to the West Indies, Australia and South Africa, in which he
happily deploys the discourses of racism and imperialism. But for all
these novelists, the Empire repeatedly appears at the margins of their
texts: as the source of exotic interest or sudden wealth, with the threat
of personal or sexual licence, as Utopian exit-route from domestic
impasse, or as the place from which the repressed returns – convict
(*Great Expectations*), madwoman (*Jane Eyre*) or avenging victims of colon-
ialist theft (*The Moonstone*).

Said's argument, then – or at least, part of its rich complexity – is that
the ordinary processes of culture, especially visible in the novel, contributed to a particular imaginative mapping of the world in which Britain
naturally assumed primacy, and by which the practices of imperialism
came to taken for granted. We can go farther than this in considering

the role of certain cultural forms in forwarding imperialism. Martin Green has argued, by contrast, that '... the adventure tales that formed the light reading of Englishmen for two hundred years and more after *Robinson Crusoe* were, in fact, the energizing myth of English imperialism'.[13] Green's argument is also a complex one, and 'adventure novels' include for him both the sober, Protestant, technologically can-do and progressive kind exemplified by *Robinson Crusoe,* and 'romances' – more atavistic, idealistic, drawing on pre-modern cultural models. In the course of the nineteenth century, but above all in its final Imperialist phase, the 'romance' variant of the adventure novel became dominant: 'adventure took the place of fable; and the adventure took on the characteristics of romance. Children's literature became boys' literature; it focused its attention on the Empire and the Frontier; and the virtues it taught were dash, pluck, and lion-heartedness, not obedience, duty, and piety'.[14] In this account, one specific cultural form, the 'adventure novel', was crucial in providing the imaginative energy by which empire could be sustained and expanded.

In fact, we can see that the cultural forms explicitly associated with empire, and which habitually romanticise and propagandise *for* empire, represent in one sense a regression to more archaic cultural forms than, for example, the novel of sober domestic realism, or the complex 'double' poem characteristic of the mid-nineteenth century. The adventure novel, romance, heroic poetry, even epic, are characteristically forms which emerge from more hierarchical, more aristocratic and more military phases of social history than the modern, industrial, rationalistic world of the steam-train, the electric telegraph, standardised time and by-law housing. One explanation for the success of these imperialist cultural forms (or better, these cultural forms remade for Imperialism) is that they provide an imaginative escape from the drabness of an overwhelmingly grey and rationalised world – this is certainly the defence offered by the writer Andrew Lang (1844–1912) in the 1880s, defending the masculine romances of Stevenson and Haggard.[15] But more generally, the success of these forms, and the Imperialist ideology which that can readily be made to carry, testify just as much to a decline in confidence, a failure to sustain faith in bourgeois reform, a loss of belief in the once more dominant ideas of classical political economy and the internationalism of free trade. As Patrick Brantlinger observes,

although the equation is far from exact, imperialism as an element in British culture grew increasingly noisy, racist, and self-conscious as faith in free trade and liberal reformism declined. The militant imperialism of the late Victorian and Edwardian years thus represents a national (indeed, international) political and cultural regression, a social atavism . . . both economic and cultural.[16]

While it is important to recognise that this cultural 'atavism', or reversion to ancestral or primitive forms, need not have only one political inflection – as all the cultural work of the revolutionary socialist and anti-imperialist William Morris testifies – nevertheless there is a profound affinity between these archaic cultural forms and the militaristic demands of empire.

A recent, comprehensive history of the British Empire, by P. J. Cain and A. G. Hopkins, has suggested that its fundamental expansionist dynamic is to be explained by the peculiarities of English economic and social history in the eighteenth and nineteenth centuries. According to this account, the dominant formation in English society in this period can be described as 'gentlemanly capitalism', by which is meant the particularly close integration of the landed elite with the City throughout the two centuries. As a result, the economic imperatives of banking, shipping, insurance and commerce dominated over industrial capital – even when Britain was the 'workshop of the world'. In a more specifically cultural context, the importance of the notion of 'gentlemanly capitalism' is that it suggests an affinity between the recruitment of the 'aristomilitary caste' (Martin Green's phrase) and the ultimately aristocratic cultural forms which energised them.[17] The resurgence of atavistic cultural forms at the end of the century is less surprising if the dominant fraction of English society had never been deeply penetrated by the mentality of bourgeois modernity.

Nevertheless, a shift towards a more overtly Imperialist culture did occur towards the end of the century. For example, the critic Joseph Bristow has spoken of 'an aesthetics of a new kind of militaristic masculinity' becoming more pervasive from the 1870s, especially in writing for boys. Juvenile literature occupied a very substantial part of all publishing in this period – 19 per cent in 1882, with 18 per cent of library borrowings ten years later.[18] Bristow's argument describes, for example, the hugely popular novels of G. A. Henty (1832–1902), which recount episodes of British military history, and indeed of contemporary events like the two campaigns in the Sudan in 1884–85 and 1898, in a manner which elevates pluck and manliness as essential qualities in winning empire.[19] A comparable aesthetic – though more richly realised – can be seen in the new type of masculine romance represented by the novels of Rider Haggard (*King Solomon's Mines* [1886], *She* [1887], *Allan Quatermain* [1887]) and Robert Louis Stevenson (*Treasure Island* [1883]) and, in a less culturally prestigious but just as important a form, the many magazines for boys founded in the late nineteenth century, of which the most well known is the *Boy's Own Paper* (founded 1879). These novels and stories are not all simply the same; several of them, particularly the novels of Haggard and Stevenson, display complexities and anxieties which are notably absent from the stories of Henty or the boys' magazines. But they do all see the world beyond England as a space in which the manly virtues can be fittingly exercised. Adventure happens abroad.

In addition to these examples taken from narrative fiction, the late nineteenth century saw the production of a quantity of patriotic and Imperialist verse, ranging wildly in quality and in the verse idioms on which it drew. The following sample from the *Boy's Own Paper* of 1888 could be endlessly matched:

> Come, boys, let us tell of the heroes
> Who have fought and dar'd to die
> For St. George and merry England
> In the brave days long gone by,
> Who have swell'd their country's glory,
> And made the foeman flee,
> The patriot, prince, and soldier,
> The mariner bold and free.
>
> Tell how England won her glory,
> Tell how England won her fame
> We'll sing aloud for we are proud,
> Proud of our English name.[20]

The better-known verse of writers like W. E. Henley (1849–1903) and Henry Newbolt (1862–1938) represent an explicit attempt to write heroic poetry for boys, and to direct their imaginations towards Britain's imperial history and her contemporary imperial destiny. This can be seen in poems like Newbolt's 'Admirals All' ('Effingham, Grenville, Raleigh, Drake, / Here's to the bold and free!'), or 'Vitaï Lampada' ('Play up! play up! and play the game!'), 'Clifton Chapel', or 'The Schoolfellow':   CRICKET.

Our game was his but yesteryear;
  We wished him back; we could not know
The self-same hour we missed him here
  He led the line that broke the foe.

Blood-red behind our guarded posts
  Sank as of old the dying day;
The battle ceased; the mingled hosts
  Weary and cheery went their way:

'To-morrow well may bring,' we said,
  'As fair a fight, as clear a sun.'
Dear lad, before the word was sped,
  For evermore thy goal was won.[21]

This makes the connection between the world of the public school, the
playing-field and the imperial context in a way that is charged with a
genuine pathos (though perhaps bathos would better describe that last
line). The high point of this kind of patriotic and imperialist verse is
undoubtedly Kipling's 'Recessional' (1897), which manages to mix
Christian humility with its patriotic fears of imperial decline:

God of our fathers, known of old,
  Lord of our far-flung battle-line,
Beneath whose awful hand we hold
  Dominion over palm and pine –
Lord God of Hosts, be with us yet,
Lest we forget – lest we forget![22]

These are public, unironic, high-minded poems, that seek a dignified
style to go with the large and important topics they are addressing.
They contrast interestingly with a group of poems which draw deliber-
ately on a more vernacular register, of which the best-known are
Kipling's 'Barrack-room Ballads' (1892), but which also include some
of Newbolt's poems such as 'Drake's Drum' and 'San Stefano (A Ballad
of the Bold Menelaus)'.

Equally unironic and high-minded was the tradition of history painting, dominated by military and imperial themes throughout the
nineteenth century, but given much wider popular currency by the
new technologies of mass reproduction employed by papers such as

the *Illustrated London News*. There was a well-established tradition of idealising military art in the nineteenth century that looked back to such famous canvases as Benjamin West's *Death of Wolfe* (1771) – carried forward by such popular triumphs of Royal Academy art as

Figure 6 W.G. Joy, *General Gordon's Last Stand* (1984)

Calling the roll after an engagement, Crimea (1874) by Elizabeth Thompson (later Lady Butler), or her equally famous *Scotland for Ever!* (1881). These pictures draw on a visual language of unequivocal heroism, emphasising the uniformed masculine figure in attitudes of (partly vulnerable) attack. This older tradition of pictorial art was extended with little difficulty into more obviously Imperialist subjects, where the enemies of the British soldier were no longer other Europeans, but the black and brown peoples against whom Britain waged its interminable 'little wars'. In this continuation, where the worked-up sketches of war artists as they appear in the illustrated papers are as important as the great canvases of the Academy, the heroic white military figure now rises above a sea of black bodies, be they from the Sudan or from the Zulu wars. The most famous picture in this line is G. W. Joy's picture of Gordon at Khartoum, defending himself heroically against the Mahdist hordes with only a revolver (Figure 6).

These poems and paintings were certainly popular in the sense that the poems were widely read, forming part of school poetry anthologies, while the paintings were frequently reproduced. The poems especially can be compared to songs of the music-hall, the cultural institution in which popular Imperialism took on its most visible – and audible – expression. Indeed, the very word 'jingoism' was coined as a result of a music-hall song from 1878, inciting popular support for an aggressive anti-Russian policy in the Balkans. Throughout the last two decades of the century, the music-hall provided a succession of popular songs and spectacles on patriotic and Imperialist themes, typically giving them a demotic twist by celebrating the common soldier and seaman as the winners and defenders of empire:

> It's the soldiers of the Queen, my lads,
> Who've been, my lads, who've seen my lads,
> In the fight for England's glory, lads,
> Of its world wide glory let us sing.[23]

Thus goes a song of 1881. Popular patriotism of this kind was no new thing, of course, and the music-hall drew on traditions going back well into the eighteenth century. What was distinctive about this highly commercialised and indeed highly capitalised system of entertainment was the way that it effectively blotted out other traditions within demotic culture, some of them strongly anti-militarist; so that, while the music-hall did allow some space for parody (for example, of the 'By Jingo' song of

1878), this was overwhelmingly a space in which popular militarism and Imperialism were propagated.

Though we think of the music-hall as a 'popular' cultural institution, it was of course internally differentiated, and in the West End had a vociferous aristocratic audience. But the most powerful institution for the inculcation of Imperialist values for the ruling elite in the later nineteenth century was undoubtedly the public school. Many public schools had direct connections with the military, their task being to prepare young men for service in the Empire. More generally, all the schools sought to create an ethos which combined institutional and patriotic loyalties, calling on the boyish enthusiasms of their scholars – with inevitably partial results.

The danger of arguments which insist on the pervasiveness of Imperialism as an ideology, however, is that they can suggest too readily that culture, and even specific cultural forms, were the instigating causes of imperialism as a practice. This is a curious variant of Imperialism's own self-image: that empire was part of a civilising mission, by which 'primitive' or Oriental peoples were somehow to be set free from priestcraft, tyranny or superstition by being placed under British rule. On the contrary, the fundamental dynamic of British imperial expansion was economic, powered by the peculiarities of British capitalist development, and the dominance, even in the world's first industrial nation, of the alliance of commerce and agriculture centred on London and the South-East of England.[24] Yet there is no final contradiction in recognising that economic motivations are accompanied by a panoply of cultural forms, in which the individual agents of empire work out their destinies with varying degrees of idealism, cynicism, cupidity, conviction, naivety, intelligence and ignorance.

Furthermore, it is important to remember that cultural and ideological forms do not automatically produce the results that their authors intend, or that subsequent readers or critics deduce. Especially in a society characterised by a diverse and even contradictory culture, there are always cultural resources to draw on to enable the 'subjects' of ideology to resist or renegotiate the hegemonising claims that are made upon them. Some of these complexities can be gauged from considering the writings of even the most evidently Imperialist writers from the end of the century, in the work of Rudyard Kipling, Rider Haggard or Henry Newbolt. Kipling takes the Empire as his almost exclusive topic; his *Stalky & Co.*, a collection of school stories from the 1890s, explicitly considers the means by which boys are to be turned into effective Imperial

military officers, being based on Kipling's own experiences at the United
Services College at Westward Ho! in Devon. One continuous theme in
them is the inadequacy of any direct or immediate effort at propagandis-
ing the boys. In one, 'The Flag of Their Country', the boys are given a
patriotic address by a Conservative politician to encourage them to join
a newly established cadet-corps, during which he unfurls the national
flag; the immediate effect is to disgust the boys with this explicit patriotism, so that those who have already joined the corps resign. The boys
learn rather by indirection and negative example from their peers and
their masters – they learn whom to admire and whom to despise. Thus,
in another of the stories, 'Regulus', the boys learn *despite* their sarcastic
Latin master, who is elsewhere a butt of their bad behaviour. Here, he is
conducting a class on Horace's Odes, in particular the story of Regulus,
the Roman hero who argued in effect for his own death when persuading
the Roman Senate that the captured soldiers from whom he was an envoy
should not be ransomed from Carthage:

> 'Regulus *was* in earnest. He was also engaged at the same time in
> cutting his own throat with every word he uttered. He knew Carthage
> which (your examiners won't ask you this so you needn't take notes)
> was a sort of God-forsaken nigger Manchester. Regulus was not
> thinking about his own life. He was telling Rome the truth. He was
> playing for his side. Those lines from the eighteenth to the fortieth
> ought to be written in blood.'[25]

It is precisely at moments such as this, when the master has departed
from the official curriculum, that the boys can assimilate some of the
'true' values of that curriculum, so that the great patriotic themes of
Horace can become available to them (one of the boys remarks at the
end of the class that 'When King's really on tap he's an interestin' dog'
[p.165]). In this scene, the contemptuous and racist reference to Manchester (symbol of trading England), combining with still wider contempt for the scientific part of the curriculum recently introduced at
the college, suggests further aspects of that unofficial curriculum. Altogether, though public schools were undoubtedly institutions for instil-
ling imperialist values into the boys who attended them, the informal
mechanisms by which it did so cannot simply be read off from the curriculum provided.

Part of the strength of Kipling's writing – if strength it be – is its assimilation of such complexities in a wider rhetorical economy that remains

committed to empire. He recognises, in other words, that any successful hegemonising project will have to concede at least some things to the opposition, if only to make its hegemonic claims more complete (*Stalky & Co.*, for instance, allows its boys to be especially scornful of goody-goody books for boys, like F. W. Farrar's *Eric, or Little by Little* [1858]). Equally complex, though finally more equivocal, are the tales of Joseph Conrad (1857–1924), which are at once romances or adventure stories, and elaborate self-conscious meditations on the meaning of adventure. Conrad wrote a series of novels and short stories in the 1890s which took imperial settings and the British merchant marine service as their topic: *Almayer's Folly* (1895), *An Outcast of the Islands* (1896), *The Nigger of the Narcissus* (1897), *Youth* (1898) and *Heart of Darkness* (1899). These books are characterised by a number of contradictory commitments – by an ideal of service as exemplified in the British Merchant Navy; by disgust with the high-sounding ideological justifications and racial complacency of European imperialism; by a deployment of a racial typology in the characterisation and the disposition of narrative interest; and by hostility towards the actual practice of imperialism, especially when it is practised by Europeans other than the British. These contradictions are resolved in differing ways in the novels, the form permitting Conrad both to suggest his allegiances (to the simple, if exacting, duties of a sailing ship, for example) and to intimate also the limitations of such loyalties. Thus *An Outcast of the Islands* recounts a story of racial and mercantile conflict and competition, but it does so from a multiplicity of different viewpoints – English, Dutch, Malay, Arab, male and female – that awards no priority to any single perspective on events. Similarly, and more famously, *Heart of Darkness* offers both a ferocious critique of Belgian imperialism in the Congo, and a map of the world cognate to the imperialist mentality, as the narrator of the story adventures into the heart of Africa – a journey which is also into the savage past of humanity. These ambiguities are constitutive of the novels as Conrad uses the form, and suggest how the contentions surrounding imperialism at the end of the century can enter into the very fabric of the cultural forms that address it.

Conrad's novels make a convenient concluding-point for this consideration of nineteenth-century ideas of ethnicity, race and empire, for these notions, and the oppositions that formed around them, combine in telling and complex ways in his stories. Much of the cultural production that I have surveyed, however, does not even have the saving grace of complexity, the faultline of race marking a dismal limit to the century's artistic sympathies, across which writers only ventured in opprobrious fantasy – projections of Celtic sensibility, of Oriental barbarism or of African savagery – that served the social, political and perhaps psychological needs of the metropolitan centre. At the end of the century the British Empire was still expanding – it reached its greatest geographical extent in the 1930s – but its real nemesis, as of many of the cultural forms which sustained it, was not long to wait in 1900. The Great War was only fourteen years away.

CONCLUSION

Cultural history does not follow a timetable conveniently laid out in centuries, any more than social history does. Indeed, I have been suggesting throughout this book that the historical rhythms of the various forms and conventions of culture are partly distinct from those of other elements of the social order. It is for this reason that we cannot speak of a *Zeitgeist* for the nineteenth century, or any portion of it, such as the 'Victorian age', since every period of history is characterised by multiple and contradictory ways of thinking, seeing and feeling. It is rare indeed that there comes a moment at which, across a whole range of social and cultural forms, matters appear decisively to alter.

Such a change did not occur in 1900, still less on the death of Queen Victoria on 22 January 1901, however much that event seemed to mark, for her contemporaries, the end of an epoch. Nor, despite Virginia Woolf's claim to the contrary, did human nature change in 1910 as the Georgians took over from the Edwardians. But perhaps such a change did occur with the Great War of 1914–18, an event which marked a terminal point for aspects of the nineteenth-century English social order and many of the cultural forms that accompanied them. Most evidently, it marked the end for Britain as the dominant world power; but even in relation to matters we have been considering in this book, the War appears as a transitional moment. Thanks to it, women's suffrage was achieved in 1919. As a result of it, the greatest ever transfer of English farming-land occurred, meaning the end of the system of landlord, tenant farmer and landless labourer that had dominated the previous century in the countryside. Above all, the war produced a loss of confidence in whatever cultural and intellectual certainties had survived from the nineteenth century. In the wake of the war in 1922, in a remarkable evocation and emptying-out of cultural meanings, T. S. Eliot could write, symptomatically, of England – London especially – as *The Waste Land*.

Even the cataclysm of the Great War, however, did not obliterate many of the forms of life that we have been considering in this book. In some respects, in fact, the war only accelerated trends that were already in motion long before the beginning of the twentieth century. The very text that I have just brought forward as exemplifying the sense of cultural crisis that accompanied the First World War, *The Waste Land*, draws upon intimations of the city, and cultural forms, that were pioneered in the nineteenth century. More generally, as some of the previous period's substantial characteristics persisted – a deeply class-divided society, with little effective emancipation for women, in control of an empire until the middle of the twentieth century – we should not be surprised to see the same faultlines persisting also, however differently articulated in new cultural technologies.

But this is not only a story of unconsidered recurrence, in which unchanging conditions of life throw up unaltered cultural negotiations of them. Such a story could certainly be told; it has been uncomfortable to watch, for example, how nineteenth- century debates over poverty have reappeared in strikingly similar terms at the end of the twentieth century, even down to discussions over the morality of giving to street-beggars. However, we can look at this from the other way about. Cultural forms and genres, I have been suggesting, are ways of negotiating social relations, historically created resources which people use to make sense of their lives and to manage their place in the world in relation to others. If this is so, then we can assume that the cultural forms of the nineteenth century – even with that estranging distance which now separates us from the period – will continue to provide a resource for us as we embark upon the twenty-first.

NOTES AND REFERENCES

1 Introduction: 'Society' and 'Cultural Form'

1 See especially, *Culture and Society* (Chatto & Windus, London, 1958), *Keywords: A Vocabulary of Culture and Society* (Fontana, n.p., 1983) and *Culture* (Fontana, n.p., 1981).
2 George Eliot, 'The Natural History of Social Life', in *Essays of George Eliot*, edited by Thomas Pinney (Routledge and Kegan Paul, London, 1963).
3 John Ruskin's views on these matters are powerfully expressed in *Unto this Last* (1862); this can be contrasted with John Stuart Mill's *Liberty* (1859).
4 Raymond Williams, *The Long Revolution* (Chatto & Windus, London, 1961).
5 See especially, M. M. Bakhtin, *The Dialogic Imagination: Four Essays*, edited by Michael Holquist; translated by Caryl Emerson and Michael Holquist (University of Texas Press, Austin, 1981); and V. N. Vološinov, *Marxism and the Philosophy of Language*, translated by Ladislav Matejka and I. R. Titunik (Academic Press, New York, 1986).
6 See *George Eliot: The Critical Heritage*, edited by David Carroll (Routledge, London, 1971); especially the review of *The Mill on the Floss* by E. S. Dallas, pp. 131–7.
7 Charles Dickens, *Bleak House* (1852–53), ch. 47.
8 'Legible symbolic configuration': see Martin Meisel, *Realisations: Narrative, Pictorial and Theatrical Arts in Nineteenth-century England* (Princeton University Press, Princeton, 1983), p. 45.
9 These examples are taken from the *Official Descriptive and Illustrated Catalogue of the Great Exhibition*, 3 vols. (1851), I: 467; II: plates 56, 63.
10 Raymond Williams, 'The Bloomsbury Fraction', in *Problems in Materialism and Culture* (Verso, London, 1980), pp. 145–69.
11 See Isobel Armstrong, *Victorian Poetry: Poetry, Poetics, and Politics* (London, Routledge, 1993).

12 Benedict Anderson, *Imagined Communities: Reflections on the Origin and Spread of Nationalism*, revised edn (Verso, London, 1991).
13 See *The Dialogic Imagination*, pp. 342–8.

2 Connections: Culture and the Social Order

1 Quoted in Owen Chadwick, *The Victorian Church*, 2 vols. (Adam and Charles Black, London, 1970), I: 515.
2 *Ibid.*, II: 151.
3 See Doreen M. Rosman, *Evangelicals and Culture* (Croom Helm, London, 1984).
4 See Chadwick, *The Victorian Church*, II: 56–7, for these figures.
5 Rev. Legh Richmond, *Annals of the Poor* (J. Briddon, Ryde, *c*.1830), p. 122.
6 Rosman, *Evangelicals and Culture*, p. 33.
7 See Beth Tobin, *Superintending the Poor; Charitable Ladies and Paternal Landlords in British Fiction, 1770–1860* (Yale University Press, New Haven and London, 1993); and Leonore Davidoff and Catherine Hall, *Family Fortunes: Men and Women of the English Middle Class 1780–1850* (Hutchinson, London, 1987),
8 See, for example, Richard Price, 'Does the notion of Victorian England make any sense?', in *Cities, Class and Communication; Essays in Honour of Asa Briggs*, edited by D. Fraser (Harvester Wheatsheaf, Brighton, 1990); and 'Historiography, Narrative and the Nineteenth Century', *Journal of British Studies* 35 (1996), 220–56. Michael Mason, in *The Making of Victorian Sexual Attitudes* and *The Making of Victorian Sexuality: Sexual Behaviour and Its Understanding* (both Oxford University Press, Oxford, 1994), argues against the notion that Evangelicalism was responsible for Victorianism, if by the latter is meant, narrowly, an attitude of prudish or high-minded disapproval of sexuality.
9 John Tulloch, *Movements of Religious Thought in the Nineteenth Century* (Leicester University Press, Leicester, 1971), p. 105.
10 J. H. Newman, *Parochial and Plain Sermons* (n.p., London, 1908–18), I: 320. Quoted in *The Oxford Movement*, edited by Eugene R. Fairweather (Oxford University Press, New York, 1964), p. 21.
11 See Chadwick, *The Victorian Church*, I: 220.
12 Joseph Arch, *From Ploughtail to Parliament: an Autobiography* (The Cresset Library, London, 1986). See especially ch. 1, 'Childhood'.
13 Matthew Arnold, *Literature and Dogma*, in *Dissent and Dogma*, edited by R. H. Super (University of Michigan Press, Ann Arbor, 1968), p. 363.
14 Matthew Arnold, *The Popular Education of France*, in *Democratic Education*, *Complete Prose Works of Matthew Arnold*, edited by R. H. Super (University of Michigan Press, Ann Arbor, 1962), II: 385. The quoted phrase appeared in the 1861 edition only.
15 I allude here of course to Arnold's *Culture and Anarchy* (1869).
16 Carlyle's spiritual autobiography is *Sartor Resartus* (1838); *Past and Present* (1843) addresses explicitly the problem of authority in a secular state.
17 For the 'moral economy', see Eric Hobsbawm and George Rudé, *Captain Swing* (Lawrence and Wishart, London, 1969).

18 John Stuart Mill, *Autobiography* (1873).
19 George Eliot, 'The Natural History of German Life' (1856), in *Selected Essays, Poems and Other Writings*, edited by A. S. Byatt and Nicholas Warren (Penguin, London, 1990), p. 170.
20 Charles Dickens, *Bleak House* (Penguin, Harmondsworth, 1975), pp. 49–50.
21 See Peter K. Garrett, *The Victorian Multiplot Novel: Studies in Dialogic Form* (Yale University Press, New Haven and London, 1980).
22 W. M. Thackeray, *The Newcomes* (1853–55), ch. XXIV.

3 Divisions: Cultural and Social Challenges

1 Henry Mayhew, *London Labour and the London Poor*, selections made and introduced by Victor Neuburg (Penguin, London, 1985), p. 303.
2 Mayhew's writing is more fully discussed in Chapter 5 below.
3 There is an implicit argument here with the most important piece of social and cultural history written in English since the war, E. P. Thompson's *The Making of the English Working Class* (Gollancz, London, 1963).
4 Robert Roberts, *The Classic Slum* (Manchester University Press, Manchester, 1971).
5 David Vincent, *Bread, Knowledge and Freedom: A Study of Nineteenth-Century Working Class Autobiography* (Methuen, London, 1981), p. 128.
6 Thomas Cooper, *The Life of Thomas Cooper*, with an introduction by John Saville (Leicester University Press, Leicester, 1971), p. 59.
7 Vincent, *Bread, Knowledge and Freedom*, p. 166.
8 *The Poorhouse Fugitives: Self-taught Poets and Poetry in Victorian Britain*, edited by Brian Maidment (Carcanet Press, Manchester, 1987), pp. 18, 136.
9 Quoted in Elizabeth Gaskell, *Mary Barton* (Oxford University Press, Oxford, 1987), p. 128.
10 Samuel Bamford, *Passages in the Life of a Radical* (Oxford University Press, Oxford, 1984), p. 146.
11 Cobbett's writing is further discussed in Chapter 4 below.
12 See, for this tradition, Edward Royle, *Victorian Infidels: The Origins of the British Secularist Movement, 1791–1866* (Manchester University Press, Manchester, 1974), pp. 9–58.
13 Barbara Taylor, *Eve and the New Jerusalem: Socialism and Feminism in the Nineteenth Century* (Virago, London, 1983).
14 William S. Villiers Sankey, 'Rule Britannia!', in *An Anthology of Chartist Literature*, edited by Yu. V. Kovalev (Literature in Foreign Languages Publishers, Moscow, 1956), p. 78.
15 Benjamin Stott, 'Song for the Millions', in Kovalev, ed., *An Anthology of Chartist Literature*, p. 106.
16 *Workman's Times*, 20 Feb. 1892, p.6. Quoted in Stephen Yeo, 'A new life: the religion of socialism in Britain 1883–1896', *History Workshop Journal* 4 (Autumn 1977), 5–56.
17 Raymond Williams, 'The Bloomsbury Fraction', in *Problems in Materialism and Culture* (Verso; London, 1980), pp. 145–69.

18   Harold Perkin, *The Origins of Modern English Society* (Routledge and Kegan Paul, London, 1972), chs. 7 and 8.

19   John Ruskin, *Praeterita, Complete Works of John Ruskin*, edited by E. T. Cook and Alexander Wedderburn, 39 vols. (George Allen, London, 1908), XXXV: 13.

20   Fiona MacCarthy, *The Simple Life: C. R. Ashbee in the Cotswolds* (Lund Humphries, London, 1981).

4   Rural England

1   Eric Hobsbawm and George Rudé, *Captain Swing* (Lawrence and Wishart, London, 1969).

2   William Cobbett, *Rural Rides* (Penguin, Harmondsworth, 1967), pp. 226–7.

3   John Clare, *The Parish; A Satire*, edited by Eric Robinson (Penguin, Harmondsworth, 1986), pp. 33–4.

4   'The new-fashioned farmer', in *The Painful Plough*, edited by Roy Palmer (Cambridge University Press, Cambridge, 1973), p. 14.

5   Joseph Arch, *From Ploughtail to Parliament: an Autobiography* (The Cresset Library, London, 1986), p. 9.

6   Quoted in Pamela Horn, *Labouring Life in the Victorian Countryside* (Alan Sutton, Stroud, 1987), p. 59.

7   Fred Kitchen, *Brother to the Ox: The Autobiography of a Farm Labourer* (Penguin, Harmondsworth, 1983), pp. 59–63, 148–51.

8   Leonore Davidoff and Catherine Hall, *Family Fortunes: Men and Women of the English Middle Class 1780–1850* (Hutchinson, London, 1987), *passim*.

9   Samuel Taylor Coleridge, 'Frost at Midnight' (1798).

10   W. B. Yeats, 'The Lake Isle of Innisfree' (1893).

11   See John Barrell, *The Dark Side of the Landscape: The Rural Poor in English Painting 1730–1840* (Cambridge University Press, Cambridge, 1980).

12   The various traditions of representations of rural life are discussed in Karen Sayer, *Women of the Fields: Representations of Rural Women in the Nineteenth Century* (Manchester University Press, Manchester, 1995).

13   Oscar Wilde, 'The Soul of Man under Socialism', in *Plays, Prose Writings and Poems* (Everyman's Library, London, 1975), p. 281.

14   George Eliot, 'The Natural History of German Life' (1856), in *Selected Essays, Poems and Other Writings*, edited by A. S. Byatt and Nicholas Warren (Penguin, London, 1990), p. 111.

15   For a full account of late nineteenth-century theories of degeneration, see William Greenslade, *Degeneration, Culture and the Novel 1880–1940* (Cambridge, Cambridge University Press, 1994).

16   Martin Wiener, *English Culture and the Decline of the Industrial Spirit, 1850–1980* (Cambridge University Press, Cambridge, 1981)

17   See Ebenezer Howard, *Garden Cities of Tomorrow* (Attic Books, Builth Wells, 1985). (First published 1902.)

5   Understanding the City

1   R. J. Morris and Richard Rodger, 'An Introduction to British Urban History, 1820–1914', in *The Victorian City: A Reader in British Urban History, 1820–1914*, edited by R.J. Morris and Richard Rodger (Longman, London, 1993), pp.1–39. Figures for the nineteenth century are relatively secure compared to previous centuries, if only because of the institution of the national census on a decennial basis from 1801 onwards. Nevertheless, they are still open to interpretation, if only because, in this instance, definitions of what constituted a city or an urban settlement changed in the course of the century. Changing urban boundaries also affect the statistics.

2   P. J. Cain and A. G. Hopkins, *British Imperialism: Innovation and Expansion 1688–1914* (Longman, London and New York, 1993), p. 115.

3   *Ibid.*, pp. 2–3. Alun Howkins, in *Reshaping Rural England; a Social History 1850–1925* (HarperCollins, London, 1991), has rightly suggested some caution about assuming majority urban experience in mid-century England, pointing out that many of those considered 'urban' on the basis of the census would have been living in traditional small country towns relatively unaffected by industrialism.

4   See H. J. Dyos and Michael Wolff, 'The Way We Live Now', in *The Victorian City; Images and Realities*, edited by H. J. Dyos and Michael Wolff, 2 vols. (Routledge and Kegan Paul, London, 1973), 2: 893–907, for a contrast between the eighteenth- and nineteenth-century cities along these lines.

5   Asa Briggs, 'The Human Aggregate', in Dyos and Wolff, eds., *The Victorian City*, pp. 83–104, 87–8.

6   See Michael Wolff and Celina Fox, 'Pictures from the Magazines', in Dyos and Wolff, eds., *The Victorian City*, pp. 559–82. The illustrations are reproduced between pp. 572 and 573. Wolff and Fox offer these illustrations as evidence of a more active social conscience to be found in lesser-known journals like the *Illustrated Times*.

7   Thomas Carlyle, 'Chartism', in *English and Other Critical Essays* (J. M. Dent and Sons, London, n.d.), pp. 165–238, p. 170.

8   George Eliot, 'The Natural History of German Life' (1856), in *Selected Essays, Poems and Other Writings*, edited by A. S. Byatt and Nicholas Warren (Penguin, London, 1990).

9   Charles Dickens, *Dombey and Son* (1847–48), ch. 47.

10   See, for the 'Condition-of-England novel', Raymond Williams, *Culture and Society 1780–1950* (Penguin, Harmondsworth, 1961), ch. 5, 'The Industrial Novels', pp. 99–119; Louis Cazamian, *The Social Novel in England 1830–1850*, translated by Martin Fido (Routledge, London, 1973); Sheila M. Smith, *The Other Nation: The Poor in English Novels of thd 1840s and 1850s* (Clarendon Press, Oxford, 1980).

11   This apparently arbitrary conjunction of writing and painting seems less arbitrary in the light of Martin Meisel's great work *Realisations*, which traces the connections between writing, pictures and indeed theatre, from the late eighteenth century to the late nineteenth century.

12 This painting is closely modelled on an illustration Fildes provided for the *Graphic* 1 (1869), 9. See the illustrations between pp. 572–3 in Michael Wolff and Celina Fox, 'Pictures from the Magazines', in Dyos and Wolff, eds., *The Victorian City*, pp. 559–82.

13 Elizabeth Gaskell, *Mary Barton*, edited by Edgar Wright (Oxford; Oxford University Press, 1987), p. 96.

14 George Gissing, *The Nether World* (Oxford, Oxford University Press, 1992), p. 280.

15 Charles Booth, *Life and Labour of the People in London*, 1st ser., revised edn, 5 vols. (Macmillan, London, 1902).

16 See n. 8, Chapter 1, above.

17 G. W. M. Reynolds, *The Mysteries of London*, edited by Trefor Thomas (Keele University Press, Keele, 1996), pp. 4–5.

18 Gustave Doré and Blanchard Jerrold, *London: A Pilgrimage* (Grant and Co., London, 1872), p. 25.

19 *Ibid.*, between pp. 138 and 139.

20 See Roger Sales, 'Pierce Egan and the Representation of London', in *Reviewing Romanticism*, edited by Philip W. Martin and Robin Jarvis (Macmillan, London, 1992), pp. 154–69.

21 E. P. Thompson, 'Mayhew and the *Morning Chronicle*', introduction to *The Unknown Mayhew: Selections from the Morning Chronicle 1849–1850*, edited by E. P. Thompson and Eileen Yeo (Penguin, Harmonsdworth, 1971).

22 Peter Bailey, 'Ally Sloper's Half-Holiday: Comic Art in the 1880s', *History Workshop Journal* 16 (Autumn 1983), 4–32.

23 Andrew Mearns, *The Bitter Cry of Outcast London*, edited with an introduction by Anthony S.Wohl (Leicester, Leicester University Press, 1970), p. 55.

24 See Gareth Stedman Jones, *Outcast London: A Study in the Relationship between Classes in Victorian Society* (Clarendon Press, Oxford, 1971); Judith R. Walkowitz, *City of Dreadful Delight: Narratives of Sexual Danger in Late-Victorian London* (Virago, London, 1992).

25 E. P. Hennock, 'Poverty and Social Theory in England: The Experience of the Eighteen-Eighties', *Social History* 1 (January 1976), 67–91.

26 Benjamin Brierley, 'Out of Work', in *Tales and Sketches of Lancashire Life*, 6 vols. (John Heywood, Manchester, 1882–86), VI: 76–7.

27 M. J. Daunton, *House and Home in the Victorian City; Working-Class Housing 1850–1914* (Edward Arnold, London, 1983).

28 F. Engels, *The Condition of the Working Class in England*, translated and edited by W. O. Henderson and W. H. Chaloner (Basil Blackwell, Oxford, 1971).

29 See Walkowitz, *City of Dreadful Delight*.

6 Gender and Cultural Forms

1 Leonore Davidoff and Catherine Hall, *Family Fortunes: Men and Women of the English Middle Class 1780–1850* (Hutchinson, London, 1987), p. 319.

2 See below, Chapter 7, pp. 171–2. For the general contrast between 'adventure fiction' and domestic realism, see Martin Green, *Dreams of Adventure, Deeds of Empire* (Routledge and Kegan Paul, London, 1980).

3 Alfred Tennyson, *The Princess*, in *The Poems of Tennyson*, edited by Christopher Ricks (Longman, London, 1969), pp. 741–844, p. 806.

4 *Ibid.*, pp. 814–15.

5 Elizabeth Barrett Browning, *Aurora Leigh* (Tauchnitz, Leipzig, 1872), p. 21.

6 *Ibid.*, p. 171.

7 *The Poems of Arthur Hugh Clough*, edited by F. L. Mulhauser (Oxford University Press, Oxford, 1974), p. 52.

8 *Ibid.*, p. 82.

9 George Meredith, 'Modern Love', in *Poems I* (Archibald, Constable and Co., Westminster, 1898), p. 27.

10 Robert Browning, *Poetical Works, 1833–1864* (Oxford University Press, London, 1970), pp. 567–8.

11 Christina Rossetti, *Selected Poems*, edited by C. H. Sisson (Carcanet, Manchester, 1984), pp. 92–3.

12 *The Poems of Coventry Patmore*, edited by Frederick Page (Oxford University Press, Oxford, 1949), p. 62.

13 *Ibid.*, p. 138.

14 Judith R. Walkowitz, *City of Dreadful Delight: Narratives of Sexual Danger in Late-Victorian London* (Virago, London, 1992).

15 Elaine Showalter, *Sexual Anarchy* (Bloomsbury, London, 1991).

16 Beatrice Webb, *My Apprenticeship*, with an introduction by Norman MacKenzie (Cambridge University Press, Cambridge, 1979), p. 179.

7 Ethnicity, Race and Empire

1 Linda Colley, *Britons: Forging the Nation 1707–1837* (Pimlico, London, 1992).

2 M. A. G. Ó Tuathaigh, 'The Irish in Nineteenth- Century Britain', in *The Irish in the Victorian City*, edited by Roger Swift and Sheridan Gilley (Croom Helm, London, 1985), pp. 13–36, p. 15.

3 Matthew Arnold, 'On the Study of Celtic Literature', in *Lectures and Essays in Criticism, Complete Prose Works of Matthew Arnold*, edited by R. H. Super (University of Michigan Press, Ann Arbor, 1962), III: 346–7.

4 Robert Young, *Colonial Desire; Hybridity in Theory, Culture and Race* (Routledge, London, 1995).

5 See *ibid.* for the full implications of this debate.

6 Thomas Carlyle, 'The Nigger Question', in *English and Other Critical Essays* (Everyman's Library, Dent, London, n.d.), p. 309.

7 V. G. Kiernan, *The Lords of Human Kind: European Attitudes to the Outside World in the Imperial Age* (Penguin, Harmondsworth, 1972), p. 49.

8 Patrick Brantlinger, *Rule of Darkness: British Literature and Imperialism, 1830–1914* (Cornell University Press, Ithaca and London, 1988), ch. 7, 'The Well at Cawnpore: Literary Representations of the Indian Mutiny of 1857'.

9 Charles Dickens, *The Letters of Charles Dickens*, edited by Walter Dexter (The Nonesuch Press, London, 1938), II: 889; 4 Oct. 1857.

10 Catherine Hall, 'Competing Masculinities: Thomas Carlyle, John Stuart Mill, and the Case of Governor Eyre', in *White, Male and Middle Class: Explorations in Feminism and History* (Polity Press, London, 1992), pp. 255–95.

11 Edward Said, *Culture and Imperialism* (Chatto and Windus, London, 1993). See especially ch. 2, 'Consolidated Vision'.

12 See n. 10, Chapter 5, above.

13 Martin Green, *Dreams of Adventure, Deeds of Empire* (Routledge and Kegan Paul, London, 1980), p. 3.

14 *Ibid.*, p. 220.

15 Andrew Lang, 'Realism and Romance', *Contemporary Review* 52 (1887), 689.

16 Brantlinger, *Rule of Darkness*, p. 33.

17 P. J. Cain and A. G. Hopkins, *British Imperialism: Innovation and Expansion, 1699–1914* (Longman, London and New York, 1993).

18 Joseph Bristow, *Empire Boys: Adventures in a Man's World* (Harper Collins Academic, London, 1991), p. 47; p. 15.

19 See Guy Arnold, *Held Fast for England: G. A. Henty, Imperialist Boys' Writer* (Hamish Hamilton, London, 1980).

20 *Boy's Own Paper* 10 (1887–88), 562; words and music by Rev. W. J. Foxell. Quoted in Bristow, *Empire Boys*, p. 45.

21 Henry Newbolt, *Collected Poems 1987–1907* (Thomas Nelson and Sons, London, n.d.), p. 149.

22 Rudyard Kipling, *The Complete Verse*, with a foreword by M. M. Kaye (Kyle Cathie, London, 1990), p. 266.

23 Quoted in Penny Summerfield, 'Patriotism and Empire', in *Imperialism and Popular Culture*, edited by John M. MacKenzie (Manchester University Press, Manchester, 1986), pp. 17–49, p. 36.

24 P. J. Cain and A. G. Hopkins, *British Imperialism: Innovation and Expansion, 1699–1914* (Longman, London and New York, 1993).

25 Rudyard Kipling, *The Complete Stalky & Co.* (Oxford University Press, Oxford, 1987), p. 161.

SUGGESTIONS FOR FURTHER READING

The following suggestions are made to enable readers to pursue further aspects of the preceding chapters that interest them. The suggestions broadly follow the line of argument in the text, but only secondary material is mentioned here; all the primary texts that appear in the body of the book are annotated there.

1   Introduction: 'Society and Cultural Form'

As will be clear from the arguments in this chapter, my starting point has been the work of Raymond Williams. The most relevant of his texts to this study are *Culture and Society* (1958) and *The Long Revolution* (1961), both of which make substantial reference to the nineteenth century; also relevant, though couched in a more abstract style of argument, are *Culture* (1981) and *Marxism and Literature* (1977). Williams's *Keywords* (revised edn, 1983) is a marvel of scholarship and compression, providing short essays on a number of the key terms used in this chapter. A convenient introduction to the thought of Bakhtin can be found in my *Bakhtinian Thought: An Introductory Reader* (1995).

There are a number of social histories of the nineteenth century, in a field especially subject to controversy and revision. The seminal work remains E. P. Thompson's *The Making of the English Working Class* (1963). The central emphasis placed upon *class* by Thompson and his generation of Marxist historians has been challenged by a more recent group of scholars, who draw attention instead to other forms of self- understanding in the nineteenth century; see for example Patrick Joyce, *Visions of the People: Industrial England and the Question of Class, 1848–1914* (1991), *Democratic Subjects: The Self and the Social in Nineteenth-century England* (1994) and James Vernon, *Politics and the People: A Study in English*

191

Political Culture, c.1815–1867 (1993). Covering a roughly similar temporal range as Thompson, but with its attention on the middle class and the faultline of gender, is Leonore Davidoff and Catherine Hall, *Family Fortunes: Men and Women of the English Middle Class 1780–1850* (1987), which I refer to throughout the book; this is a wonderful example of feminist social history, connecting together a range of social, economic and gender transformations. Harold Perkin's *The Origins of Modern English Society* (1969) is still useful in its attempt to trace the history of a variety of competing class-ideals in nineteenth-century England. The three volumes of the *Cambridge Social History of England 1750–1950*, edited by F. M. L. Thompson (1990), contain substantial essays on many of the topics alluded to in this chapter.

Richard D. Altick, *The English Common Reader: A Social History of the Mass Reading Public, 1800–1900* (1957), remains a valuable account of its topic; Kate Flint's *The Woman Reader, 1837–1914* (1993) is as much a literary as a social history.

As far as the history of cultural forms is concerned, mention must certainly be made of Martin Meisel's *Realisations: Narrative, Pictorial and Theatrical Arts in Nineteenth-century England* (1983), an unduly neglected work of scholarship which traces a whole related set of aesthetic dispositions across writing, painting and the theatre from the late eighteenth century to the late nineteenth century. It can be supplemented for the history of melodrama by Peter Brooks's *The Melodramatic Imagination: Balzac, Henry James, Melodrama and the Mode of Excess* (1976), and Daniel Gerould, ed., *Melodrama* (1980). Asa Briggs, *Victorian Things* (1988), is an invaluable guide to nineteenth-century design.

J. M. Golby and A. W. Purdue, *The Civilisation of the Crowd: Popular Culture in England 1750–1900* (1984), provides an account of popular culture which stresses the successful provision of the market; it can usefully be read in conjunction with Hugh Cunningham, *Leisure in the Industrial Revolution* (1980), which also includes some discussion of the project of 'rational recreation'.

2   Connections: Culture and the Social Order

Owen Chadwick's *The Victorian Church*, (2 vols., 1970) offers a comprehensive overview, though unduly skewed towards the Church of England and its elite. Doreen M. Rosman, *Evangelicals and Culture* (1984) attempts to redress the hostile account that has been given of Evangelicalism in relation to culture; Valentine Cunningham, *Everywhere Spoken Against* (1975) has the same ambition with respect to nineteenth-century Nonconformity more generally, while Elizabeth Jay, *The Religion of the Heart: Anglican Evangelicalism and the Nineteenth-Century Novel* (1979) is important but has a narrower focus. Paternalist social attitudes are well discussed in David Roberts, *Paternalism in Early Victorian England* (1979). Arnold's cultural project is discussed in Joseph Carroll, *The Cultural Theory of Matthew Arnold* (1982).

The social history of political economy and the Philosophic Radicals can be approached through the monumental Elie Halévy, *The Growth of Philosophic Radicalism* (1928). T. R. Wright, *The Religion of Humanity: the Impact of Comtean*

Positivism on Victorian Britain (1986), gives an illuminating account of the pervasiveness of Positivism in the period. J. W. Burrow, *Evolution and Society: A Study in Victorian Social Theory* (1966), considers the impact of evolutionary ideas on nineteenth-century social thought, while Gillian Beer, *Darwin's Plots: Evolutionary Narrative in Darwin, George Eliot, and Nineteenth-Century Fiction* (1983) provides some striking textual readings of Darwin and other writers.

Two differing accounts of the history of the English language in the nineteenth century are Olivia Smith's *The Politics of Language 1791–1819* (1984) and Tony Crowley's *The Politics of Discourse: The Standard Language Question in British Cultural Debates* (1989) – though both are primarily accounts of what people thought about language than actual histories of the language itself.

Peter K.Garratt, *The Victorian Multiplot Novel: Studies in Dialogic Form* (1980) discusses the ways in which the 'large loose baggy monsters' of nineteenth-century fiction seek to comprehend the social order.

3   Divisions: Cultural and Social Challenges

Cunningham (1980) and Golby and Purdue (1984), already mentioned, give competing accounts of popular culture. There are several anthologies of ballads and other popular-cultural forms, such as Roy Palmer's *The Sound of History: Songs and Social Comment* (1988), and the same author's *A Touch on the Times: Songs of Social Change 1770 to 1914* (1974). Brian Hollingworth's *Songs of the People: Lancashire Dialect Poetry of the Industrial Revolution* (1977) has a more restricted focus. The notion of 'invented traditions' comes from the book of that name, Eric Hobsbawm and Terence Ranger, eds., *The Invention of Tradition* (1983), which contains a wealth of nineteenth- century material.

G. S. Jones in *Languages of Class: Studies in English Working Class History* (1983) gives an interesting but partial account of late nineteenth-century working-class culture. For the history of music-hall, see the essays in Peter Bailey, ed., *Music Hall: the Business of Pleasure* (1986), and J. S. Bratton, ed., *Music Hall; Performance and Style* (1986). Lucy Brown, *Victorian News and Newspapers* (1985), gives a good overview of its topic. The culture of self-improvement can be approached through David Vincent, *Bread, Knowledge and Freedom: A Study of Nineteenth-Century Working Class Autobiography* (1982), while Brian Maidment's *The Poorhouse Fugitives; Self-taught Poets and Poetry in Victorian Britain* (1987) is much more than just an anthology.

An excellent overview of explicit oppositional movements can be gained from John Belchem, *Popular Radicalism in Nineteenth-Century Britain* (1996). A class-based account of Chartism is to be found in Dorothy Thompson's *The Chartists: Popular Politics in the Industrial Revolution* (1986); it can be contrasted with Gareth Stedman Jones's *Languages of Class: Studies in English Working Class History* (1983), an account which pays due attention to the *language* of Chartism, and hence to the cultural and political forms on which it drew. Stephen Yeo, 'A new life: the religion of socialism in Britain 1883–1896', *History Workshop* 4 (Autumn 1977), 5–56, pursues the question of the 'conversion' to socialism in the 1880s and

1890s. Barbara Taylor's *Eve and the New Jerusalem: Socialism and Feminism in the Nineteenth Century* (1983), is a superb act of feminist historical recovery. E. P. Thompson's 'Mayhew and the *Morning Chronicle*' furnishes an account of the *Punch* cultural fraction in the 1840s; it forms the introduction to E. P. Thompson and Eileen Yeo, eds., *The Unknown Mayhew: Selections from the Morning Chronicle 1849–1850* (1971). There are many introductions to Pre-Raphaelitism; Timothy Hilton's *The Pre-Raphaelites* (1970) is still a good starting point.

4   Rural England

F. M. L. Thompson's *English Landed Society in the Nineteenth Century* (1963) is an excellent introduction. The nature, quality and extent of rural dispossession from the eighteenth to the nineteenth centuries are all matters of controversy; I have relied heavily on K. D. M. Snell, *Annals of the Labouring Poor; Social Change and Agrarian England 1660–1900* (1985). Eric Hobsbawm and George Rudé, in *Captain Swing* (1969) give a dramatic account of the rural disturbances of the early 1830s and the breakdown of the 'moral economy' which precipitated them.

John Lucas, *England and Englishness: Ideas of Nationhood in English Poetry* (1990), though it does not correspond to the chapter divisions of this book, nevertheless has much relevant discussion, especially concerning Clare. Similarly, Malcolm Kelsall, *The Great Good Place; The Country House in English Literature* (1993) is not confined to the nineteenth century, but has excellent accounts of the country houses in the writings of Jane Austen, Byron, Disraeli and Morris. Mark Girouard's *The Victorian Country House* (1971), *Life in the English Country House* (1978) and *The Return to Camelot: Chivalry and the English Gentleman* (1981) contain a wealth of information and argument. Beth Tobin's *Superintending the Poor; Charitable Ladies and Paternal Landlords in British Fiction, 1770–1860* (1993), gives a much bleaker account of the imaginative preparation of paternalism.

Raymond Williams, *The Country and the City* (1985) furnishes an invaluable map of the cultural forms relative to the rural. Kelvin Everest, *English Romantic Poetry* (1990) and Roger Sales, *English Literature in History; 1780–1830: Pastoral and Politics* (1983) offer accounts of Romanticism in a broadly historicising vein, and make good starting points for a topic with an enormous scholarly literature.

Two books which include much material on representations of rural life, though with very different objects of attention, are John Barrell, *The Dark Side of the Landscape; the Rural Poor in English Painting 1730–1840* (1980) and Karen Sayer, *Women of the Fields; Representations of Rural Women in the Nineteenth Century* (1995). Merryn Williams, *Thomas Hardy and Rural England* (1972), though perhaps naive in some of its assumptions, remains a good introduction.

For an account of the second half of the century, see Alun Howkins, *Reshaping Rural England; a Social History 1850–1925* (1991); this alludes as well to the creation of ideas of rurality and Englishness, also discussed in Robert Colls and Philip Dodd, eds., *Englishness: Politics and Culture 1880–1920* (1986) and G. E. Mingay, ed., *The Rural Idyll* (1989). Martin J. Weiner, in *English Culture and the Decline of the Industrial Spirit 1850–1980* (1981), gives an impressive but tendentious account of the 'southern metaphor' in English culture from the mid-nineteenth century onwards. Fiona MacCarthy, in her *William Morris: A Life for Our Time* (1994) locates Morris's ruralism in the context of Morris's life more generally.

5 Understanding the City

H. J. Dyos and Michael Wolff, eds., *The Victorian City; Images and Realities* (2 vols., 1973) is a treasure-house of scholarship and argument concerning all aspects of the nineteenth-century city. R. J. Morris and Richard Rodger, eds., *The Victorian City: A Reader in British Urban History 1820–1914* (1993) offers a useful starting point for more recent historical scholarship in this area. M. J. Daunton, *House and Home in the Victorian City; Working-Class Housing 1850–1914* (1983) suggests a transition towards more privatised forms of housing in the course of the nineteenth century, even for the working-class. Gareth Stedman Jones, *Outcast London: A Study in the Relationship between Classes in Victorian London* (1971) is an outstandingly argued account of the social relations of the capital in the second half of the century.

There is no shortage of criticism relating to Dickens and London, or to Dickens and the city, such as F. S. Scharzbach, *Dickens and the City* (1979) and Alexander Welsh, *The City of Dickens* (1971). John Lucas, *The Literature of Change: Studies in the Nineteenth-Century Provincial Novel* (1977) has an interesting discussion of Mrs Gaskell and Manchester; Chris Baldick, *In Frankenstein's Shadow: Myth, Monstruosity and Nineteenth-century Writing* (1987) tackles this (and other topics) also. *Into Unknown England 1866–1913* (1976), edited by P. J. Keating, supplies a useful introduction to, and anthology of, journalistic and social-scientific explorations of the city. Judith R. Walkowitz, *City of Dreadful Delight: Narratives of Sexual Danger in Late- Victorian London* (1992) suggests a gendered mapping of the city, making exemplary connections between cultural and material histories.

6 Gender and Cultural Forms

The explosion of feminist scholarship in the last twenty-five years has produced a wealth of material on gender and cultural forms in the nineteenth century. The books by Davidoff and Hall, and by Walkowitz, which I have already mentioned, form convenient bookends for the century; they are very highly recommended. Michael Mason, in *The Making of Victorian Sexual Attitudes* (1994) and *The Making of Victorian Sexuality: Sexual Behaviour and Its Understanding* (1994), supplies detailed and comprehensive analyses of a wide range of cultural and historical material, in the context of an argument that seeks to debunk some of the clichés concerning 'Victorian' sexuality.

Much of the writing specifically on feminism has been biographically based, such as Margaret Forster, *Significant Sisters: The Grassroots of Active Feminism* (1984). Olive Banks, *Faces of Feminism: A Study of Feminism as a Social Movement* (1981) suggests some of the different emphases within nineteenth-century feminism. The volumes in the Women's Source Library, edited by Dale Spender and Candida Ann Lacey, provide much primary material otherwise difficult of access; *Barbara Leigh Smith Bodichon and the Langham Place Group*, ed. Candida Ann Lacey (1987) is especially relevant to this chapter. For a collection of recent essays on women's history, see June Purvis, ed., *Women's History, Britain, 1850–1945: An Introduction* (1995).

There is now a substantial body of scholarship relating to gender and nineteenth-century literature. The path-breaking text is Sandra M. Gilbert and Susan Gubar, *The Madwoman in the Attic: The Woman Writer and the Nineteenth-Century Literary Imagination* (1979). For opposing views of Jane Austen, see Marylin Butler, *Jane Austen and the War of Ideas* (1975) and Margaret Kirkham, *Jane Austen, Feminism and Fiction* (1983); the question of Austen's relationship to questions of gender is discussed in Devoney Looser, ed., *Jane Austen and the Discourse of Feminism* (1995). Nancy Armstrong, *Desire and Domestic Fiction: A Political History of the Novel* (1987) and Mary Poovey, *Uneven Developments: The Ideological Work of Gender in Mid-Victorian England* (1989) provide challenging accounts of the novel in the nineteenth century, arguing strongly for the imbrication of questions of gender with class and the circuits of power. Angela Leighton and Margaret Reynolds, eds., *Victorian Women Poets, an Anthology* (1995) makes a lot of women's poetry accessible; this poetry is discussed in Angela Leighton, *Victorian Women Poets: Writing Against the Heart* (1992). Elaine Showalter's *Sexual Anarchy: Gender and Culture at the Fin de Siècle* (1991) is a stimulating and accessibly argued survey of its topic.

June Purvis, *A History of Women's Education in England* (1991) covers the period 1800–1914, and has the advantage of dealing substantially with working-class education. Penelope Byrde, *Nineteenth Century Fashion* (1992) devotes attention to the history of dress for both men and women.

7   Empire, Race and Ethnicity

Linda Colley's *Britons: Forging the Nation 1707–1837* (1994) furnishes an excellent account of the creation of the notion of 'Britain' in the eighteenth century, and its persistence into the nineteenth century. For an ambitious attempt to provide an ultimately economic explanation of Britain's imperial expansion, see P. J. Cain and A. G. Hopkins, *British Imperialism: Innovation and Expansion, 1699–1914* (1993); this is valuable also in the way the authors characterise the class-character of the British state. E. J. Hobsbawm's *The Age of Empire 1875–1914* (1987) gives a breathtaking overview of European history in the final decades of the century.

More at the level of cultural history, V. G. Kiernan's *The Lords of Human Kind: European Attitudes to the Outside World in the Imperial Age* (1972) surveys compendiously a large topic. Edward W. Said's *Culture and Imperialism* (1993) is the inescapable reference-point by an outstanding scholar, but it should not exclude attention to Martin Green, *Dreams of Adventure, Deeds of Empire* (1980) and Patrick Brantlinger, *Rule of Darkness: British Literature and Imperialism, 1830–1914* (1988). The former is a sometimes eccentric but always engaging effort to map imperialism and its accompanying cultural forms, while Brantlinger's book provides a scholarly and impressively detailed and committed survey of its field. Brian V. Street, *The Savage in Literature: Representations of 'Primitive' Society in English Fiction 1858–1920* (1975) remains valuable; Joseph Bristow, *Empire Boys: Adventures in a Man's World* (1991) is a slighter but interestingly argued account of the relations between fiction, empire and forms of masculinity in the late nineteenth century. Andrea White, *Joseph Conrad and the Adventure Tradition: Constructing and Deconstructing the Imperial Subject* (1993) includes substantial discussion of nineteenth-century travel and adventure writing as a context for its discussion of Conrad's early writing.

Roger Swift and Sheridan Gilley, eds., *The Irish in the Victorian City* (1985), includes some relevant essays; the significance of dialect and region in the formation of identity is discussed in Patrick Joyce, *Visions of the People* (1991).

Nineteenth-century racial attitudes, and the science that bolstered them, have now received substantial scholarly attention. Christine Bolt, *Victorian Attitudes to Race* (1971) is still useful; Stephen Jay Gould, in *The Mismeasure of Man* (1981) guides readers helpfully through the mistakes of nineteenth-century racial science, though unfortunately without a specifically English focus. Robert J. C. Young, *White Mythologies: Writing, History and the West* (1990) and *Colonial Desire: Hybridity in Theory, Culture and Race* (1995) provide accounts of their topics in a more poststructuralist idiom; the latter is especially challenging in the argument it makes concerning the interrelation of notions of culture and race.

INDEX